Little Nothings

The Curse of the Umbrella

D0558274

Little Nothings
The Curse of the Umbrella

LEWIS TRONDHEIM

nbm
Comics Lit

ISBN 10: 1-56163-523-5
ISBN 13: 978-1-56163-523-8
© 2006 Trondheim
Rights arranged through Sylvain Coissard Agency, France.
© 2007 NBM for the English translation
Translation by Joe Johnson
Lettering by Ortho
Printed in China

3 2 1

Comicslit is an imprint
and trademark of

NANTIER · BEALL · MINOUSTCHINE

Publishing inc.

new york

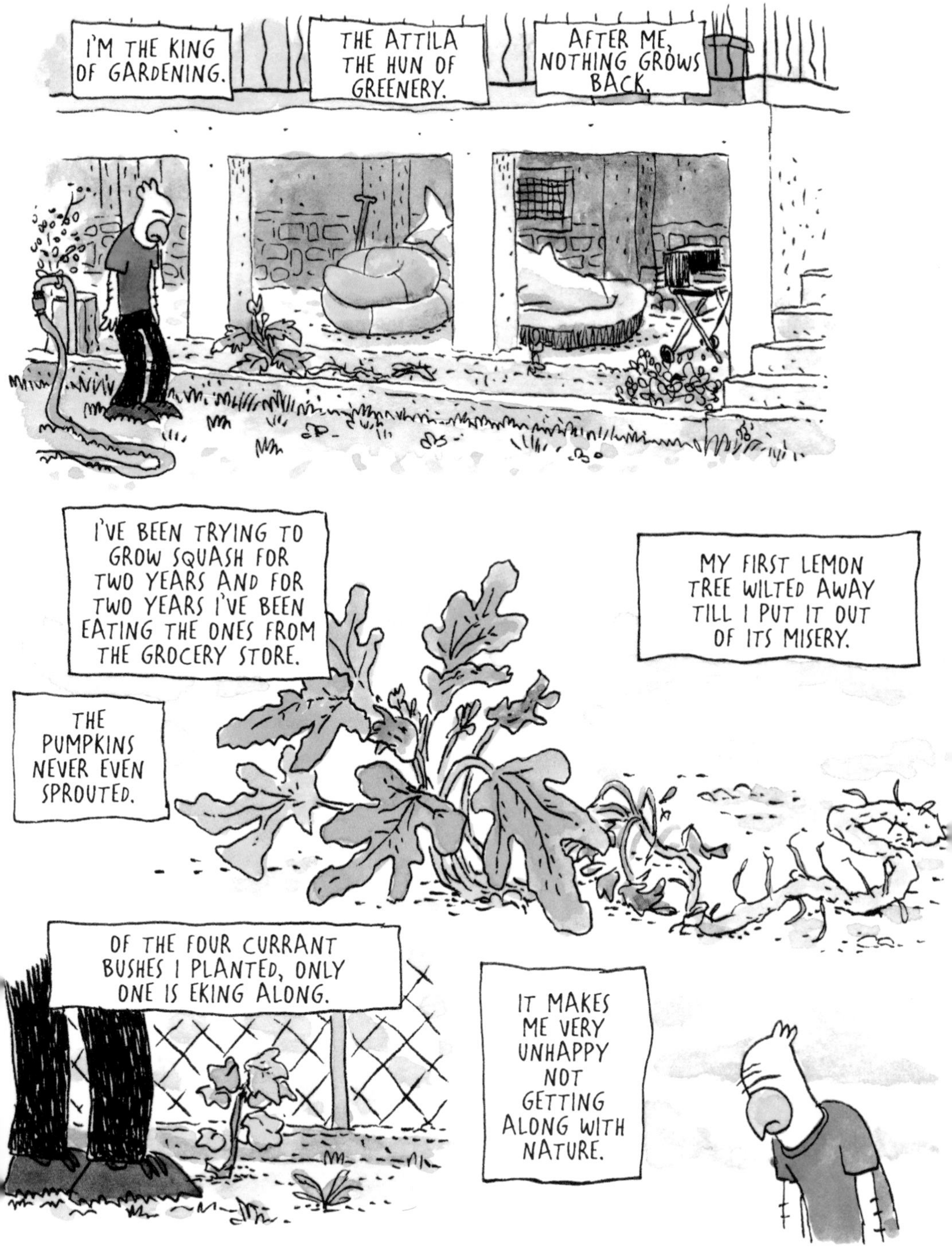
I'M THE KING OF GARDENING.
THE ATTILA THE HUN OF GREENERY.
AFTER ME, NOTHING GROWS BACK.
I'VE BEEN TRYING TO GROW SQUASH FOR TWO YEARS AND FOR TWO YEARS I'VE BEEN EATING THE ONES FROM THE GROCERY STORE.
MY FIRST LEMON TREE WILTED AWAY TILL I PUT IT OUT OF ITS MISERY.
THE PUMPKINS NEVER EVEN SPROUTED.
OF THE FOUR CURRANT BUSHES I PLANTED, ONLY ONE IS EKING ALONG.
IT MAKES ME VERY UNHAPPY NOT GETTING ALONG WITH NATURE.

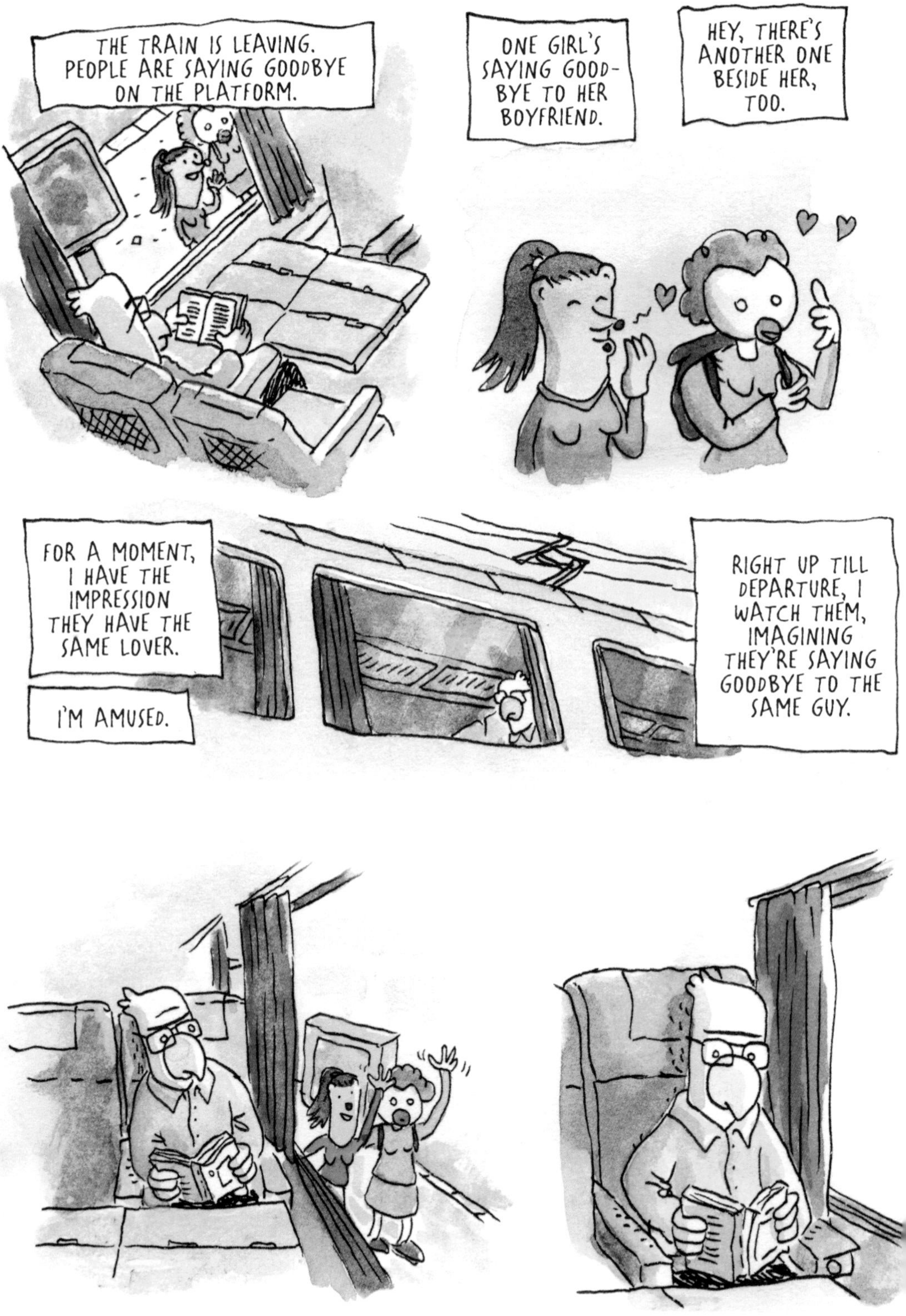
THE TRAIN IS LEAVING. PEOPLE ARE SAYING GOODBYE ON THE PLATFORM.
ONE GIRL'S SAYING GOOD-BYE TO HER BOYFRIEND.
HEY, THERE'S ANOTHER ONE BESIDE HER, TOO.
FOR A MOMENT, I HAVE THE IMPRESSION THEY HAVE THE SAME LOVER.
I'M AMUSED.
RIGHT UP TILL DEPARTURE, I WATCH THEM, IMAGINING THEY'RE SAYING GOODBYE TO THE SAME GUY.

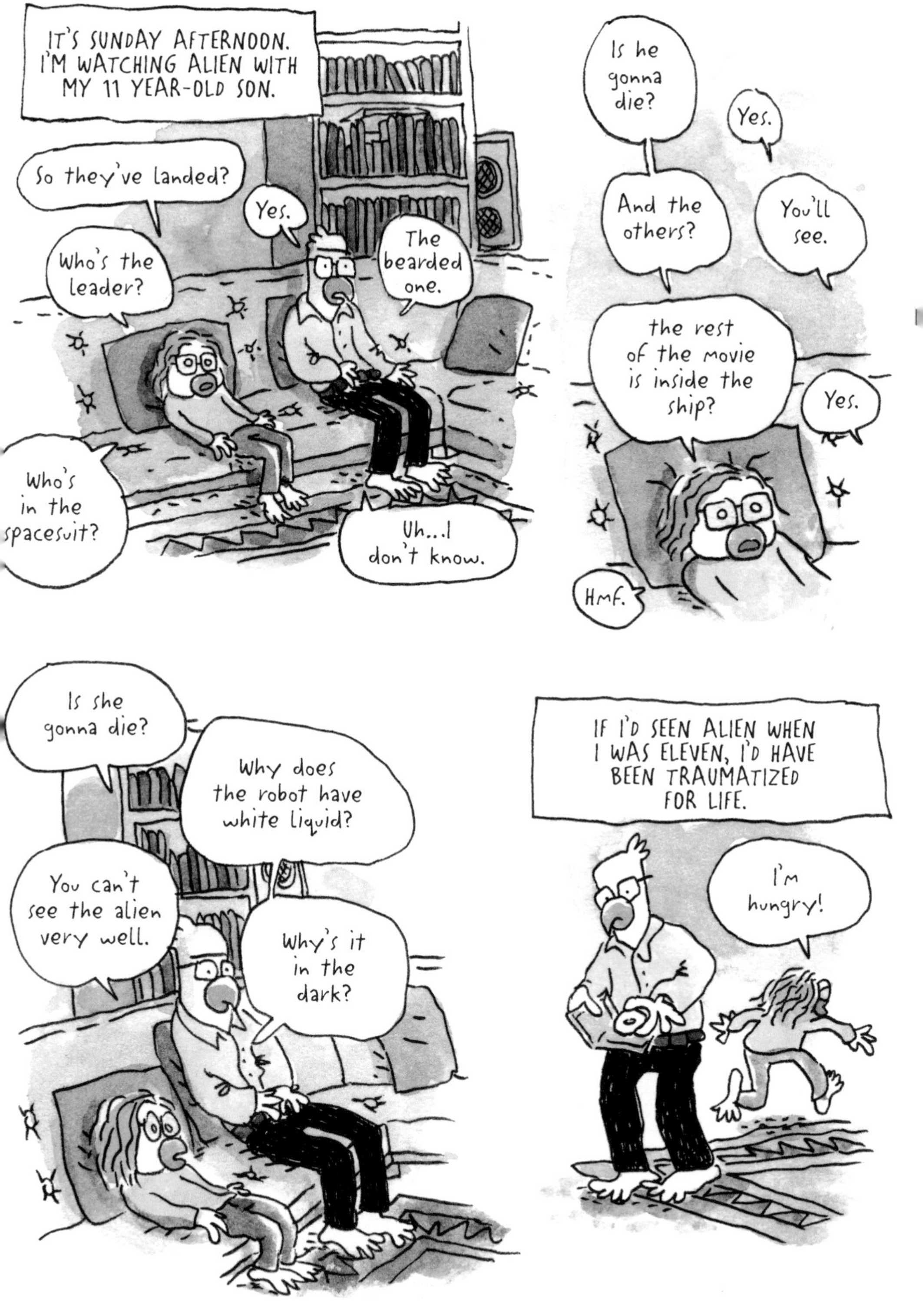
IT'S SUNDAY AFTERNOON. I'M WATCHING ALIEN WITH MY 11 YEAR-OLD SON.
So they've landed?
Yes.
Who's the leader?
The bearded one.
Who's in the spacesuit?
Uh...I don't know.
Is he gonna die?
Yes.
And the others?
You'll see.
the rest of the movie is inside the ship?
Yes.
Hmf.
Is she gonna die?
Why does the robot have white liquid?
You can't see the alien very well.
Why's it in the dark?
IF I'D SEEN ALIEN WHEN I WAS ELEVEN, I'D HAVE BEEN TRAUMATIZED FOR LIFE.
I'm hungry!

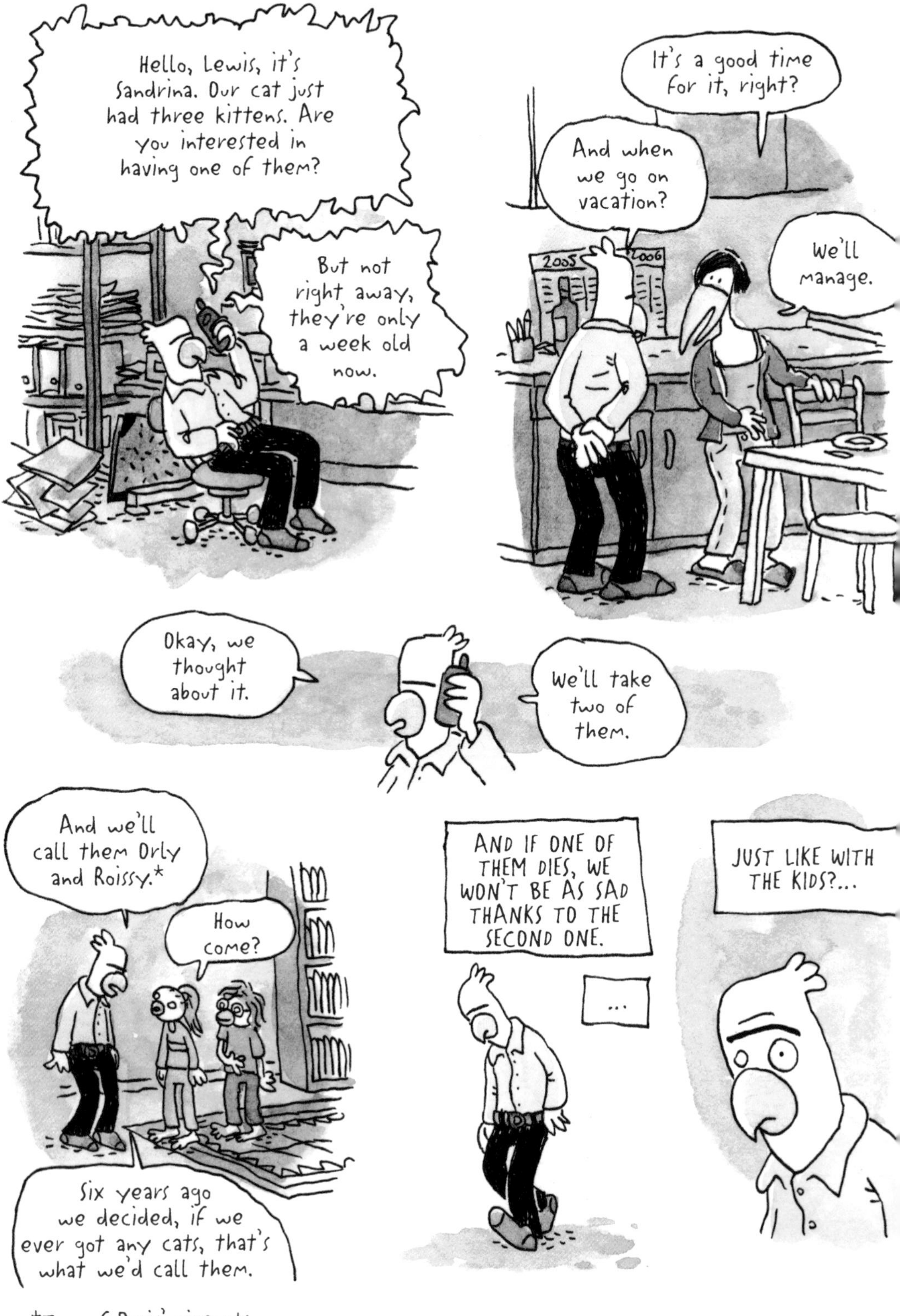
Hello, Lewis, it's Sandrina. Our cat just had three kittens. Are you interested in having one of them?
But not right away, they're only a week old now.
It's a good time for it, right?
And when we go on vacation?
We'll manage.
2005
2006
Okay, we thought about it.
We'll take two of them.
And we'll call them Orly and Roissy.*
How come?
Six years ago we decided, if we ever got any cats, that's what we'd call them.
AND IF ONE OF THEM DIES, WE WON'T BE AS SAD THANKS TO THE SECOND ONE.
...
JUST LIKE WITH THE KIDS?...

*Two of Paris' airports.

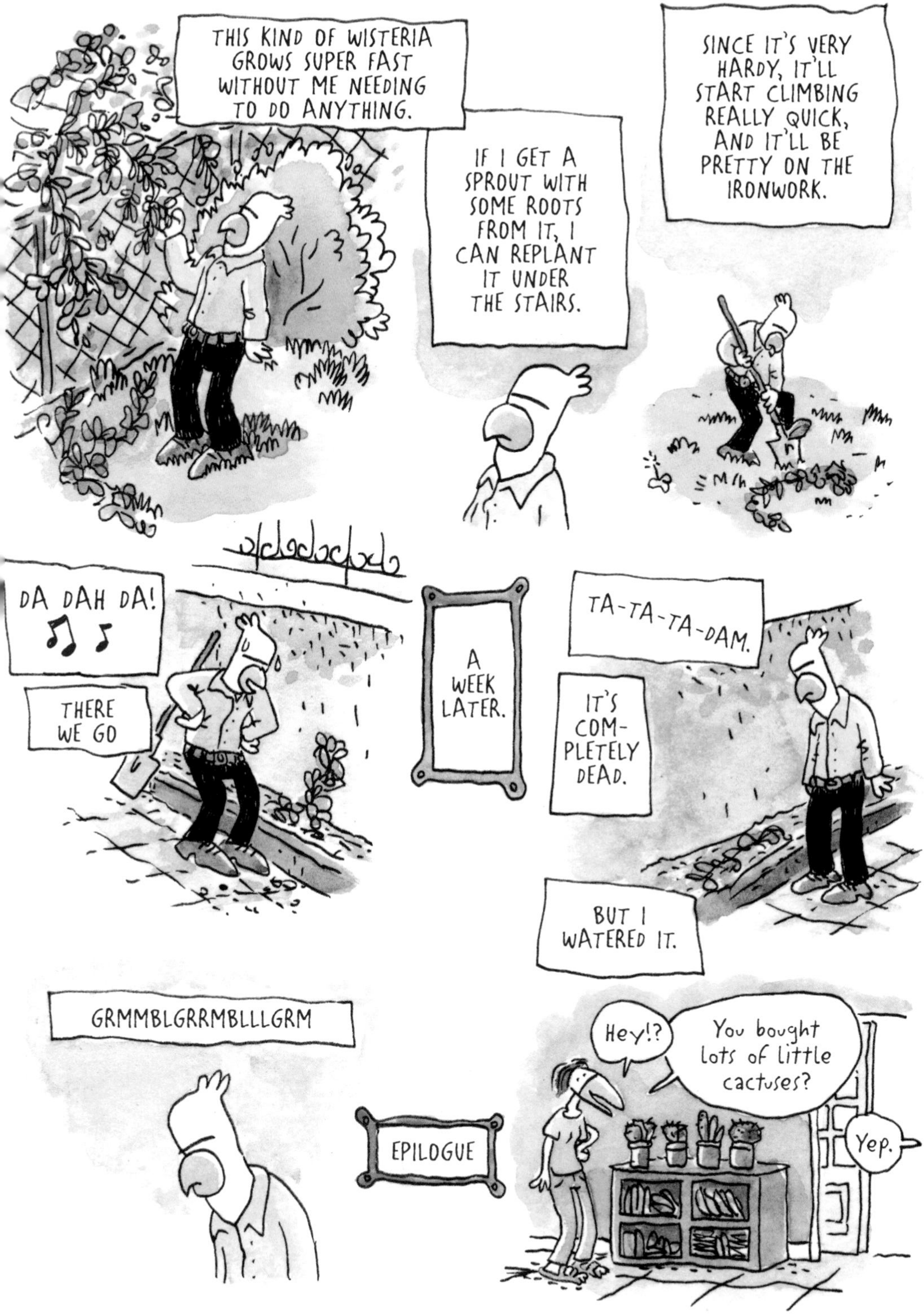
THIS KIND OF WISTERIA GROWS SUPER FAST WITHOUT ME NEEDING TO DO ANYTHING.
IF I GET A SPROUT WITH SOME ROOTS FROM IT, I CAN REPLANT IT UNDER THE STAIRS.
SINCE IT'S VERY HARDY, IT'LL START CLIMBING REALLY QUICK, AND IT'LL BE PRETTY ON THE IRONWORK.
DA DAH DA!
THERE WE GO
A WEEK LATER.
TA-TA-TA-DAM.
IT'S COM-PLETELY DEAD.
BUT I WATERED IT.
GRMMBLGRRMBLLLGRM
EPILOGUE
Hey!?
You bought lots of little cactuses?
Yep.

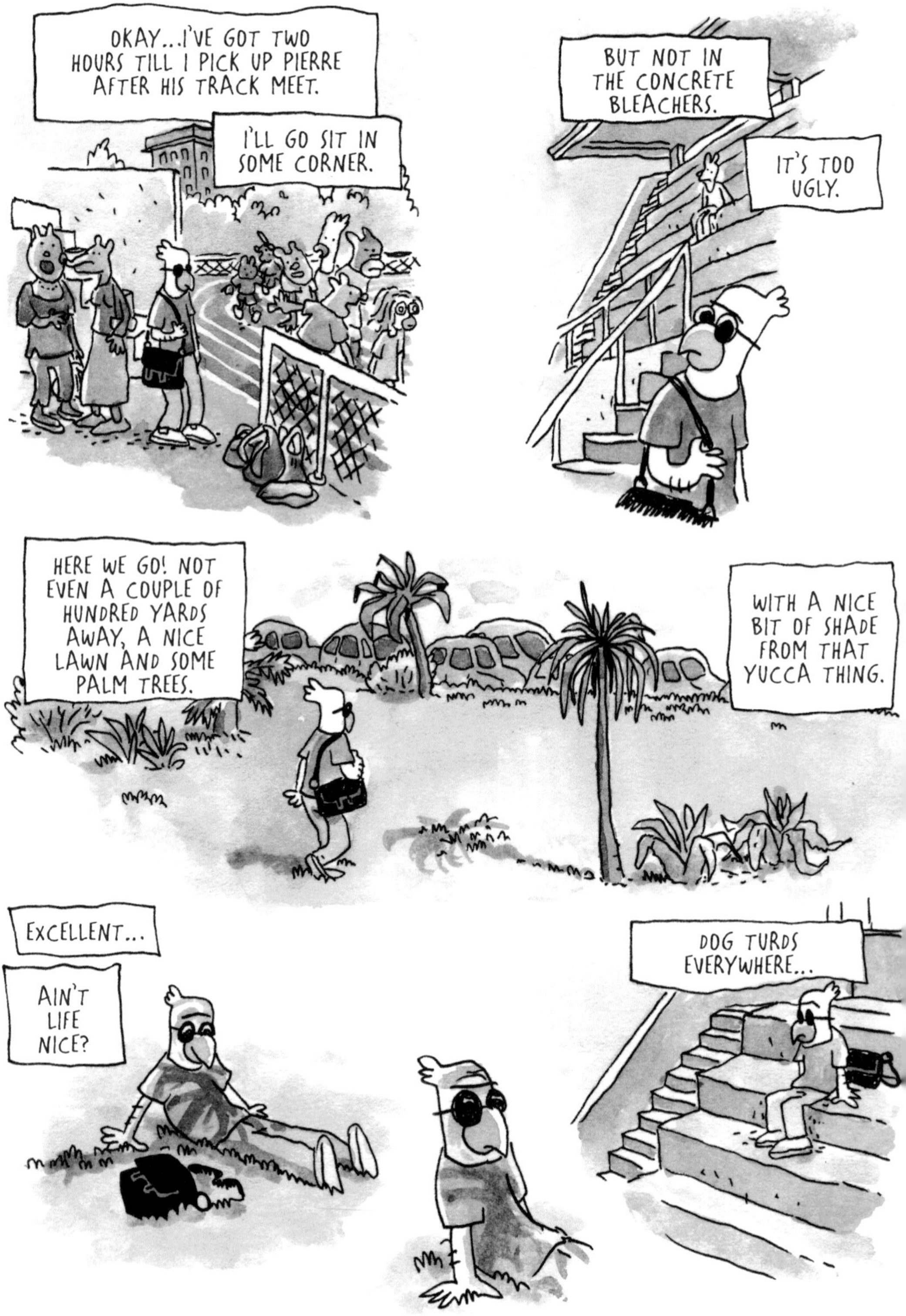
OKAY...I'VE GOT TWO HOURS TILL I PICK UP PIERRE AFTER HIS TRACK MEET.
I'LL GO SIT IN SOME CORNER.
BUT NOT IN THE CONCRETE BLEACHERS.
IT'S TOO UGLY.
HERE WE GO! NOT EVEN A COUPLE OF HUNDRED YARDS AWAY, A NICE LAWN AND SOME PALM TREES.
WITH A NICE BIT OF SHADE FROM THAT YUCCA THING.
EXCELLENT...
AIN'T LIFE NICE?
DOG TURDS EVERYWHERE...

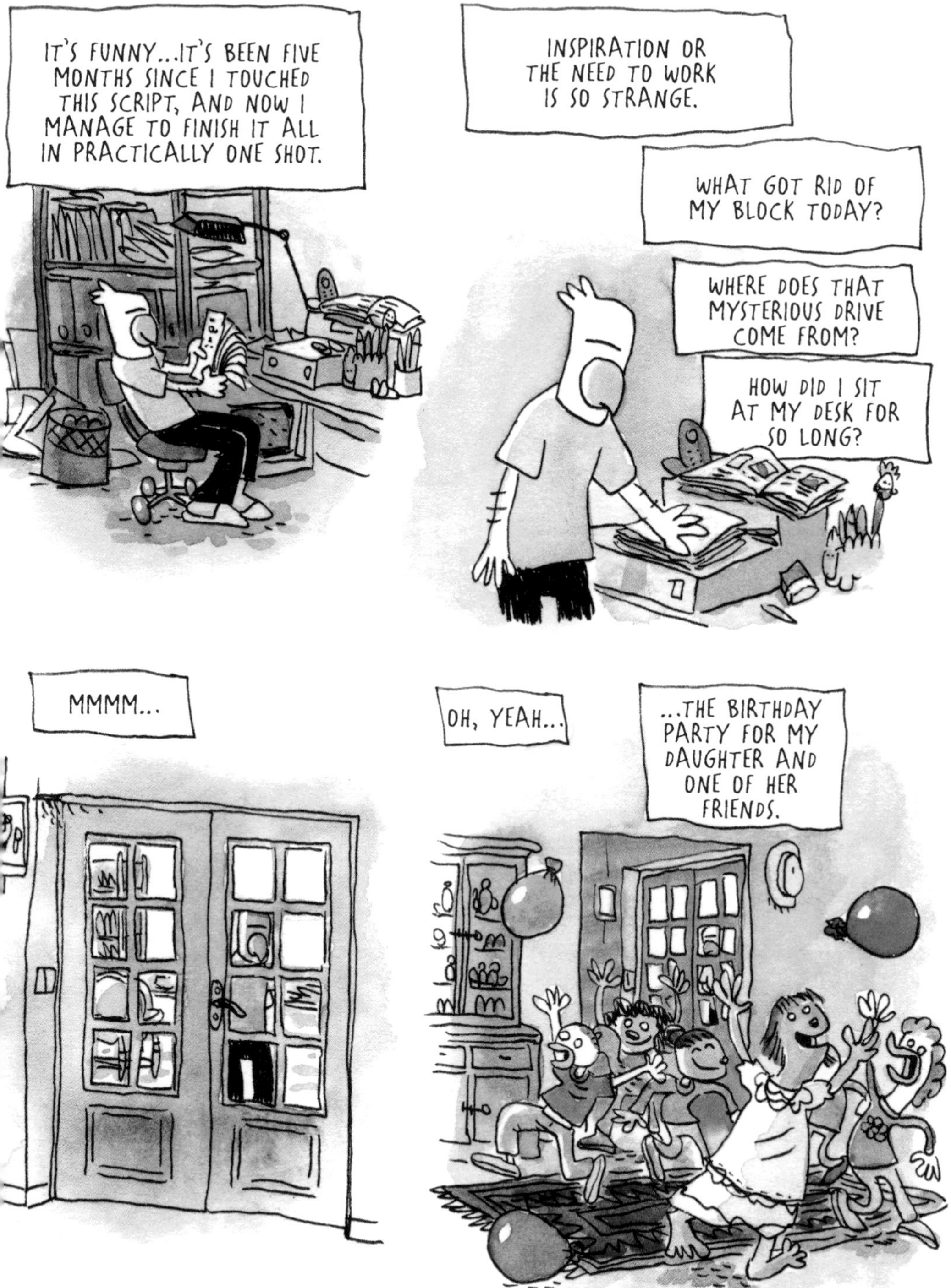
IT'S FUNNY...IT'S BEEN FIVE MONTHS SINCE I TOUCHED THIS SCRIPT, AND NOW I MANAGE TO FINISH IT ALL IN PRACTICALLY ONE SHOT.
INSPIRATION OR THE NEED TO WORK IS SO STRANGE.
WHAT GOT RID OF MY BLOCK TODAY?
WHERE DOES THAT MYSTERIOUS DRIVE COME FROM?
HOW DID I SIT AT MY DESK FOR SO LONG?
MMMM...
OH, YEAH...
...THE BIRTHDAY PARTY FOR MY DAUGHTER AND ONE OF HER FRIENDS.

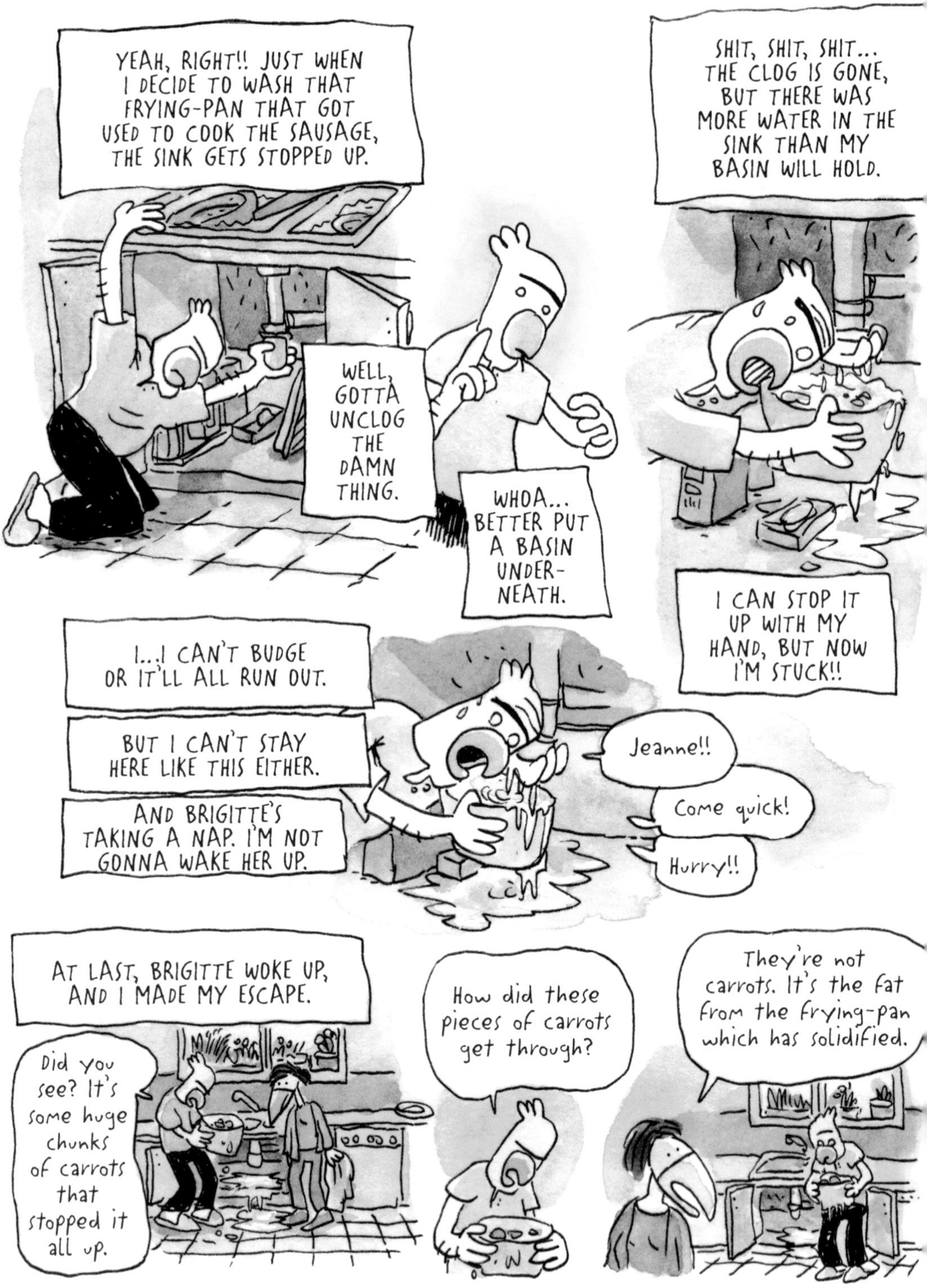
YEAH, RIGHT!! JUST WHEN I DECIDE TO WASH THAT FRYING-PAN THAT GOT USED TO COOK THE SAUSAGE, THE SINK GETS STOPPED UP.
WELL, GOTTA UNCLOG THE DAMN THING.
WHOA... BETTER PUT A BASIN UNDERNEATH.
SHIT, SHIT, SHIT... THE CLOG IS GONE, BUT THERE WAS MORE WATER IN THE SINK THAN MY BASIN WILL HOLD.
I CAN STOP IT UP WITH MY HAND, BUT NOW I'M STUCK!!
I...I CAN'T BUDGE OR IT'LL ALL RUN OUT.
BUT I CAN'T STAY HERE LIKE THIS EITHER.
AND BRIGITTE'S TAKING A NAP. I'M NOT GONNA WAKE HER UP.
Jeanne!!
Come quick!
Hurry!!
AT LAST, BRIGITTE WOKE UP, AND I MADE MY ESCAPE.
Did you see? It's some huge chunks of carrots that stopped it all up.
How did these pieces of carrots get through?
They're not carrots. It's the fat from the frying-pan which has solidified.

THREE MONTHS AGO, JOANN TOLD ME HE'D PLAYED SQUASH AND HAD HAD A GOOD TIME.

Joann + Sport = good time?

!?!!

LATER, I READ "A WIDOW FOR ONE YEAR" BY JOHN IRVING, IN WHICH SQUASH COMES UP.

Hello

SO, AFTER FOUR YEARS OF BAD-MINTON, I DECIDE TO BUY MYSELF SOME INDOOR COURT SNEAKERS.

?

Bad./squash.

AND THEN A PARENT FROM MY DAUGHTER'S SCHOOL OFFERS TO PLAY A SQUASH MATCH, EVEN THOUGH I'VE NEVER SPOKEN TO HIM ABOUT IT.

UH...OKAY. WHY NOT?

WHEN THINGS FALL TOGETHER LIKE THAT, I NEVER FIGHT IT.

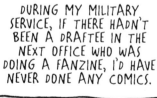

DURING MY MILITARY SERVICE, IF THERE HADN'T BEEN A DRAFTEE IN THE NEXT OFFICE WHO WAS DOING A FANZINE, I'D HAVE NEVER DONE ANY COMICS.

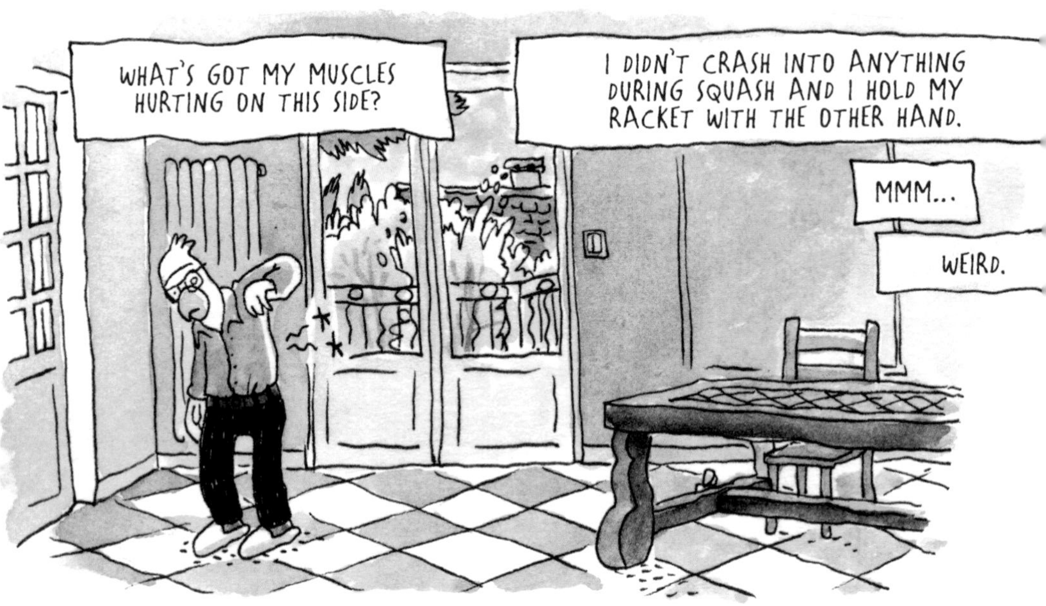
WHAT'S GOT MY MUSCLES HURTING ON THIS SIDE?
I DIDN'T CRASH INTO ANYTHING DURING SQUASH AND I HOLD MY RACKET WITH THE OTHER HAND.
MMM...
WEIRD.

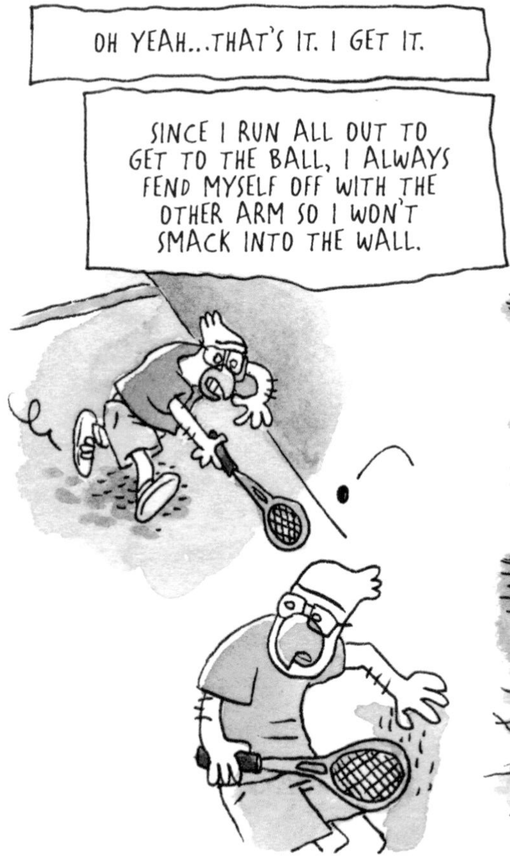
OH YEAH...THAT'S IT. I GET IT.
SINCE I RUN ALL OUT TO GET TO THE BALL, I ALWAYS FEND MYSELF OFF WITH THE OTHER ARM SO I WON'T SMACK INTO THE WALL.

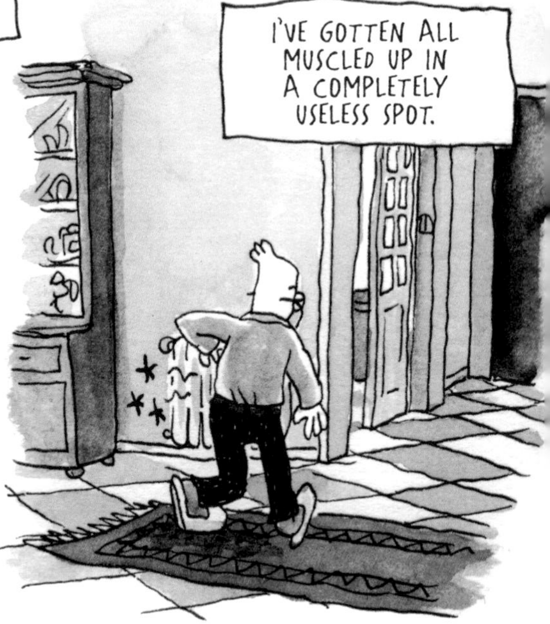
I'VE GOTTEN ALL MUSCLED UP IN A COMPLETELY USELESS SPOT.

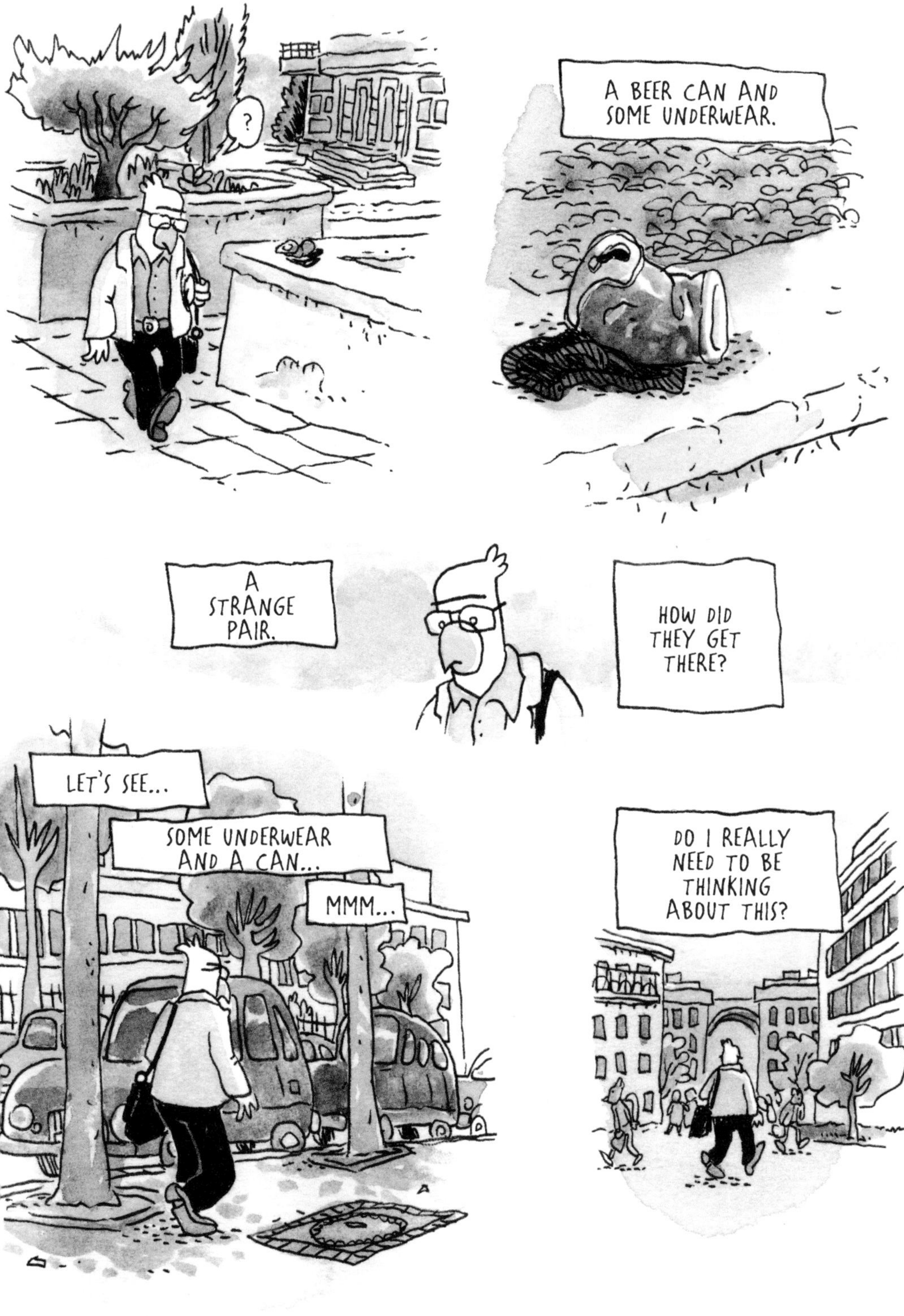
?
A BEER CAN AND SOME UNDERWEAR.
A STRANGE PAIR.
HOW DID THEY GET THERE?
LET'S SEE...
SOME UNDERWEAR AND A CAN...
MMM...
DO I REALLY NEED TO BE THINKING ABOUT THIS?

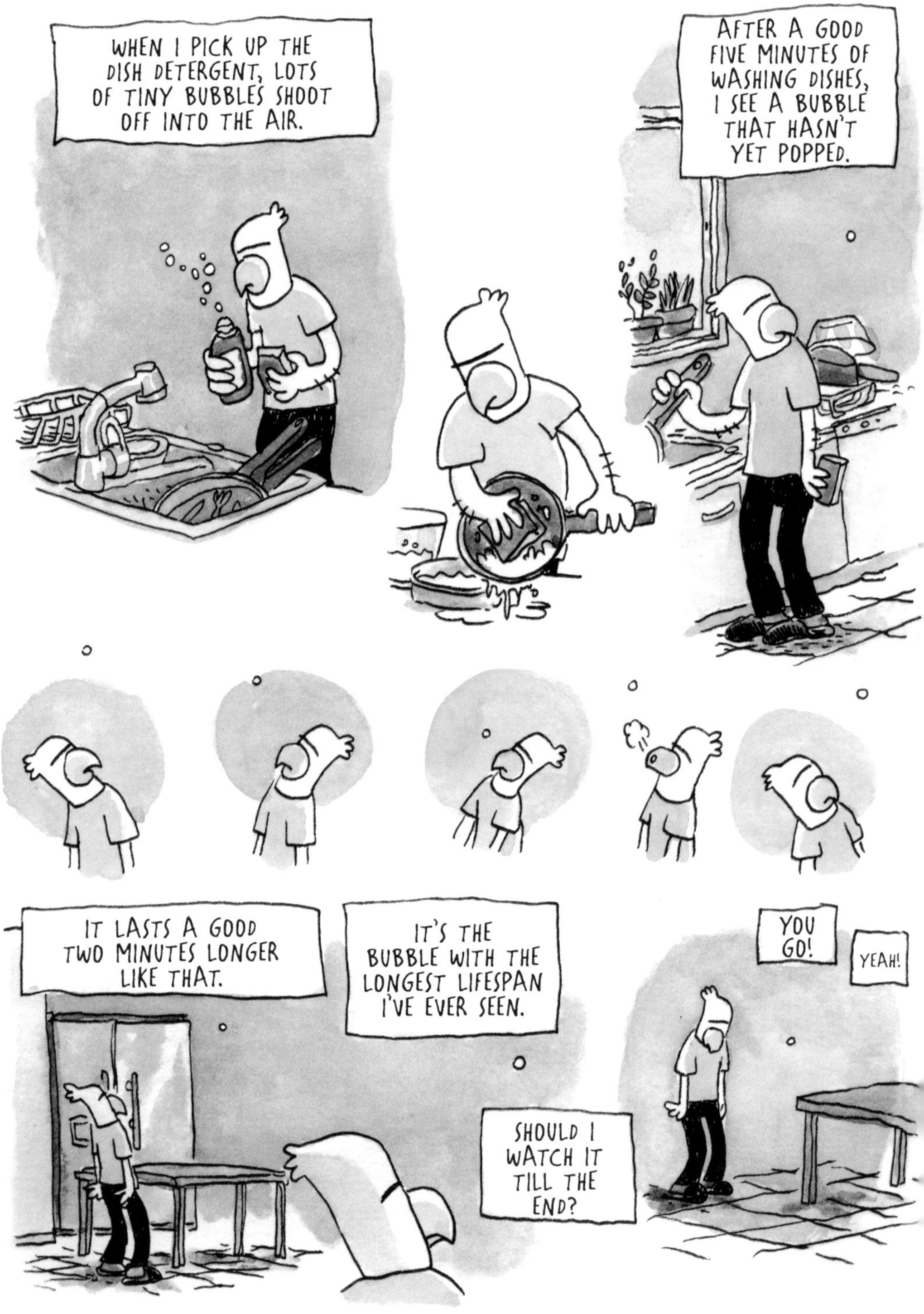
WHEN I PICK UP THE DISH DETERGENT, LOTS OF TINY BUBBLES SHOOT OFF INTO THE AIR.
AFTER A GOOD FIVE MINUTES OF WASHING DISHES, I SEE A BUBBLE THAT HASN'T YET POPPED.
IT LASTS A GOOD TWO MINUTES LONGER LIKE THAT.
IT'S THE BUBBLE WITH THE LONGEST LIFESPAN I'VE EVER SEEN.
SHOULD I WATCH IT TILL THE END?
YOU GO!
YEAH!

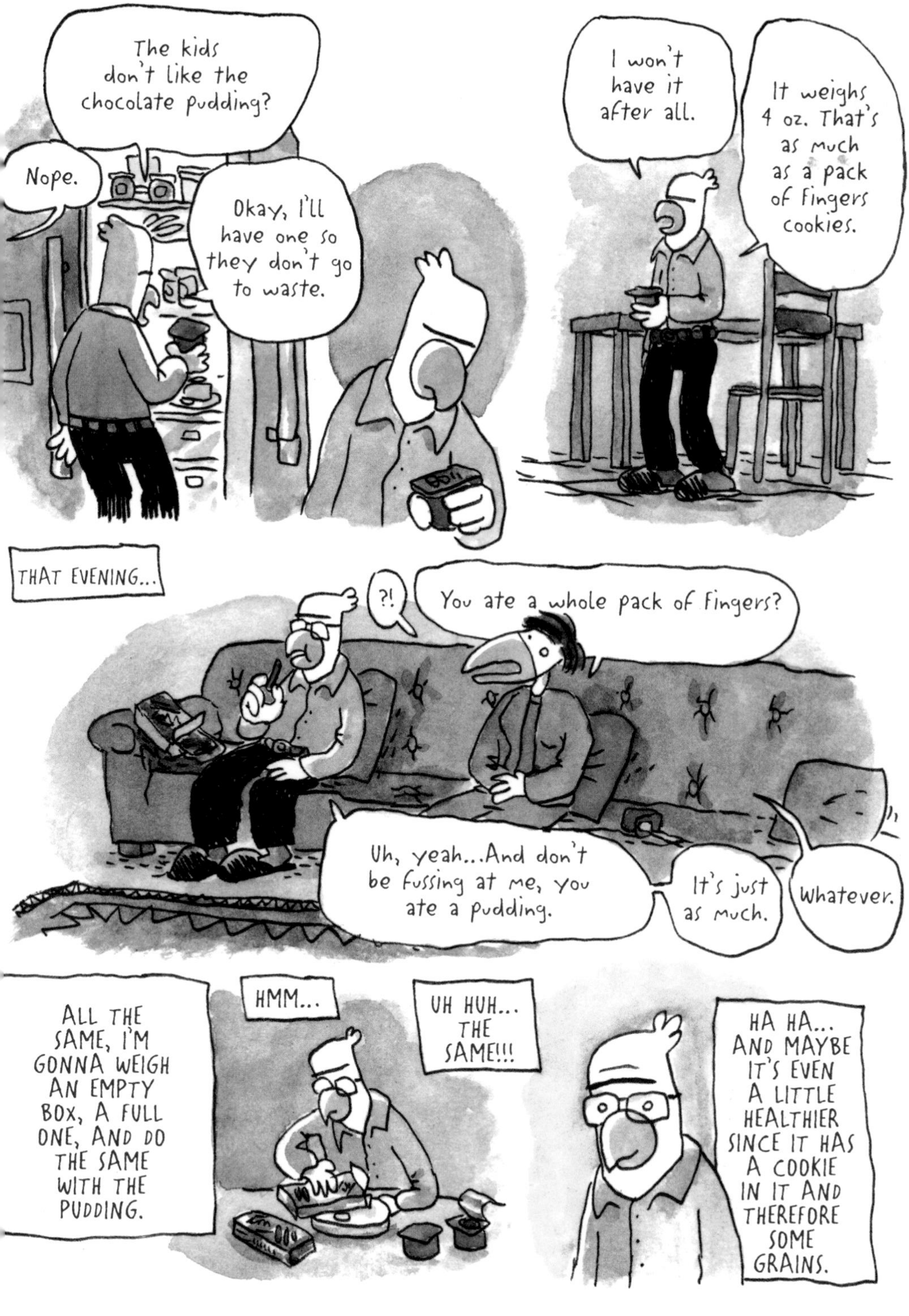
The kids don't like the chocolate pudding?
Nope.
Okay, I'll have one so they don't go to waste.
I won't have it after all.
It weighs 4 oz. That's as much as a pack of fingers cookies.
THAT EVENING...
You ate a whole pack of fingers?
?!
Uh, yeah...And don't be fussing at me, you ate a pudding.
It's just as much.
Whatever.
ALL THE SAME, I'M GONNA WEIGH AN EMPTY BOX, A FULL ONE, AND DO THE SAME WITH THE PUDDING.
HMM...
UH HUH... THE SAME!!!
HA HA... AND MAYBE IT'S EVEN A LITTLE HEALTHIER SINCE IT HAS A COOKIE IN IT AND THEREFORE SOME GRAINS.

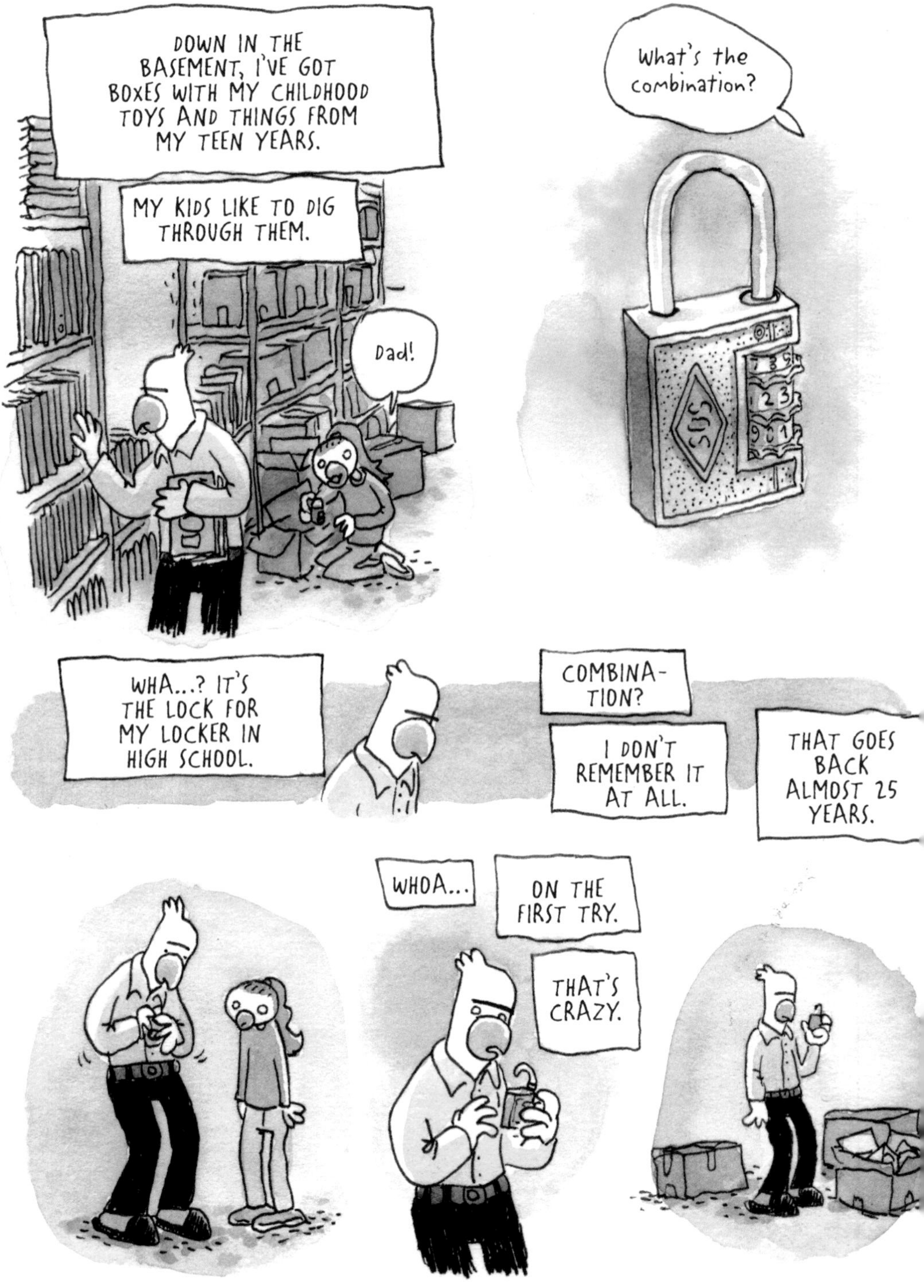
DOWN IN THE BASEMENT, I'VE GOT BOXES WITH MY CHILDHOOD TOYS AND THINGS FROM MY TEEN YEARS.
MY KIDS LIKE TO DIG THROUGH THEM.
Dad!
What's the combination?
WHA...? IT'S THE LOCK FOR MY LOCKER IN HIGH SCHOOL.
COMBINA-TION?
I DON'T REMEMBER IT AT ALL.
THAT GOES BACK ALMOST 25 YEARS.
WHOA...
ON THE FIRST TRY.
THAT'S CRAZY.

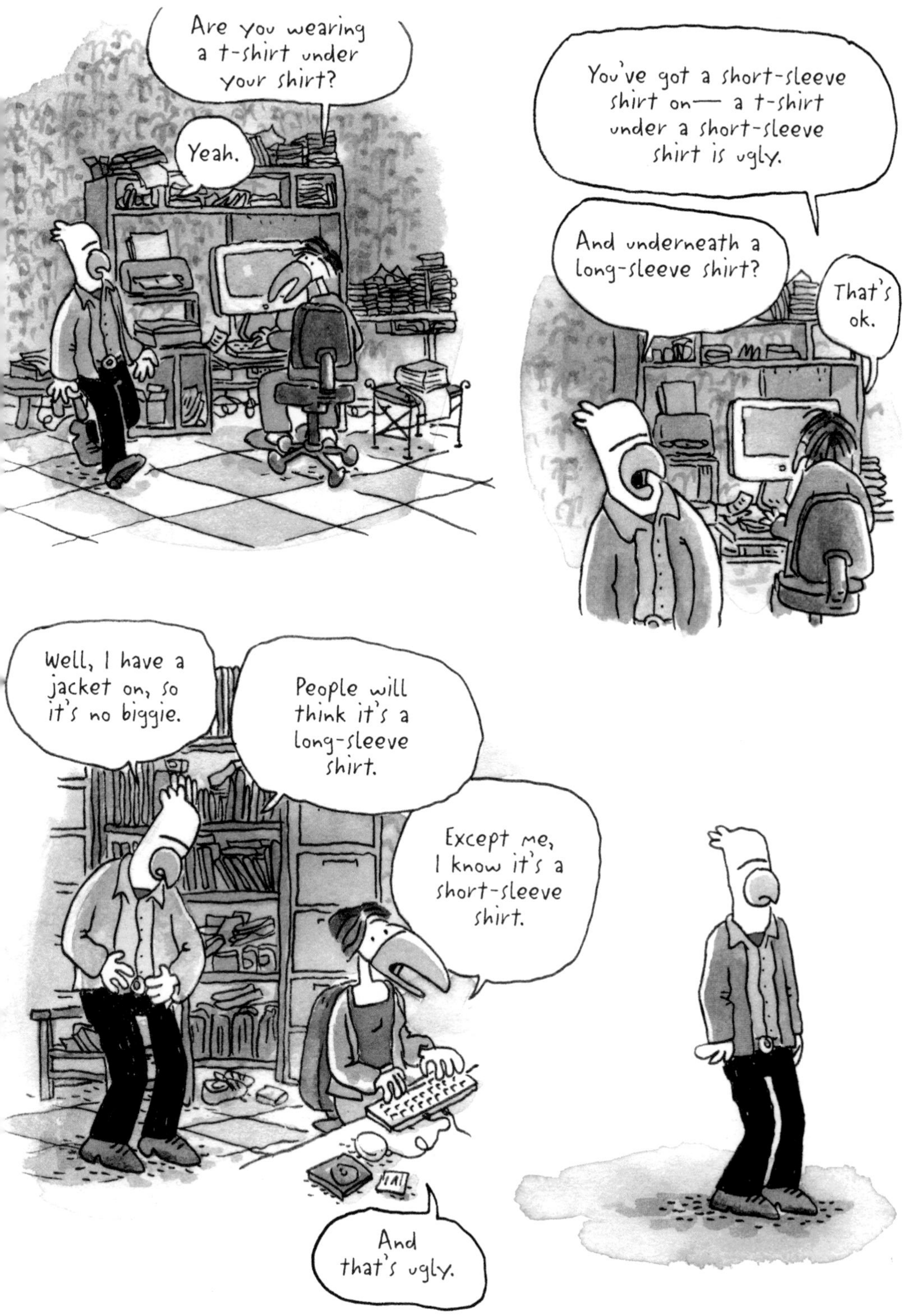
Are you wearing a t-shirt under your shirt?
Yeah.
You've got a short-sleeve shirt on— a t-shirt under a short-sleeve shirt is ugly.
And underneath a long-sleeve shirt?
That's ok.
Well, I have a jacket on, so it's no biggie.
People will think it's a long-sleeve shirt.
Except me, I know it's a short-sleeve shirt.
And that's ugly.

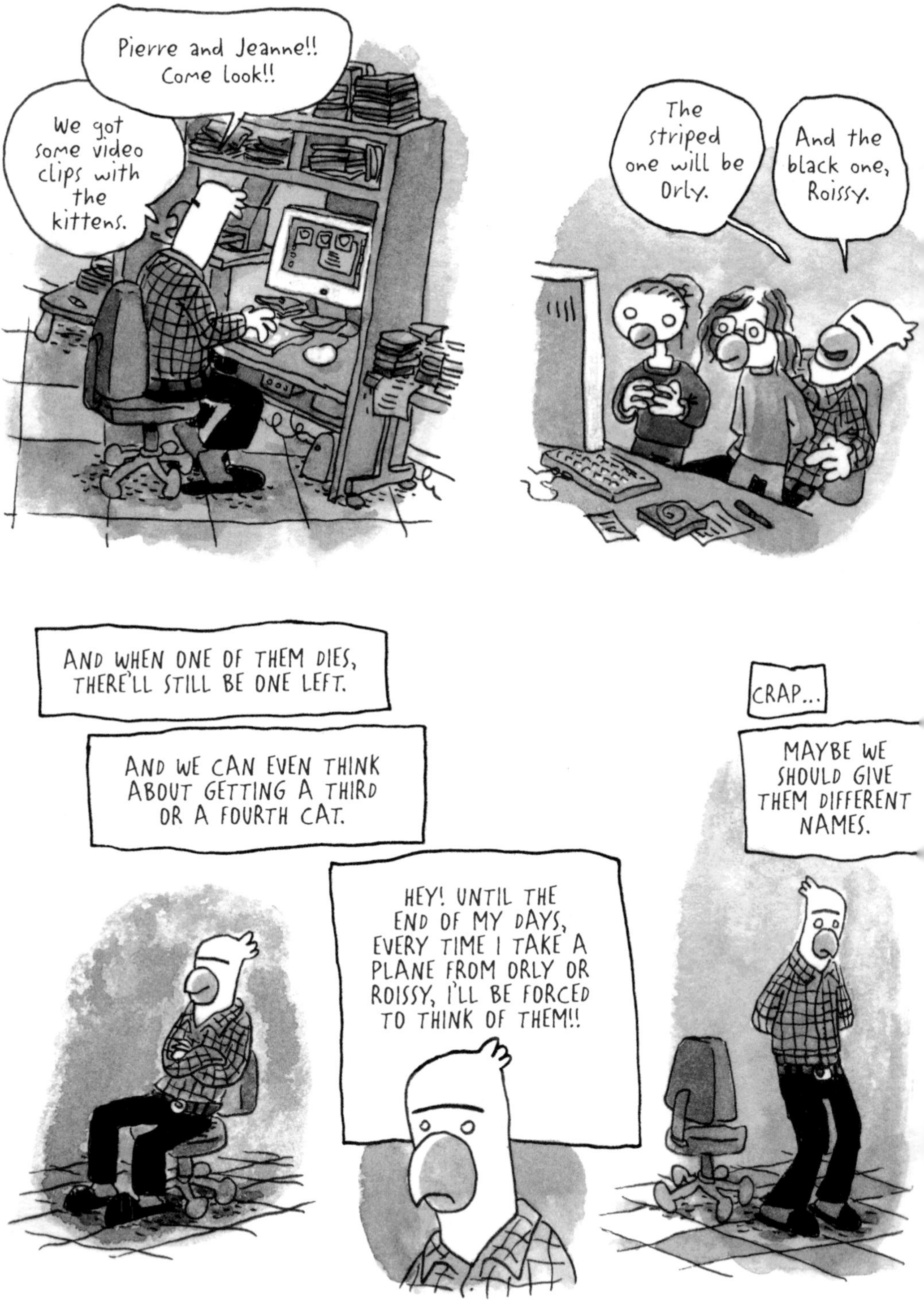
Pierre and Jeanne!! Come look!!
We got some video clips with the kittens.
The striped one will be Orly.
And the black one, Roissy.
AND WHEN ONE OF THEM DIES, THERE'LL STILL BE ONE LEFT.
AND WE CAN EVEN THINK ABOUT GETTING A THIRD OR A FOURTH CAT.
HEY! UNTIL THE END OF MY DAYS, EVERY TIME I TAKE A PLANE FROM ORLY OR ROISSY, I'LL BE FORCED TO THINK OF THEM!!
CRAP...
MAYBE WE SHOULD GIVE THEM DIFFERENT NAMES.

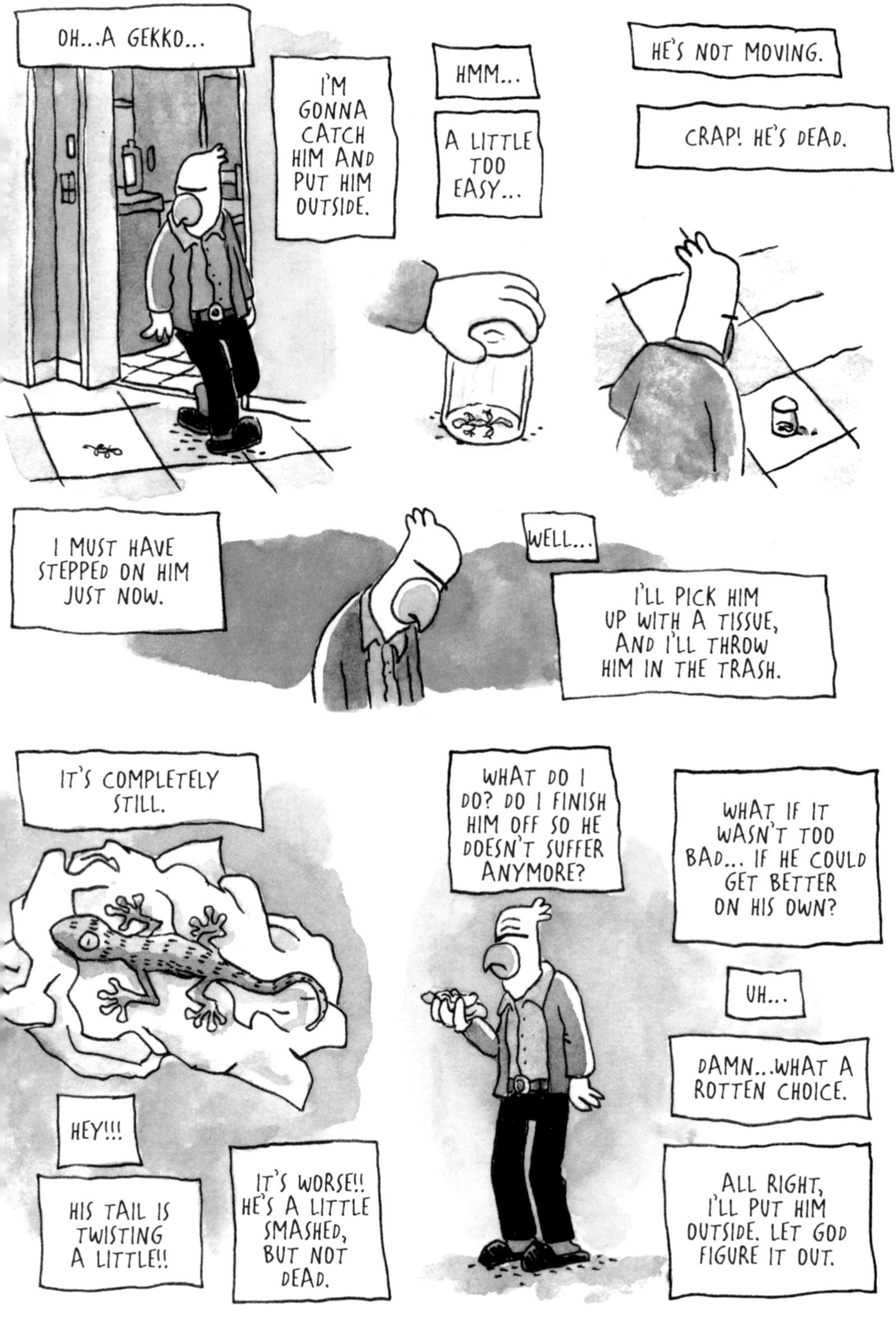
OH...A GEKKO...
I'M GONNA CATCH HIM AND PUT HIM OUTSIDE.
HMM...
A LITTLE TOO EASY...
HE'S NOT MOVING.
CRAP! HE'S DEAD.
I MUST HAVE STEPPED ON HIM JUST NOW.
WELL...
I'LL PICK HIM UP WITH A TISSUE, AND I'LL THROW HIM IN THE TRASH.
IT'S COMPLETELY STILL.
HEY!!!
HIS TAIL IS TWISTING A LITTLE!!
IT'S WORSE!! HE'S A LITTLE SMASHED, BUT NOT DEAD.
WHAT DO I DO? DO I FINISH HIM OFF SO HE DOESN'T SUFFER ANYMORE?
WHAT IF IT WASN'T TOO BAD... IF HE COULD GET BETTER ON HIS OWN?
UH...
DAMN...WHAT A ROTTEN CHOICE.
ALL RIGHT, I'LL PUT HIM OUTSIDE. LET GOD FIGURE IT OUT.

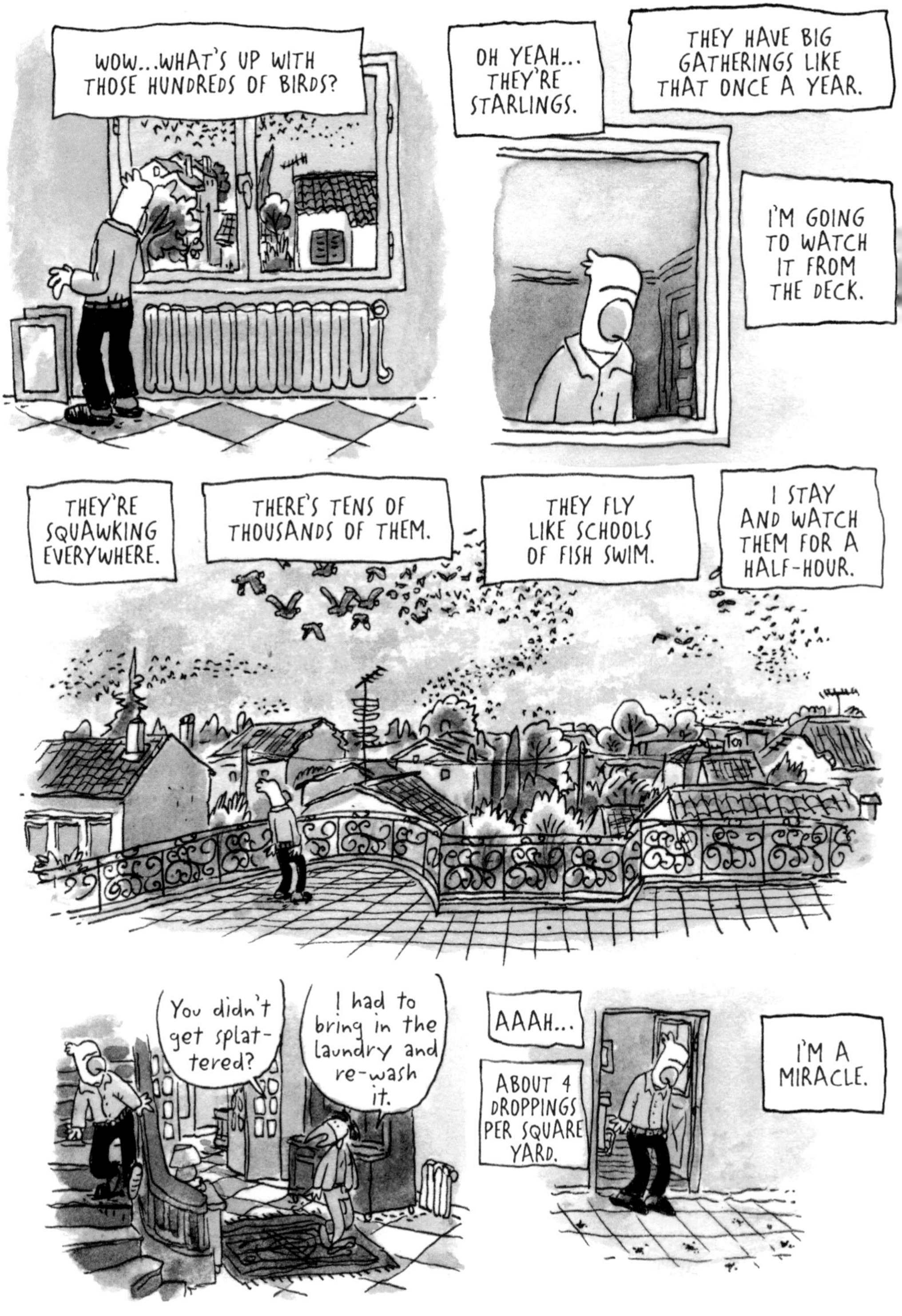
WOW...WHAT'S UP WITH THOSE HUNDREDS OF BIRDS?
OH YEAH... THEY'RE STARLINGS.
THEY HAVE BIG GATHERINGS LIKE THAT ONCE A YEAR.
I'M GOING TO WATCH IT FROM THE DECK.
THEY'RE SQUAWKING EVERYWHERE.
THERE'S TENS OF THOUSANDS OF THEM.
THEY FLY LIKE SCHOOLS OF FISH SWIM.
I STAY AND WATCH THEM FOR A HALF-HOUR.
You didn't get splattered?
I had to bring in the laundry and re-wash it.
AAAH...
ABOUT 4 DROPPINGS PER SQUARE YARD.
I'M A MIRACLE.

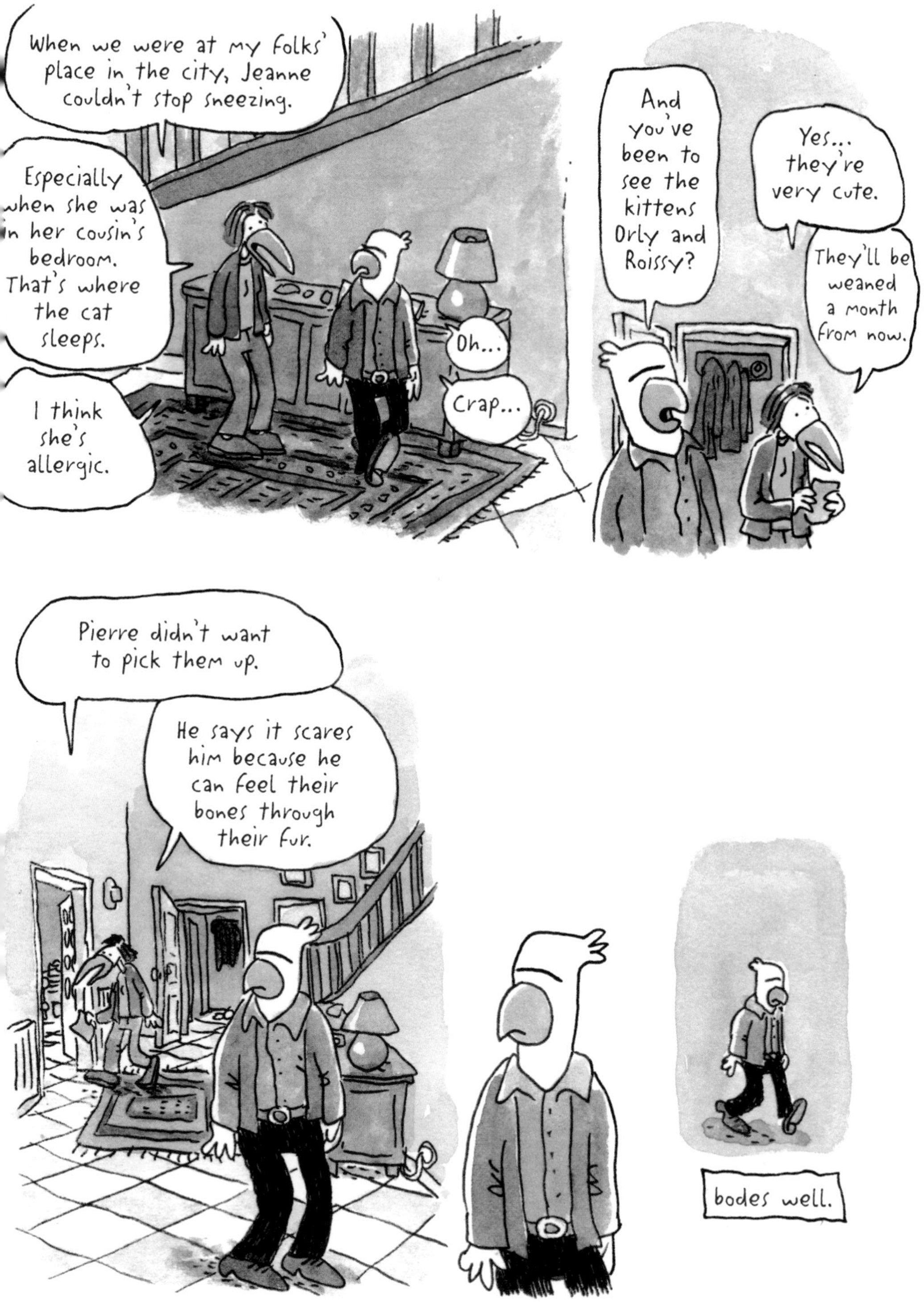
When we were at my folks' place in the city, Jeanne couldn't stop sneezing.
Especially when she was in her cousin's bedroom. That's where the cat sleeps.
I think she's allergic.
Oh...
Crap...
And you've been to see the kittens Orly and Roissy?
Yes... they're very cute.
They'll be weaned a month from now.
Pierre didn't want to pick them up.
He says it scares him because he can feel their bones through their fur.
bodes well.

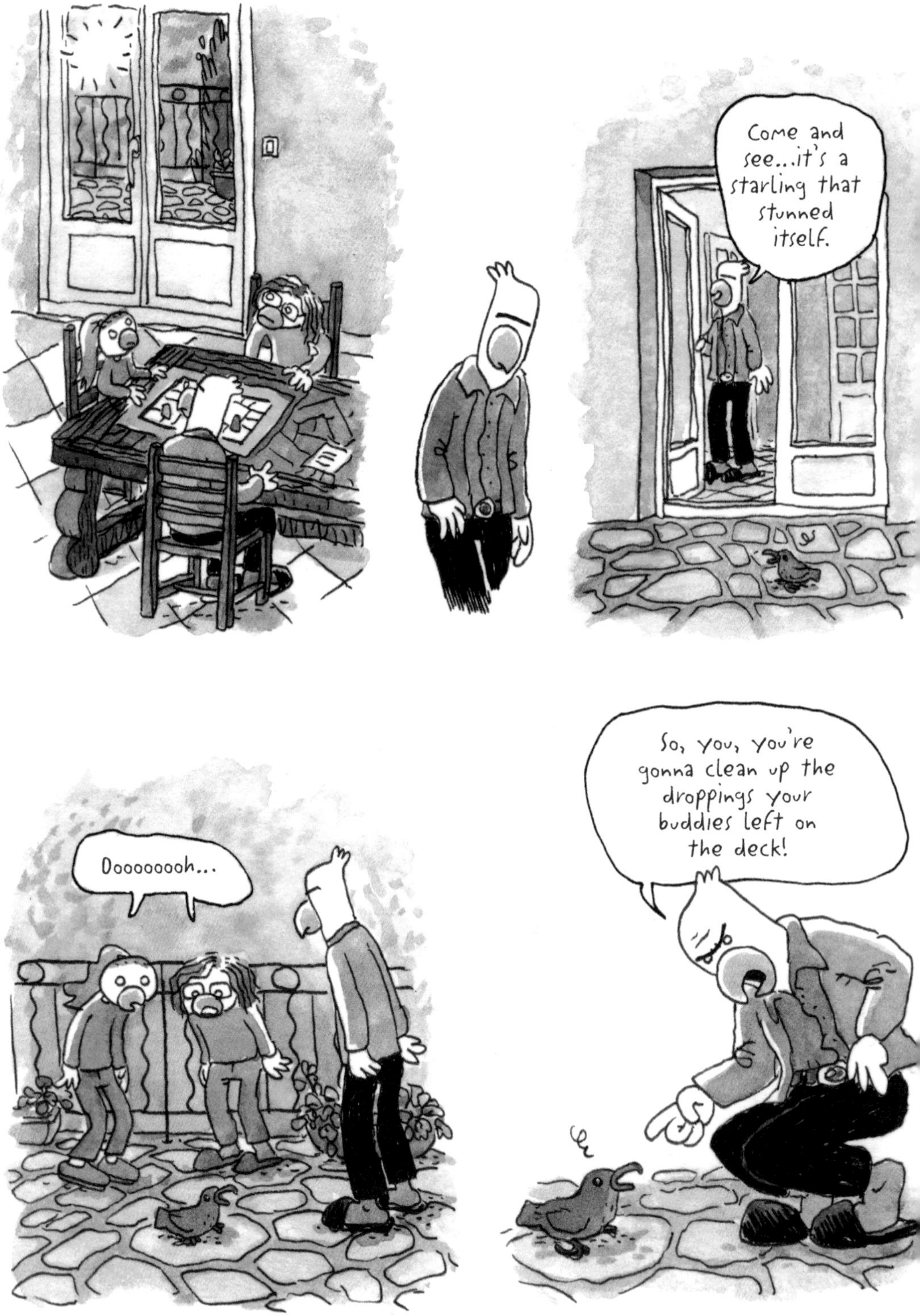

Come and see...it's a starling that stunned itself.
Doooooooh...
So, you, you're gonna clean up the droppings your buddies left on the deck!

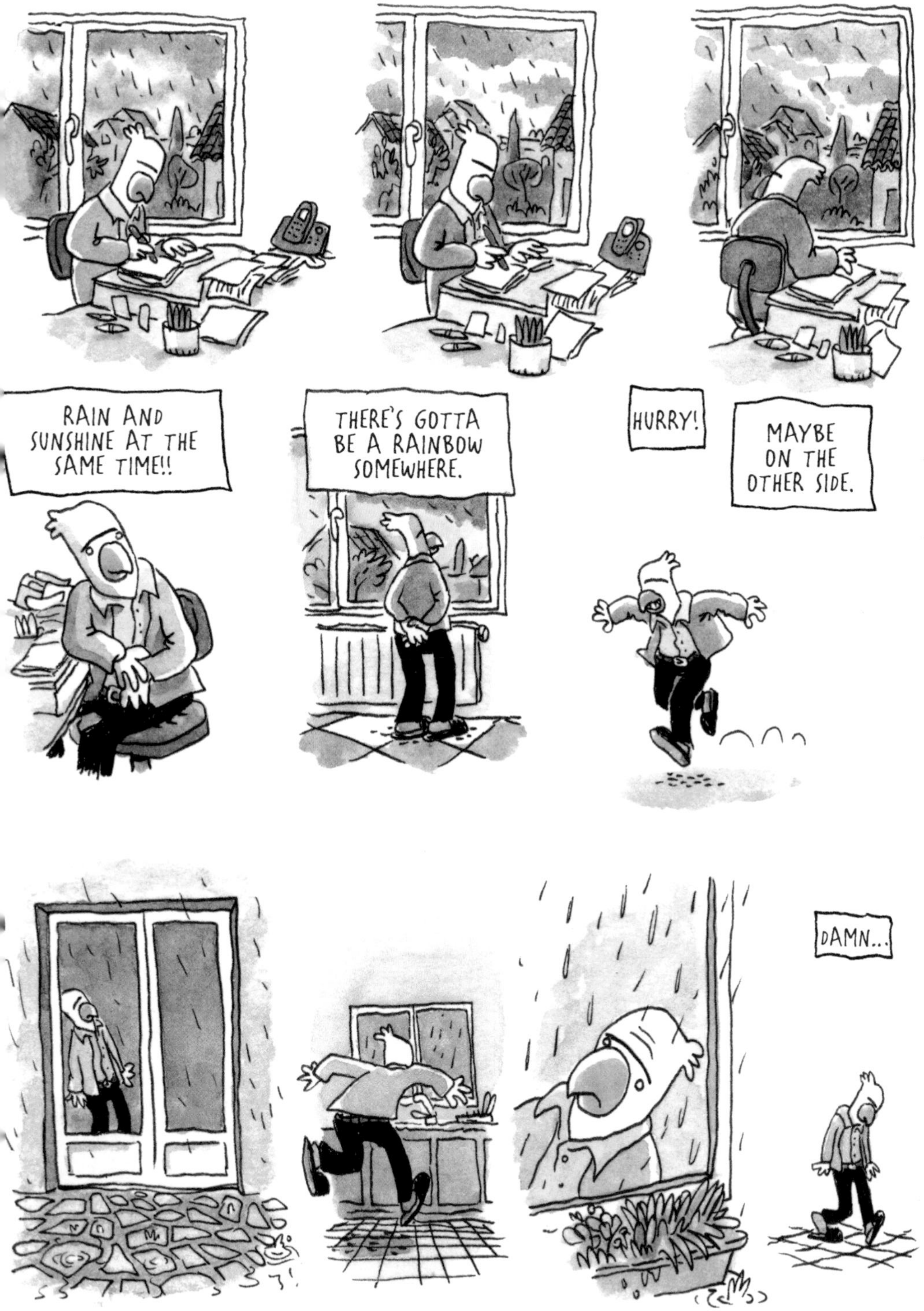
RAIN AND SUNSHINE AT THE SAME TIME!!
THERE'S GOTTA BE A RAINBOW SOMEWHERE.
HURRY!
MAYBE ON THE OTHER SIDE.
DAMN...

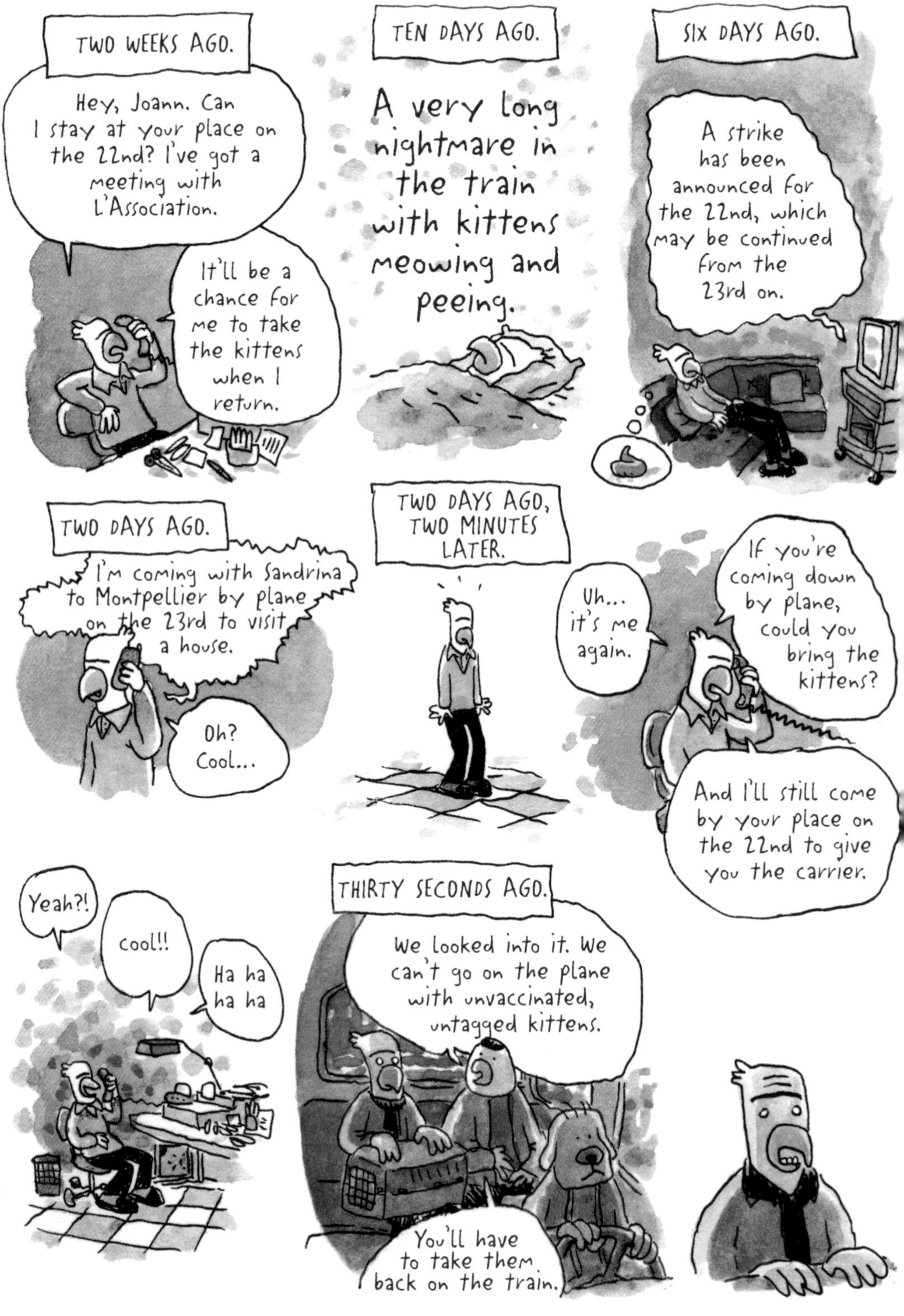
TWO WEEKS AGO.
Hey, Joann. Can I stay at your place on the 22nd? I've got a meeting with L'Association.
It'll be a chance for me to take the kittens when I return.
TEN DAYS AGO.
A very long nightmare in the train with kittens meowing and peeing.
SIX DAYS AGO.
A strike has been announced for the 22nd, which may be continued from the 23rd on.
TWO DAYS AGO.
I'm coming with Sandrina to Montpellier by plane on the 23rd to visit a house.
Oh? Cool...
TWO DAYS AGO, TWO MINUTES LATER.
Uh... it's me again.
If you're coming down by plane, could you bring the kittens?
And I'll still come by your place on the 22nd to give you the carrier.
Yeah?!
cool!!
Ha ha ha ha
THIRTY SECONDS AGO.
We looked into it. We can't go on the plane with unvaccinated, untagged kittens.
You'll have to take them back on the train.

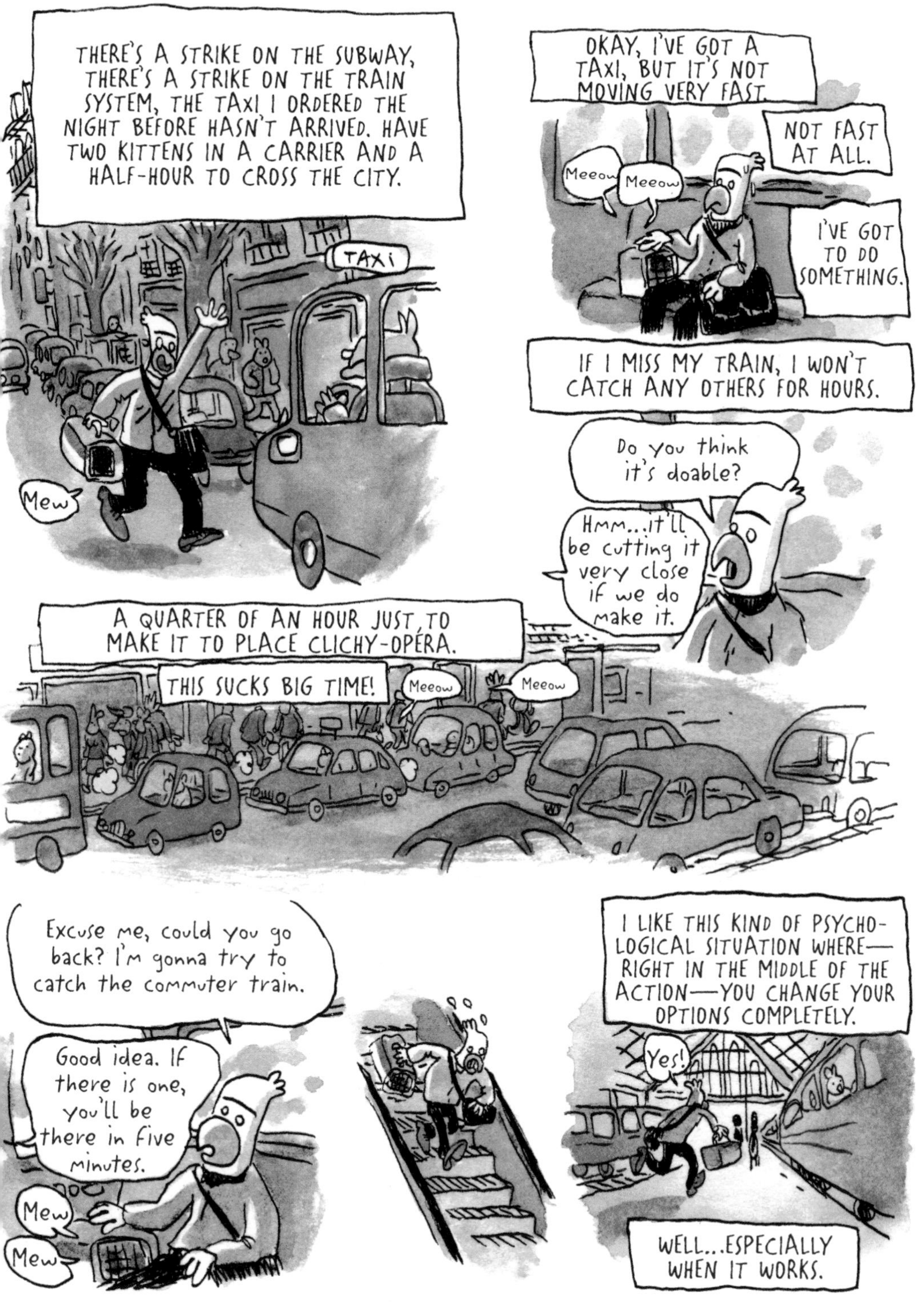
THERE'S A STRIKE ON THE SUBWAY, THERE'S A STRIKE ON THE TRAIN SYSTEM, THE TAXI I ORDERED THE NIGHT BEFORE HASN'T ARRIVED. HAVE TWO KITTENS IN A CARRIER AND A HALF-HOUR TO CROSS THE CITY.
TAXI
Mew
OKAY, I'VE GOT A TAXI, BUT IT'S NOT MOVING VERY FAST.
NOT FAST AT ALL.
Meeow
Meeow
I'VE GOT TO DO SOMETHING.
IF I MISS MY TRAIN, I WON'T CATCH ANY OTHERS FOR HOURS.
Do you think it's doable?
Hmm...it'll be cutting it very close if we do make it.
A QUARTER OF AN HOUR JUST TO MAKE IT TO PLACE CLICHY-OPÉRA.
THIS SUCKS BIG TIME!
Meeow
Meeow
Excuse me, could you go back? I'm gonna try to catch the commuter train.
Good idea. If there is one, you'll be there in five minutes.
Mew
Mew
I LIKE THIS KIND OF PSYCHOLOGICAL SITUATION WHERE—RIGHT IN THE MIDDLE OF THE ACTION—YOU CHANGE YOUR OPTIONS COMPLETELY.
Yes!
WELL...ESPECIALLY WHEN IT WORKS.

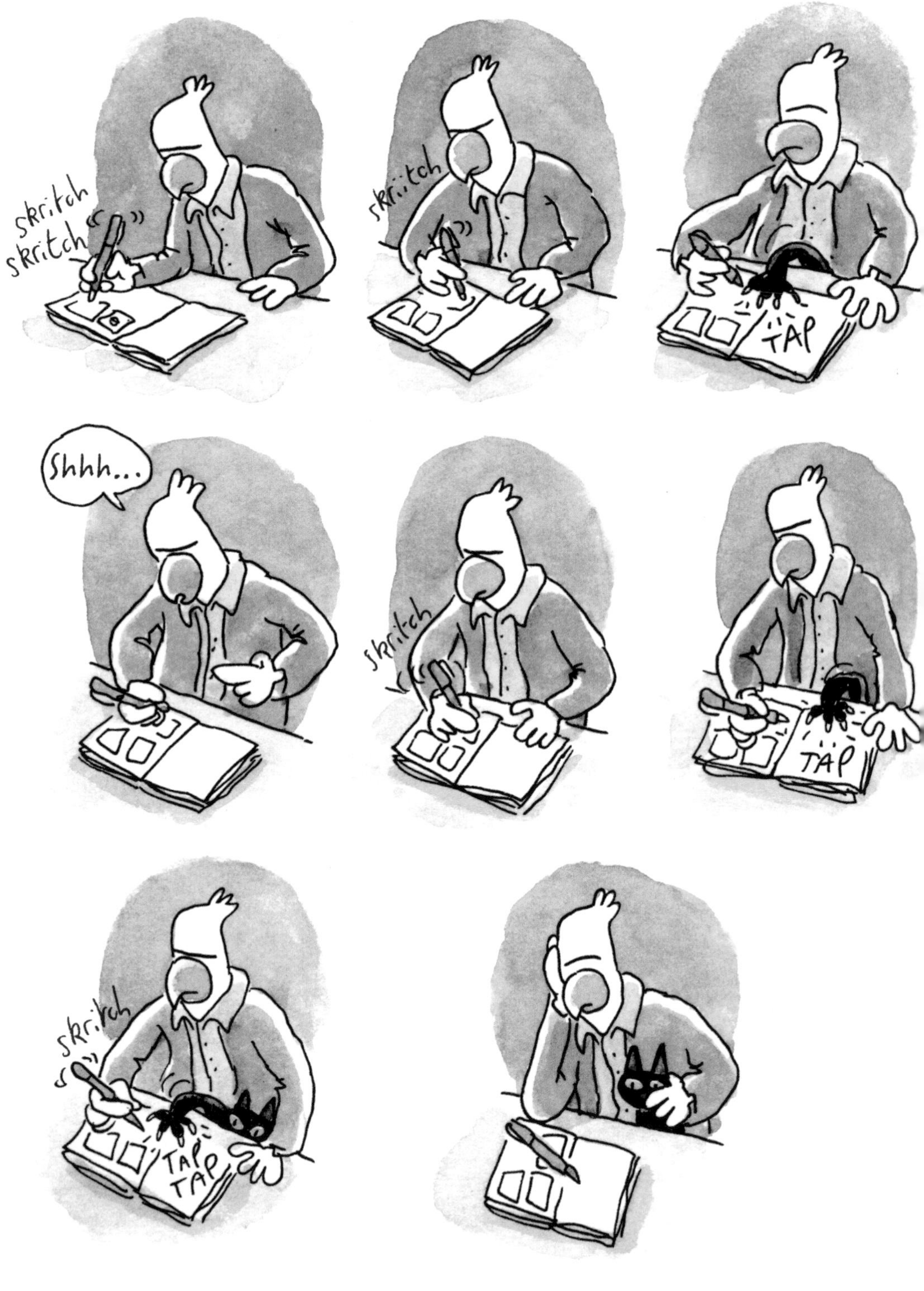
skritch
skritch
skritch
TAP
Shhh...
skritch
TAP
skritch
TAP
TAP

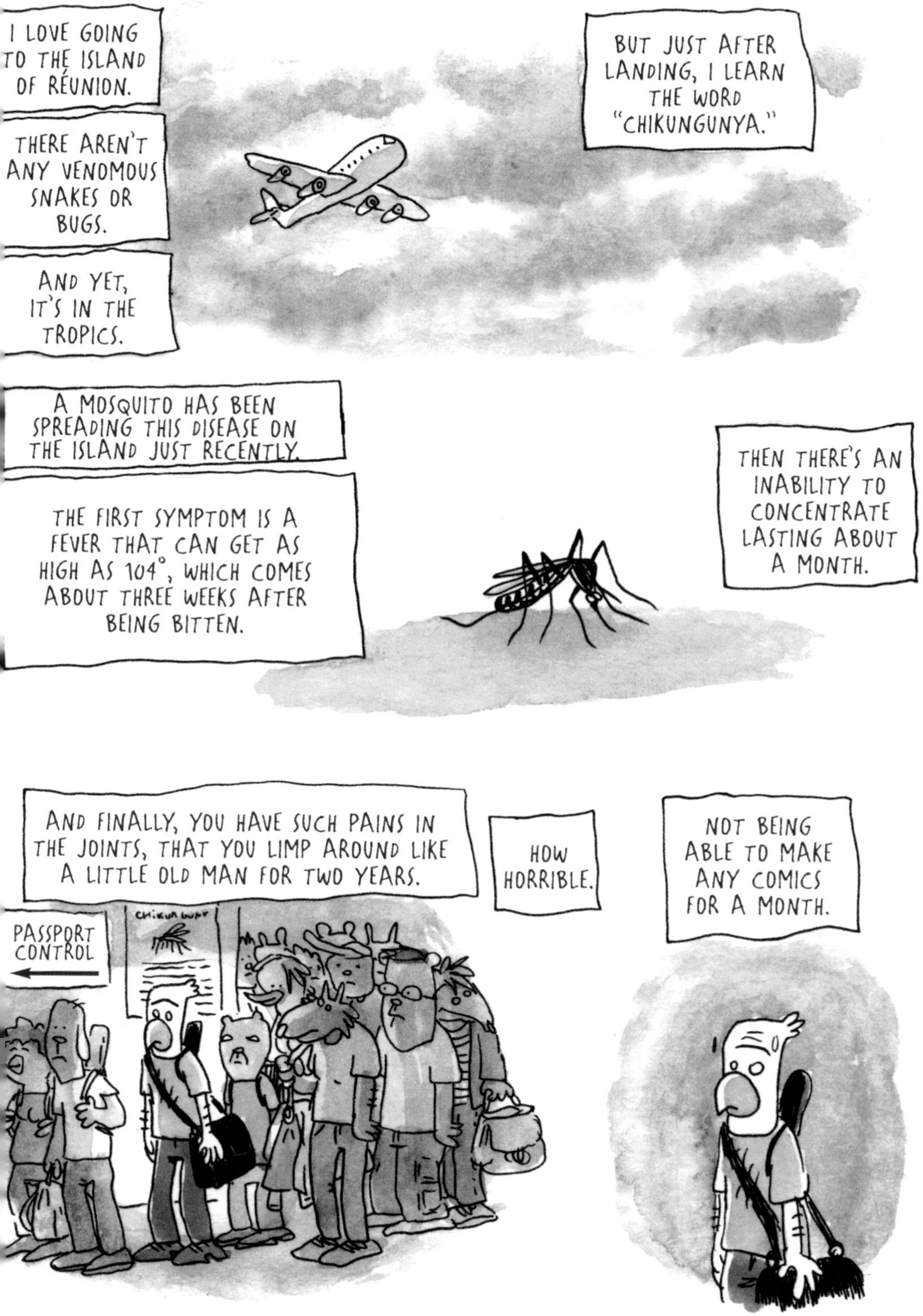

I LOVE GOING TO THE ISLAND OF RÉUNION.
THERE AREN'T ANY VENOMOUS SNAKES OR BUGS.
AND YET, IT'S IN THE TROPICS.
BUT JUST AFTER LANDING, I LEARN THE WORD "CHIKUNGUNYA."
A MOSQUITO HAS BEEN SPREADING THIS DISEASE ON THE ISLAND JUST RECENTLY.
THE FIRST SYMPTOM IS A FEVER THAT CAN GET AS HIGH AS 104°, WHICH COMES ABOUT THREE WEEKS AFTER BEING BITTEN.
THEN THERE'S AN INABILITY TO CONCENTRATE LASTING ABOUT A MONTH.
AND FINALLY, YOU HAVE SUCH PAINS IN THE JOINTS, THAT YOU LIMP AROUND LIKE A LITTLE OLD MAN FOR TWO YEARS.
HOW HORRIBLE.
NOT BEING ABLE TO MAKE ANY COMICS FOR A MONTH.
PASSPORT CONTROL

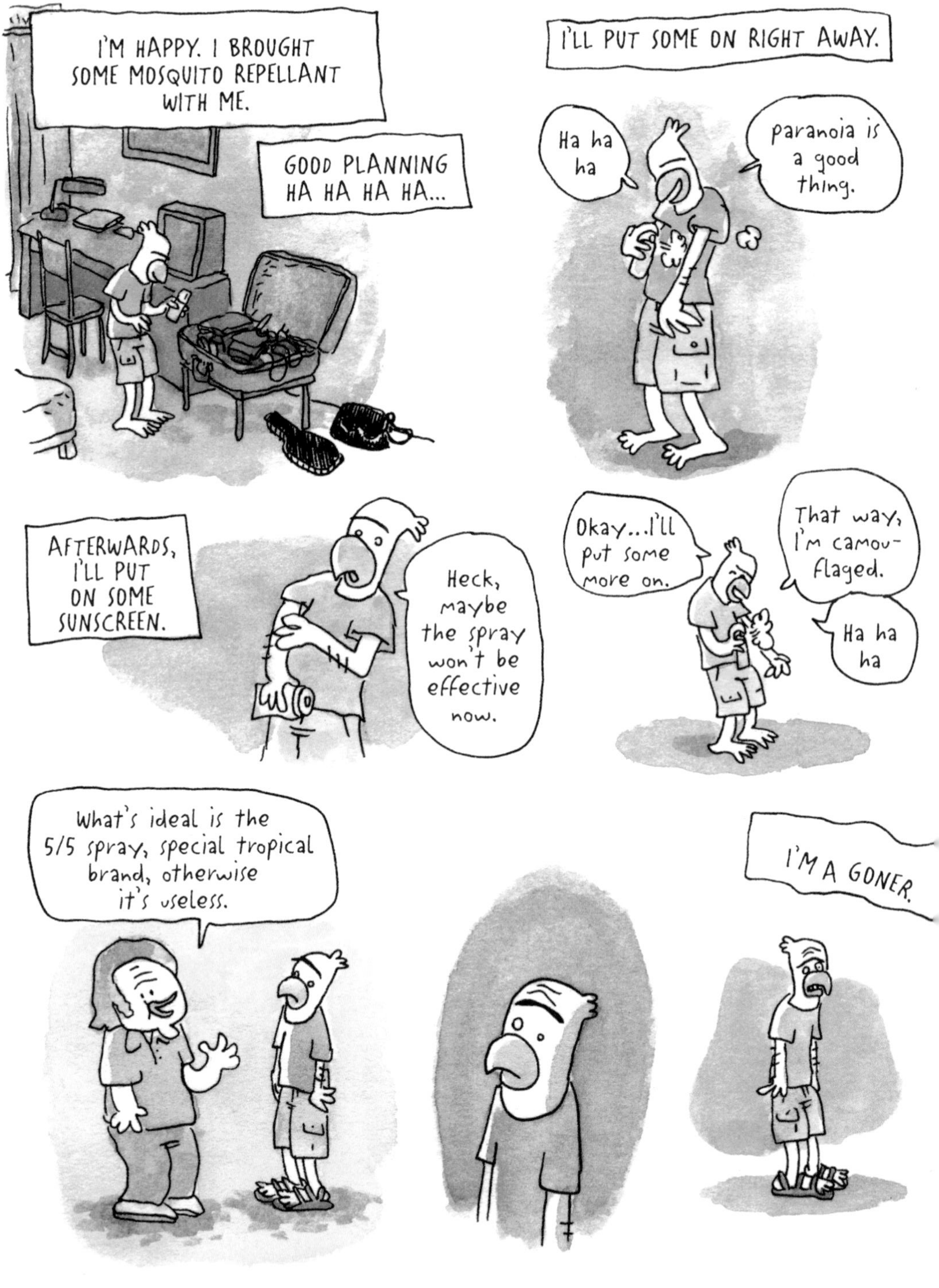
I'M HAPPY. I BROUGHT SOME MOSQUITO REPELLANT WITH ME.
GOOD PLANNING HA HA HA HA...
I'LL PUT SOME ON RIGHT AWAY.
Ha ha ha
paranoia is a good thing.
AFTERWARDS, I'LL PUT ON SOME SUNSCREEN.
Heck, maybe the spray won't be effective now.
Okay...I'll put some more on.
That way, I'm camouflaged.
Ha ha ha
What's ideal is the 5/5 spray, special tropical brand, otherwise it's useless.
I'M A GONER.

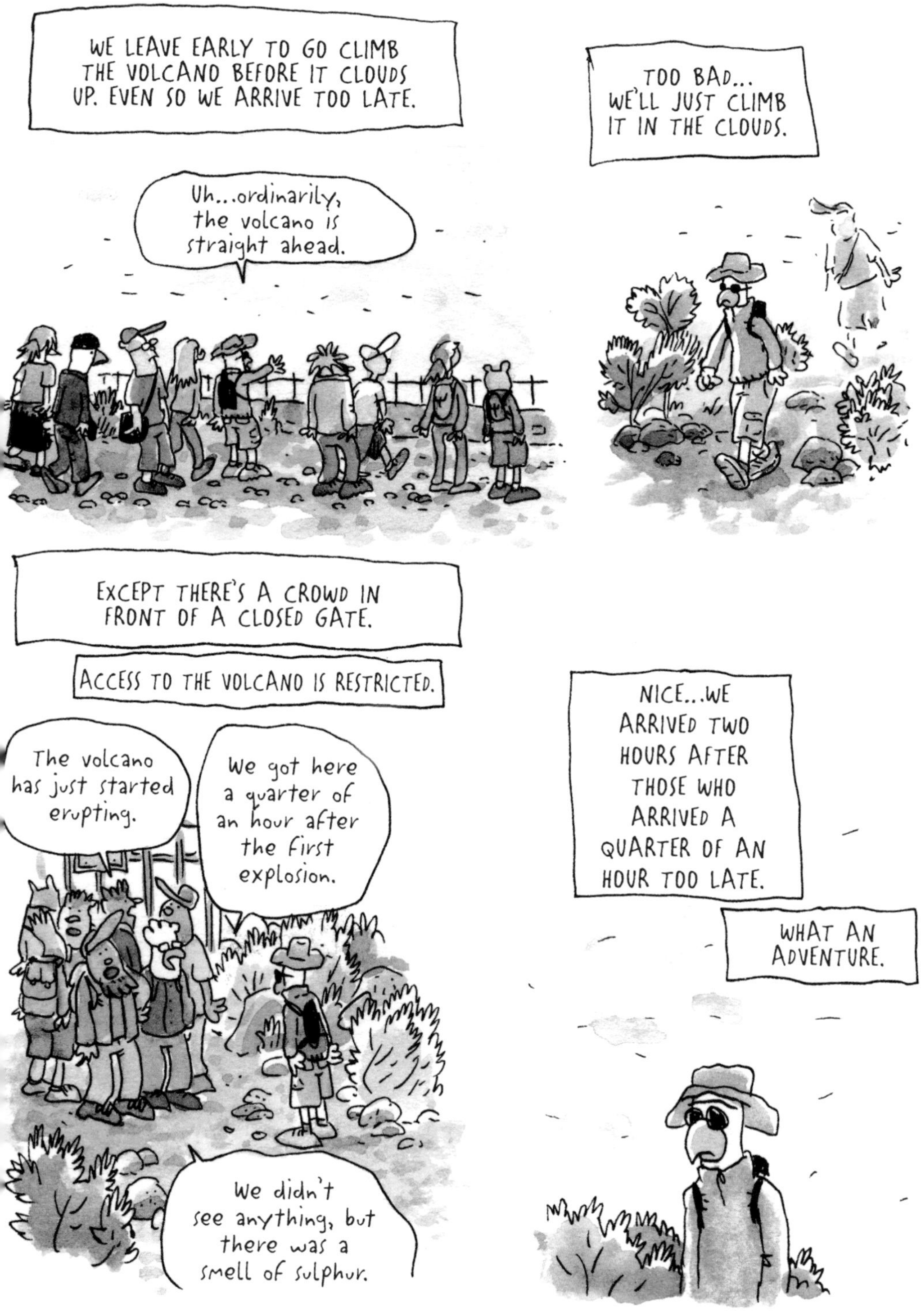
WE LEAVE EARLY TO GO CLIMB THE VOLCANO BEFORE IT CLOUDS UP. EVEN SO WE ARRIVE TOO LATE.
Uh...ordinarily, the volcano is straight ahead.
TOO BAD... WE'LL JUST CLIMB IT IN THE CLOUDS.
EXCEPT THERE'S A CROWD IN FRONT OF A CLOSED GATE.
ACCESS TO THE VOLCANO IS RESTRICTED.
The volcano has just started erupting.
We got here a quarter of an hour after the first explosion.
We didn't see anything, but there was a smell of sulphur.
NICE...WE ARRIVED TWO HOURS AFTER THOSE WHO ARRIVED A QUARTER OF AN HOUR TOO LATE.
WHAT AN ADVENTURE.

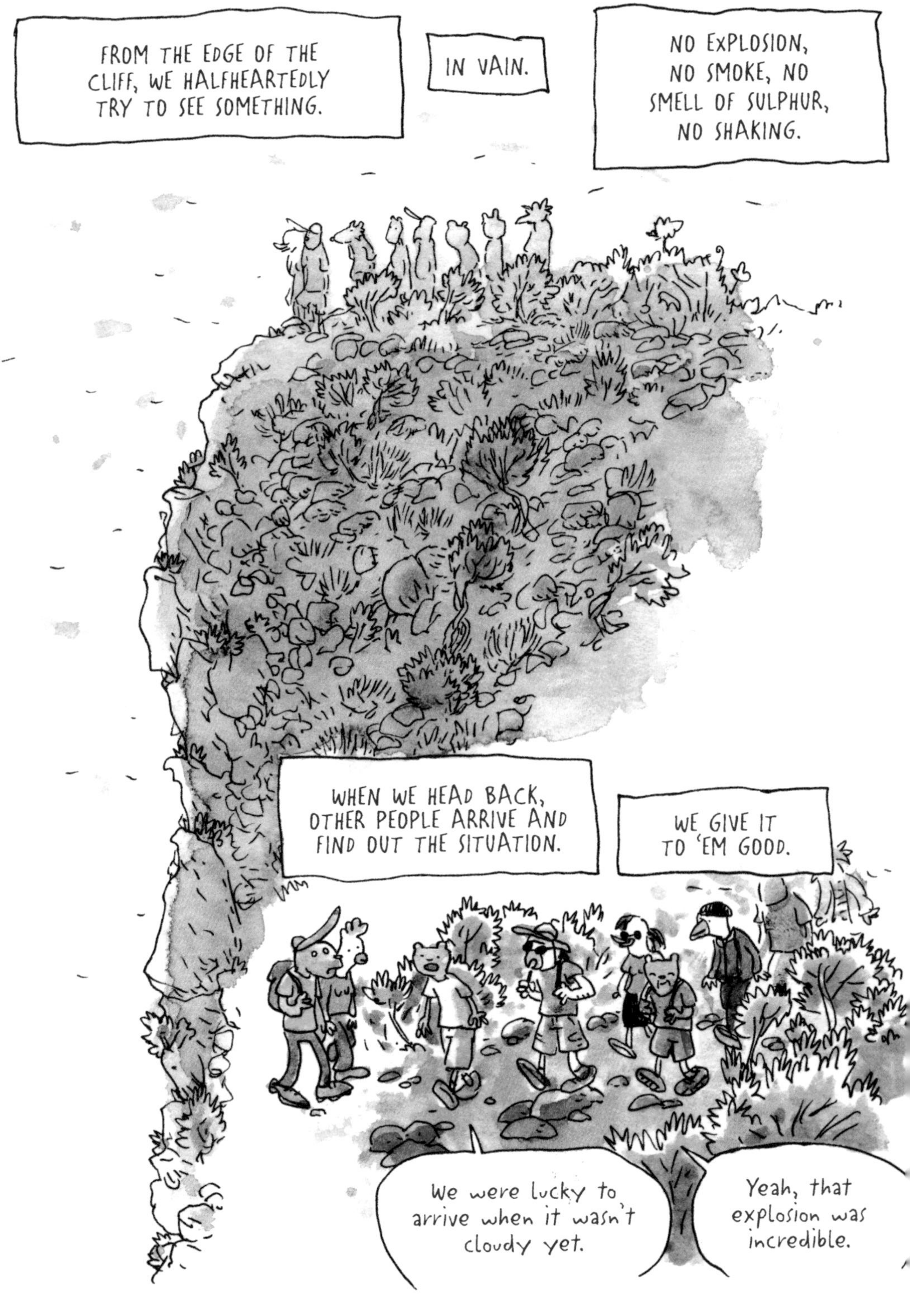
FROM THE EDGE OF THE CLIFF, WE HALFHEARTEDLY TRY TO SEE SOMETHING.
IN VAIN.
NO EXPLOSION, NO SMOKE, NO SMELL OF SULPHUR, NO SHAKING.
WHEN WE HEAD BACK, OTHER PEOPLE ARRIVE AND FIND OUT THE SITUATION.
WE GIVE IT TO 'EM GOOD.
We were lucky to arrive when it wasn't cloudy yet.
Yeah, that explosion was incredible.

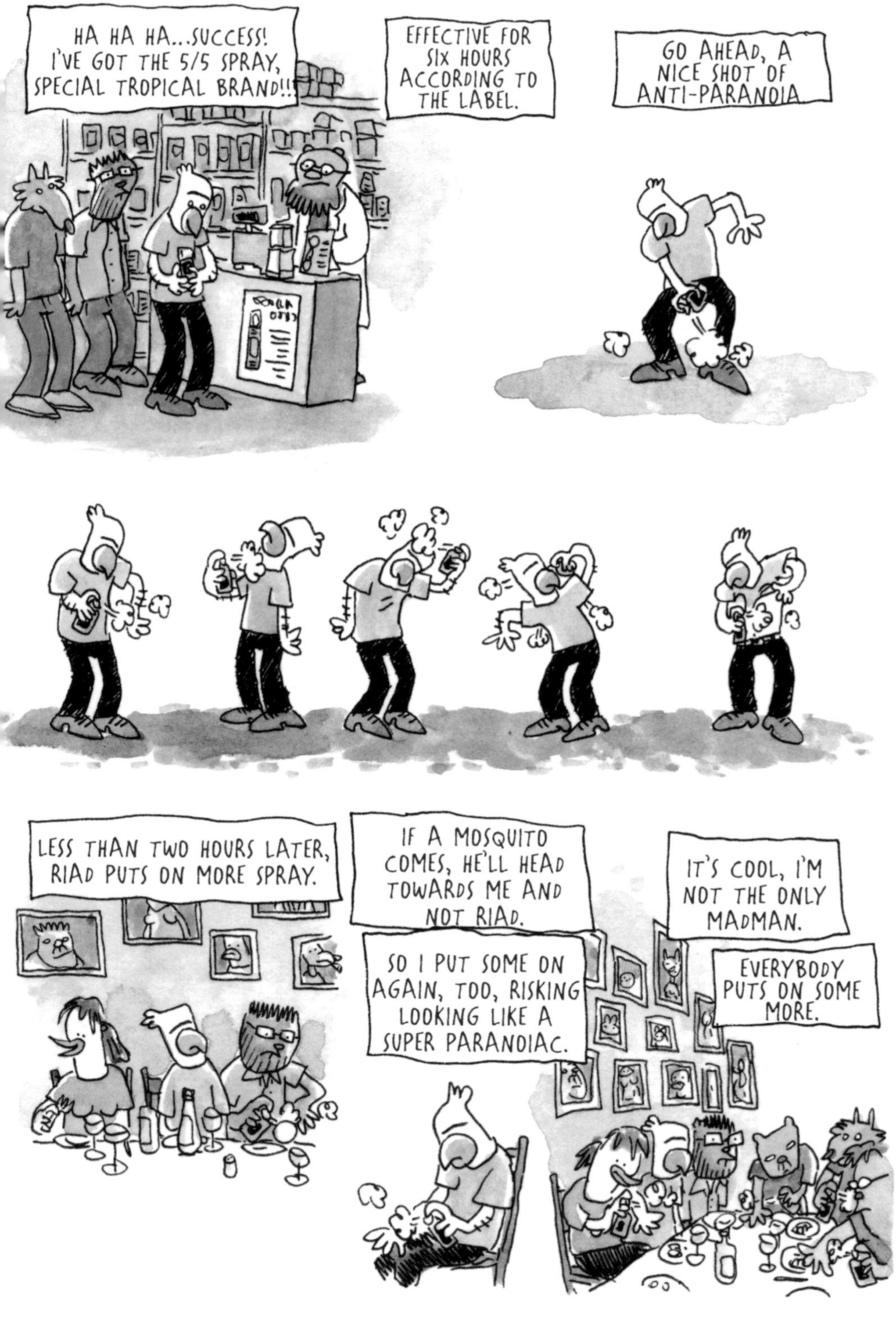

HA HA HA...SUCCESS! I'VE GOT THE 5/5 SPRAY, SPECIAL TROPICAL BRAND!!
EFFECTIVE FOR SIX HOURS ACCORDING TO THE LABEL.
GO AHEAD, A NICE SHOT OF ANTI-PARANOIA.
LESS THAN TWO HOURS LATER, RIAD PUTS ON MORE SPRAY.
IF A MOSQUITO COMES, HE'LL HEAD TOWARDS ME AND NOT RIAD.
SO I PUT SOME ON AGAIN, TOO, RISKING LOOKING LIKE A SUPER PARANOIAC.
IT'S COOL, I'M NOT THE ONLY MADMAN.
EVERYBODY PUTS ON SOME MORE.

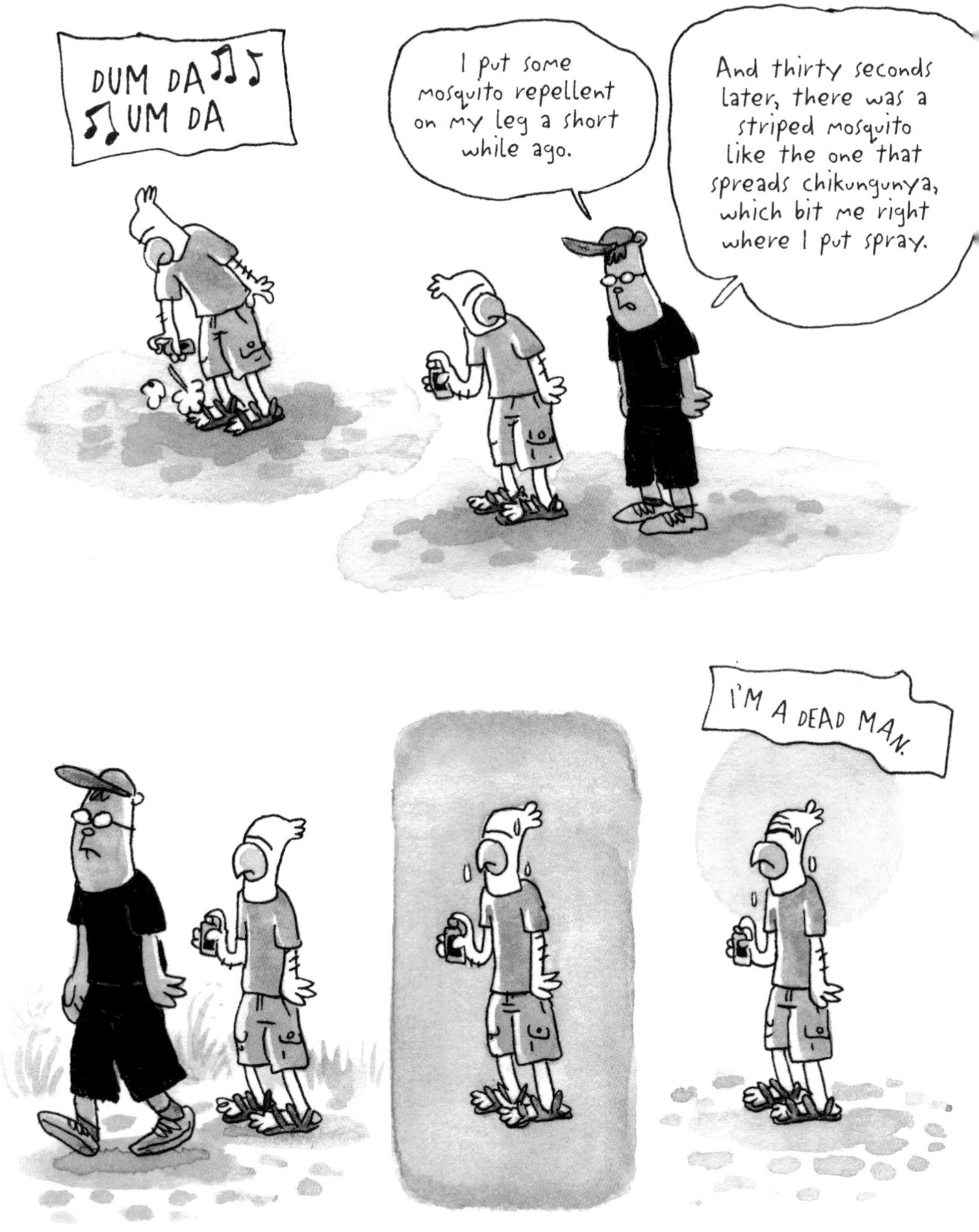
DUM DA ♫♪
♫ UM DA
I put some mosquito repellent on my leg a short while ago.
And thirty seconds later, there was a striped mosquito like the one that spreads chikungunya, which bit me right where I put spray.
I'M A DEAD MAN.

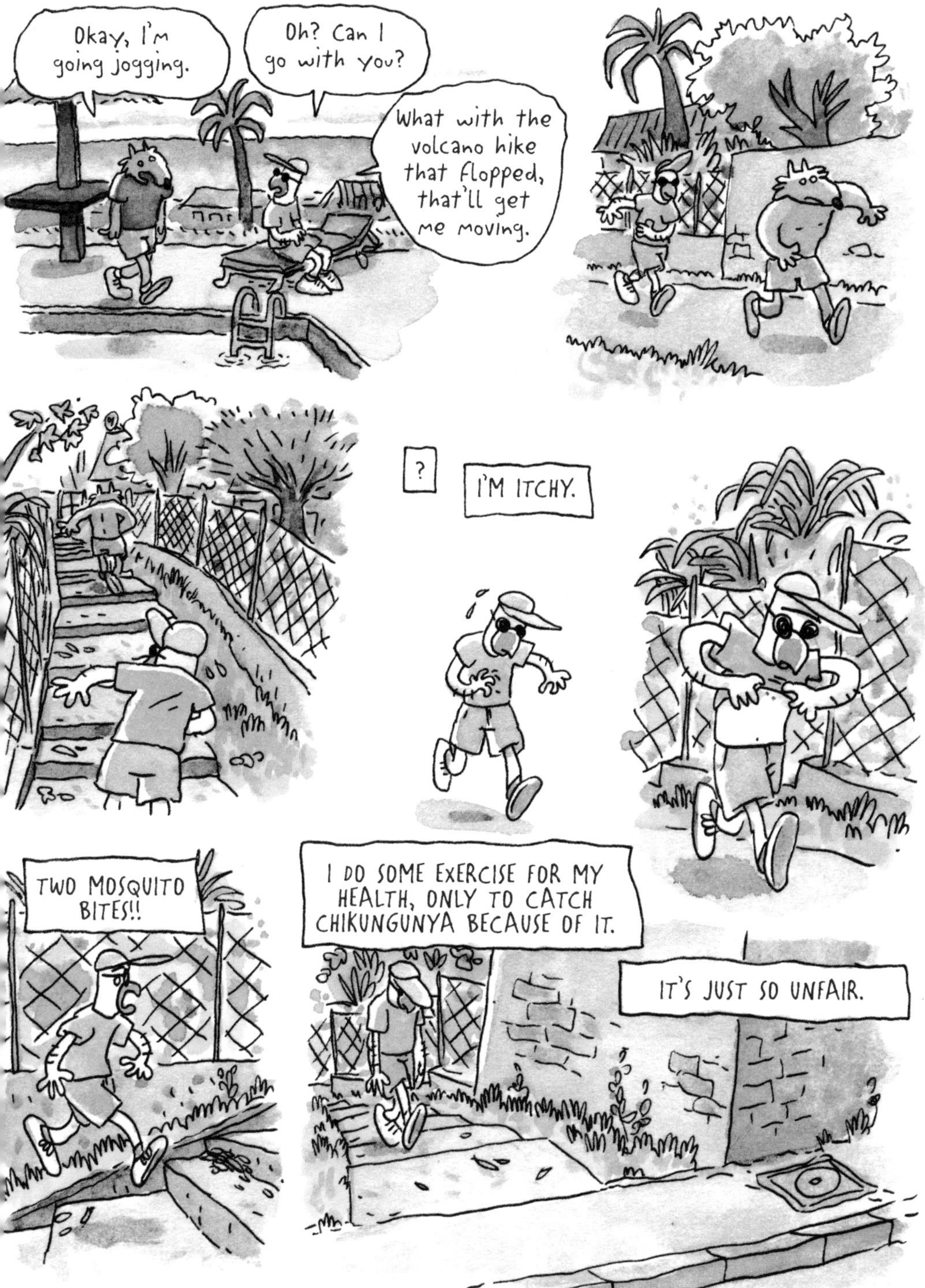
Okay, I'm going jogging.
Oh? Can I go with you?
What with the volcano hike that flopped, that'll get me moving.
?
I'M ITCHY.
TWO MOSQUITO BITES!!
I DO SOME EXERCISE FOR MY HEALTH, ONLY TO CATCH CHIKUNGUNYA BECAUSE OF IT.
IT'S JUST SO UNFAIR.

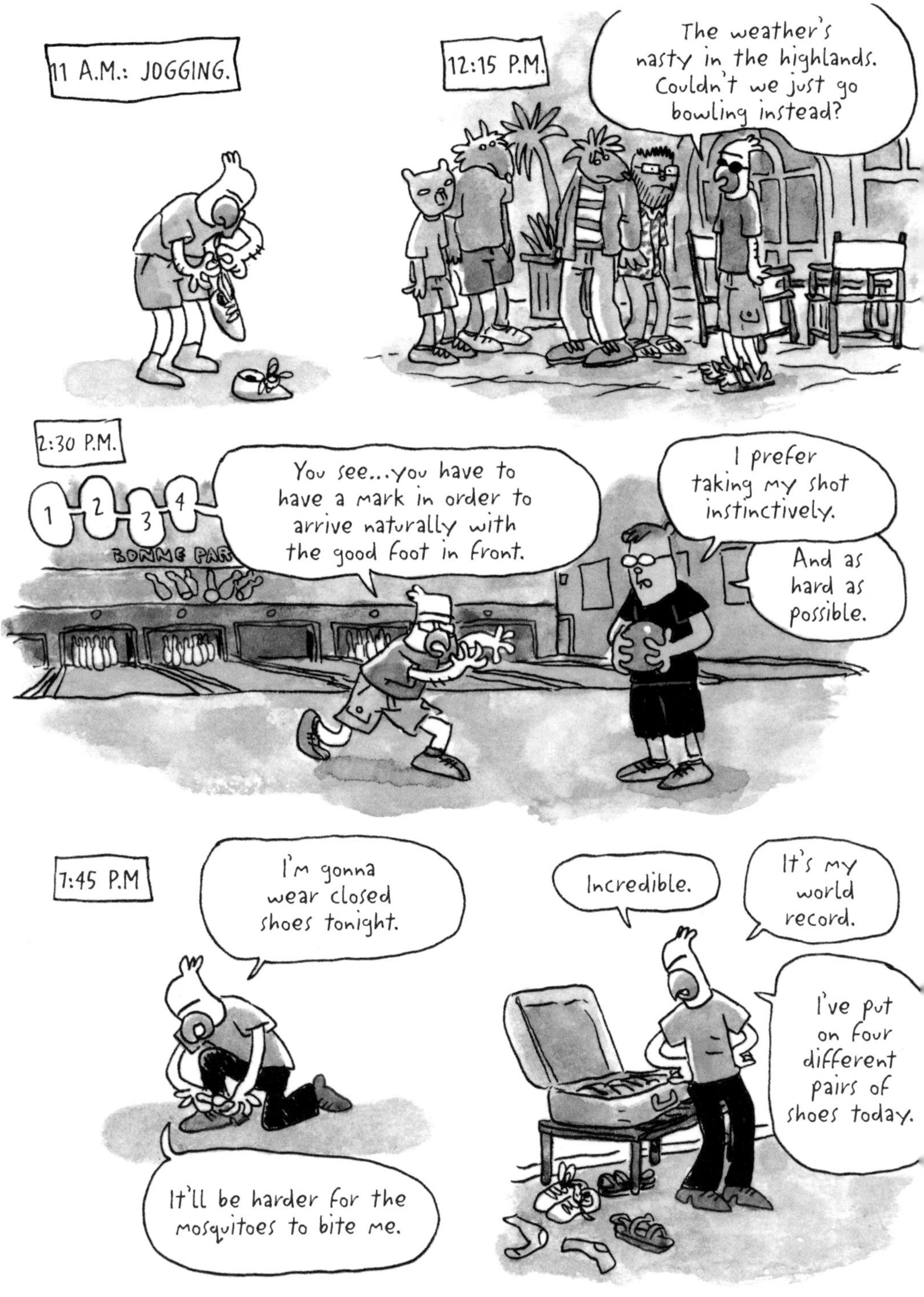
11 A.M.: JOGGING.
12:15 P.M.
The weather's nasty in the highlands. Couldn't we just go bowling instead?
2:30 P.M.
You see...you have to have a mark in order to arrive naturally with the good foot in front.
I prefer taking my shot instinctively.
And as hard as possible.
7:45 P.M
I'm gonna wear closed shoes tonight.
It'll be harder for the mosquitoes to bite me.
Incredible.
It's my world record.
I've put on four different pairs of shoes today.

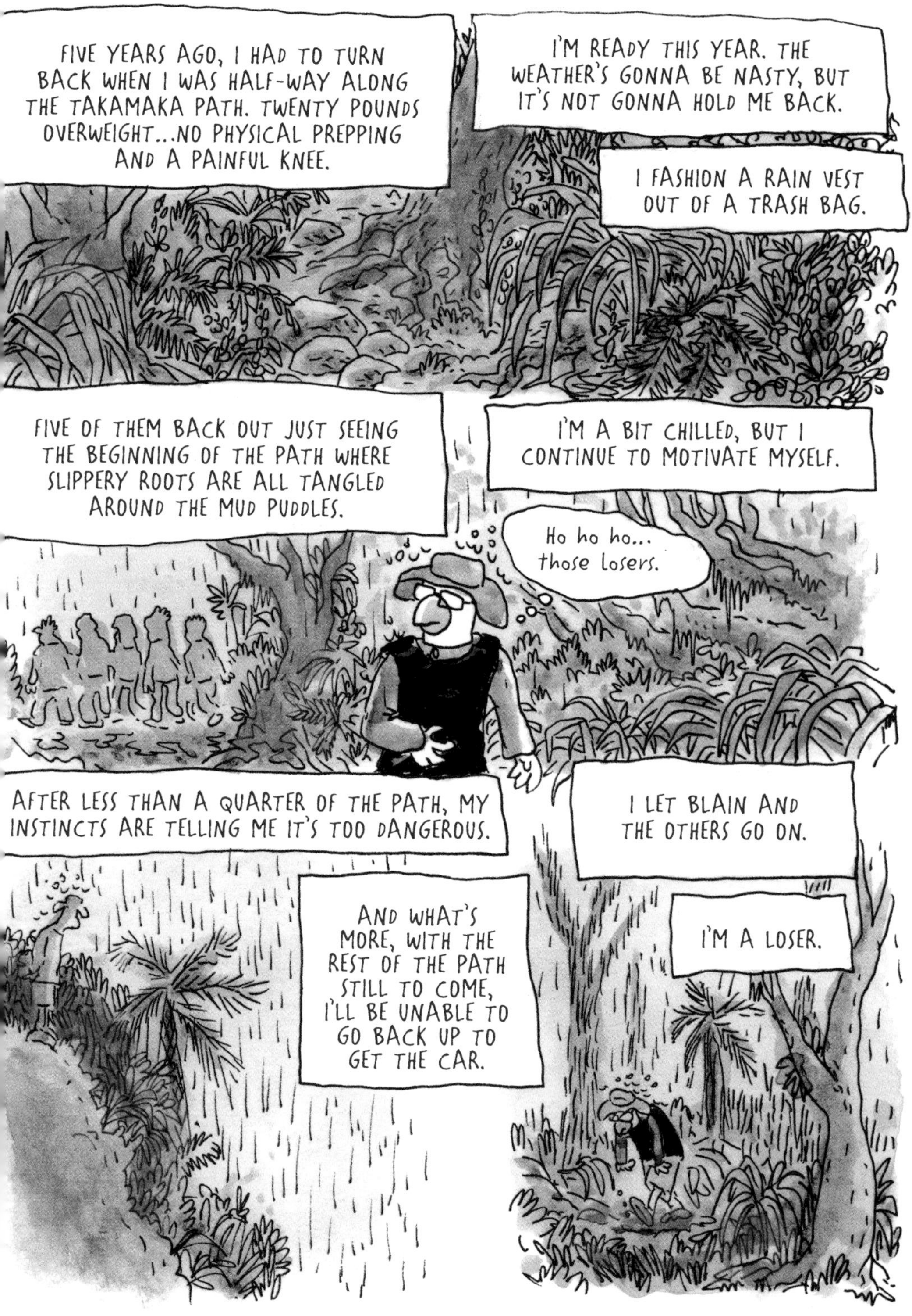
FIVE YEARS AGO, I HAD TO TURN BACK WHEN I WAS HALF-WAY ALONG THE TAKAMAKA PATH. TWENTY POUNDS OVERWEIGHT...NO PHYSICAL PREPPING AND A PAINFUL KNEE.
I'M READY THIS YEAR. THE WEATHER'S GONNA BE NASTY, BUT IT'S NOT GONNA HOLD ME BACK.
I FASHION A RAIN VEST OUT OF A TRASH BAG.
FIVE OF THEM BACK OUT JUST SEEING THE BEGINNING OF THE PATH WHERE SLIPPERY ROOTS ARE ALL TANGLED AROUND THE MUD PUDDLES.
I'M A BIT CHILLED, BUT I CONTINUE TO MOTIVATE MYSELF.
Ho ho ho... those losers.
AFTER LESS THAN A QUARTER OF THE PATH, MY INSTINCTS ARE TELLING ME IT'S TOO DANGEROUS.
AND WHAT'S MORE, WITH THE REST OF THE PATH STILL TO COME, I'LL BE UNABLE TO GO BACK UP TO GET THE CAR.
I LET BLAIN AND THE OTHERS GO ON.
I'M A LOSER.

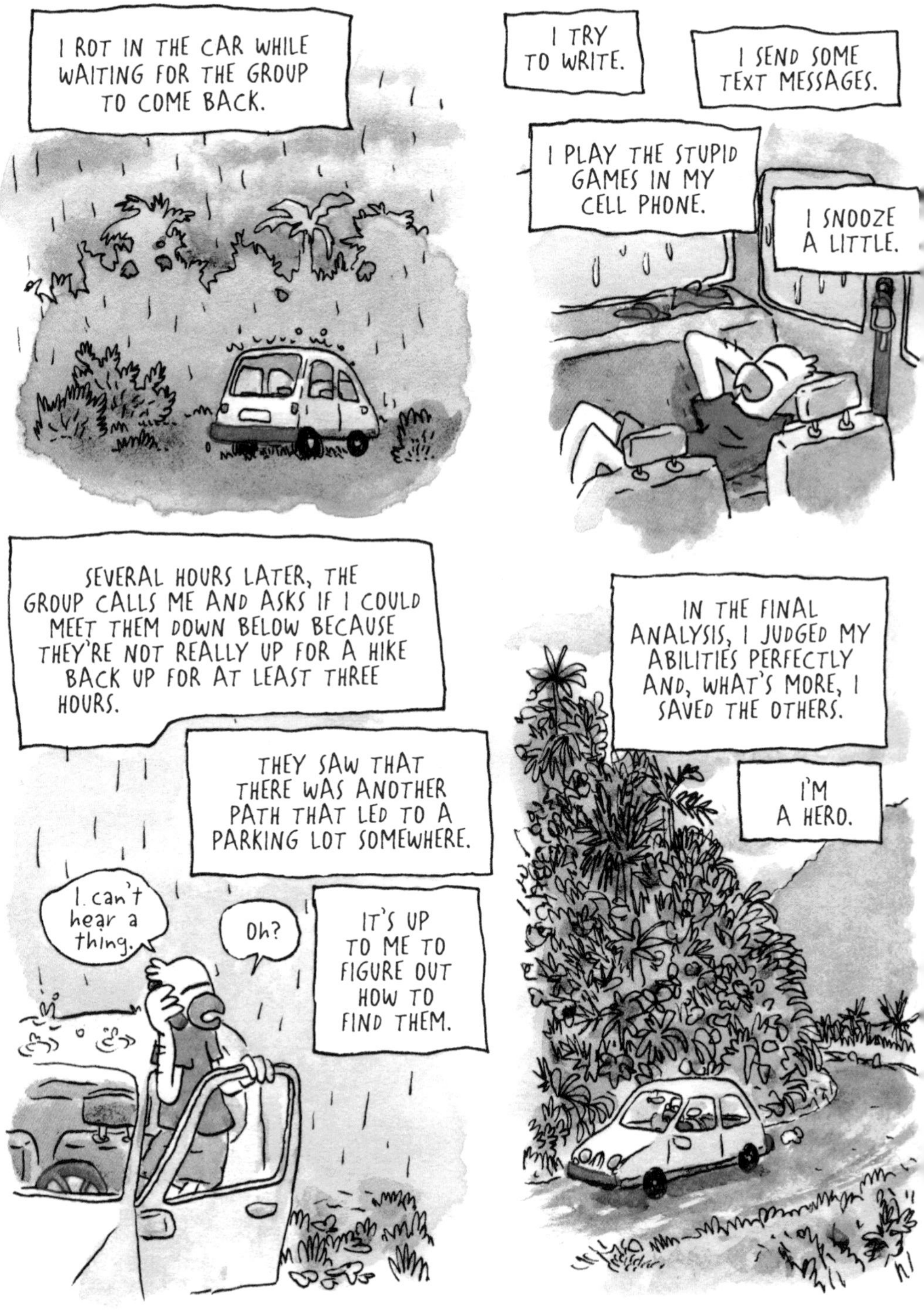
I ROT IN THE CAR WHILE WAITING FOR THE GROUP TO COME BACK.
I TRY TO WRITE.
I SEND SOME TEXT MESSAGES.
I PLAY THE STUPID GAMES IN MY CELL PHONE.
I SNOOZE A LITTLE.
SEVERAL HOURS LATER, THE GROUP CALLS ME AND ASKS IF I COULD MEET THEM DOWN BELOW BECAUSE THEY'RE NOT REALLY UP FOR A HIKE BACK UP FOR AT LEAST THREE HOURS.
THEY SAW THAT THERE WAS ANOTHER PATH THAT LED TO A PARKING LOT SOMEWHERE.
I can't hear a thing.
Oh?
IT'S UP TO ME TO FIGURE OUT HOW TO FIND THEM.
IN THE FINAL ANALYSIS, I JUDGED MY ABILITIES PERFECTLY AND, WHAT'S MORE, I SAVED THE OTHERS.
I'M A HERO.

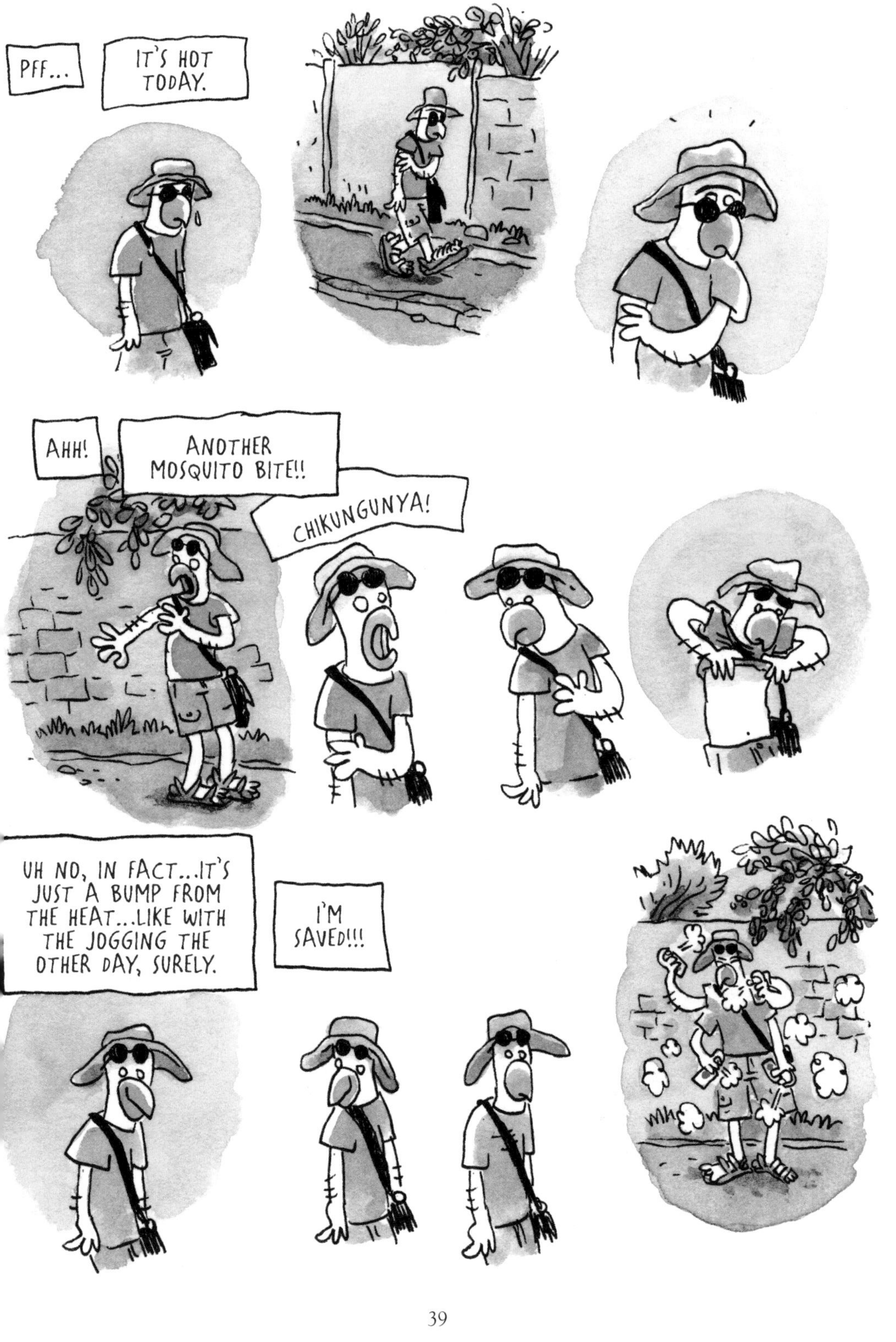
PFF...
IT'S HOT TODAY.
AHH!
ANOTHER MOSQUITO BITE!!
CHIKUNGUNYA!
UH NO, IN FACT...IT'S JUST A BUMP FROM THE HEAT...LIKE WITH THE JOGGING THE OTHER DAY, SURELY.
I'M SAVED!!!

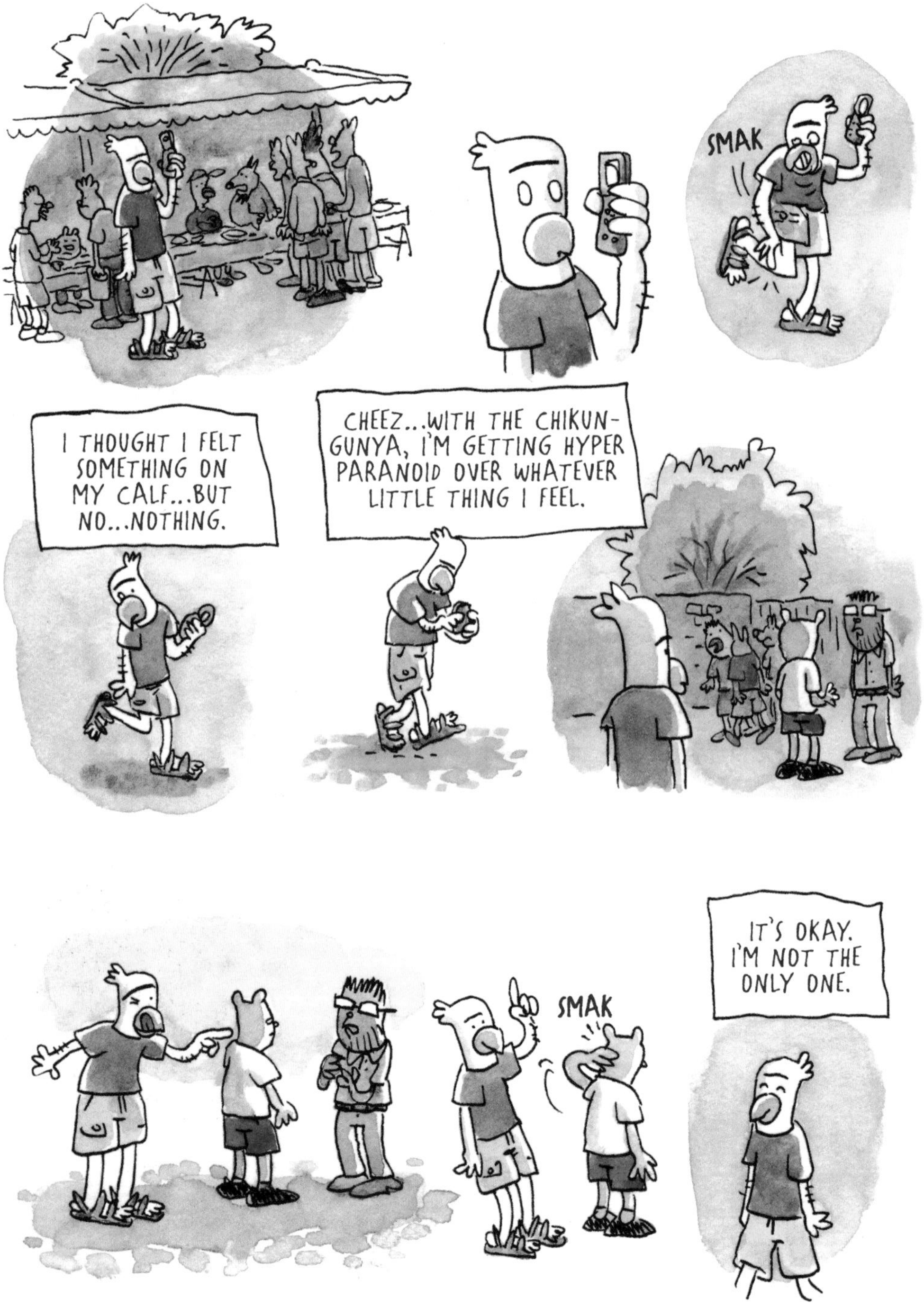
SMAK
I THOUGHT I FELT SOMETHING ON MY CALF...BUT NO...NOTHING.
CHEEZ...WITH THE CHIKUN-GUNYA, I'M GETTING HYPER PARANOID OVER WHATEVER LITTLE THING I FEEL.
SMAK
IT'S OKAY. I'M NOT THE ONLY ONE.

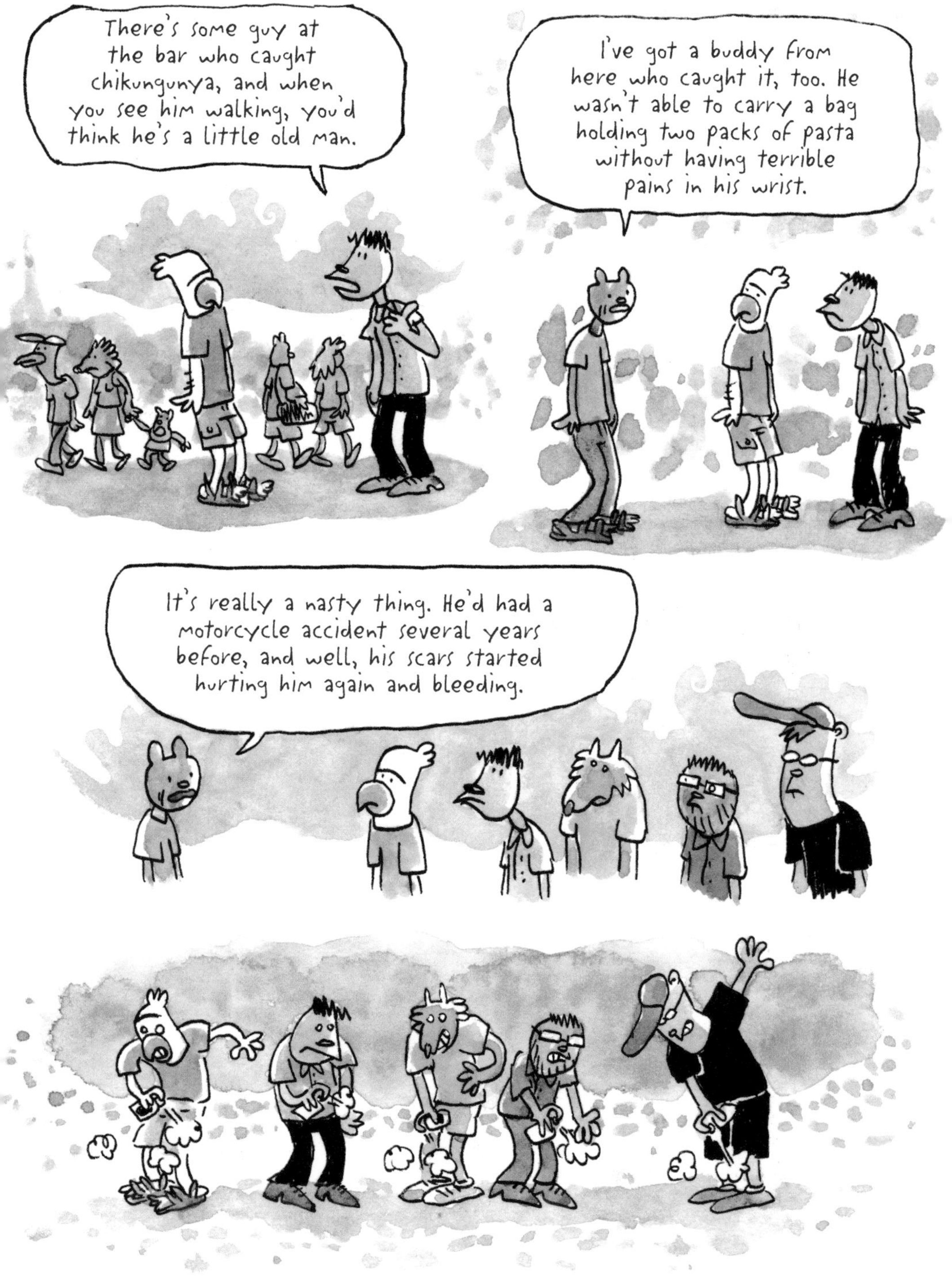
There's some guy at the bar who caught chikungunya, and when you see him walking, you'd think he's a little old man.
I've got a buddy from here who caught it, too. He wasn't able to carry a bag holding two packs of pasta without having terrible pains in his wrist.
It's really a nasty thing. He'd had a motorcycle accident several years before, and well, his scars started hurting him again and bleeding.

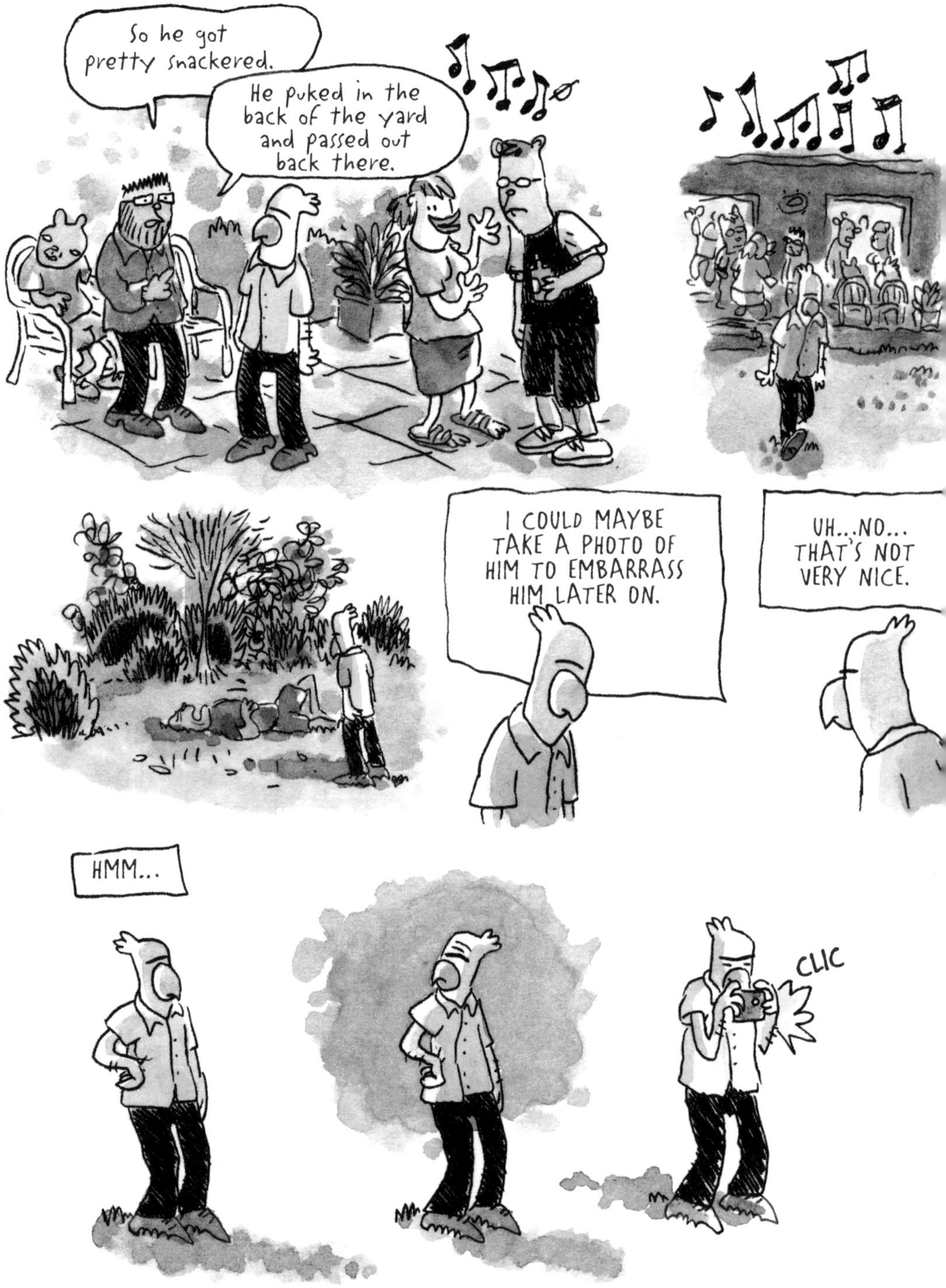

So he got pretty snackered.
He puked in the back of the yard and passed out back there.
I COULD MAYBE TAKE A PHOTO OF HIM TO EMBARRASS HIM LATER ON.
UH...NO... THAT'S NOT VERY NICE.
HMM...
CLIC

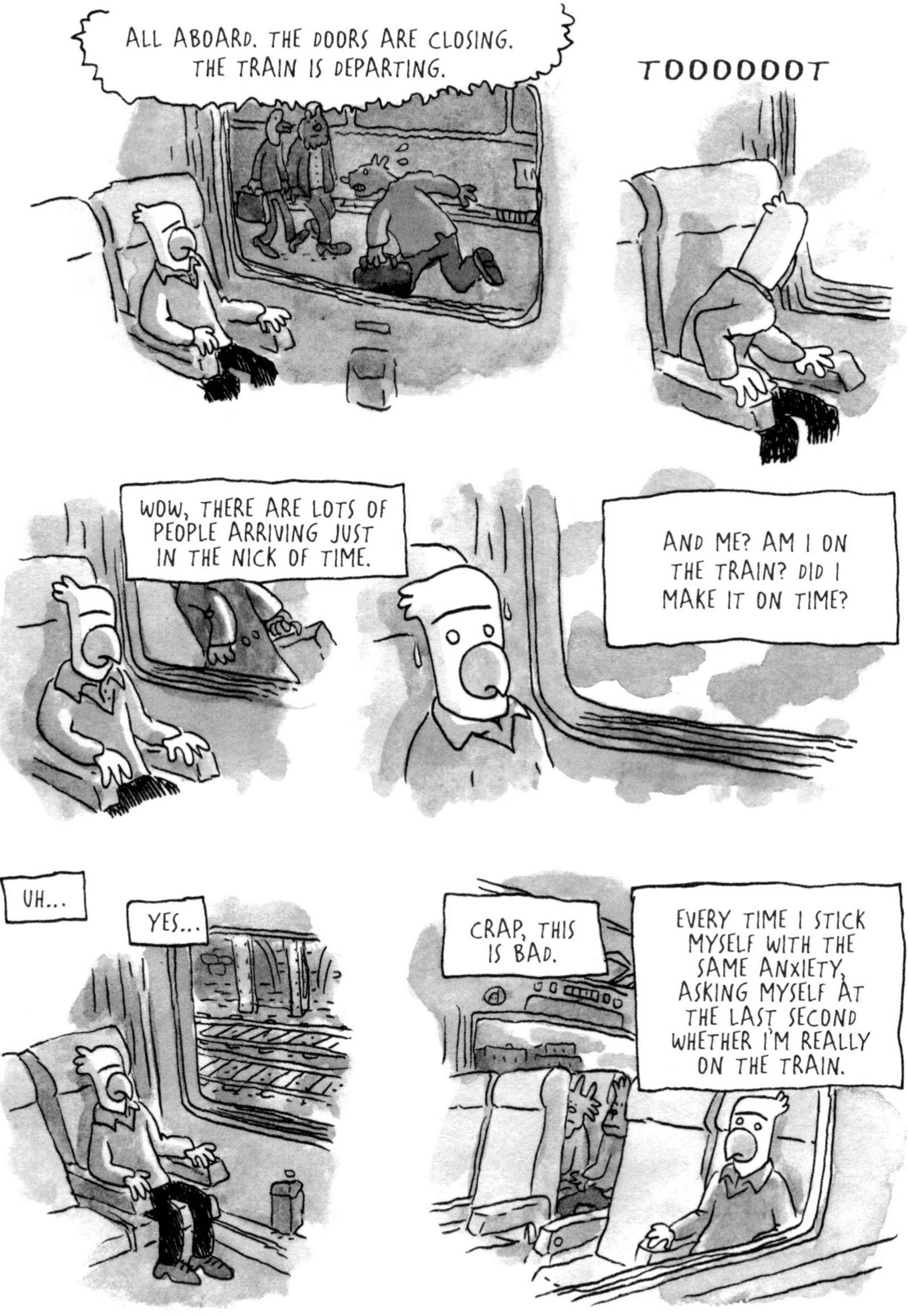
ALL ABOARD. THE DOORS ARE CLOSING. THE TRAIN IS DEPARTING.
TOOOOOOT
WOW, THERE ARE LOTS OF PEOPLE ARRIVING JUST IN THE NICK OF TIME.
AND ME? AM I ON THE TRAIN? DID I MAKE IT ON TIME?
UH...
YES...
CRAP, THIS IS BAD.
EVERY TIME I STICK MYSELF WITH THE SAME ANXIETY, ASKING MYSELF AT THE LAST SECOND WHETHER I'M REALLY ON THE TRAIN.

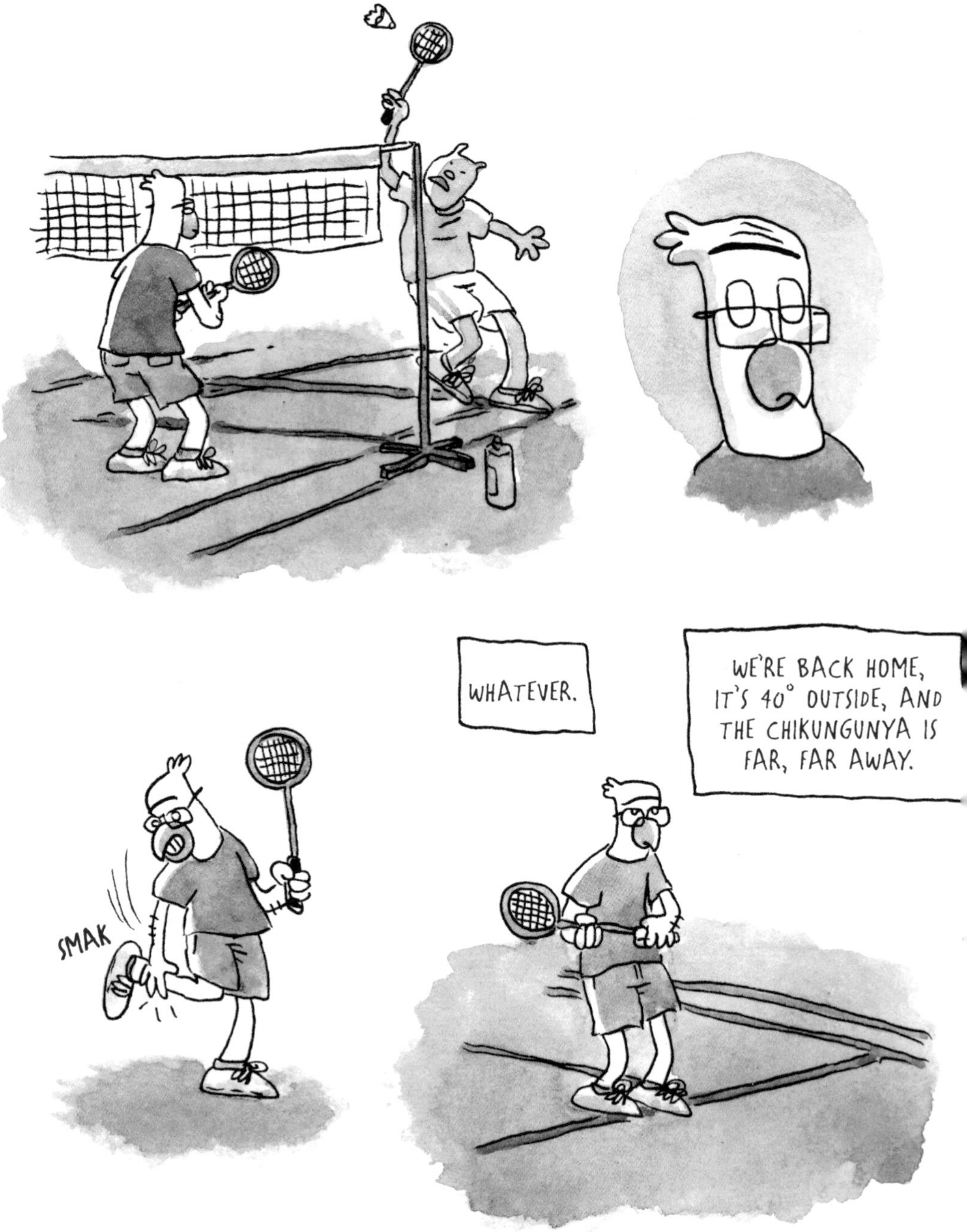
SMAK
WHATEVER.
WE'RE BACK HOME, IT'S 40° OUTSIDE, AND THE CHIKUNGUNYA IS FAR, FAR AWAY.

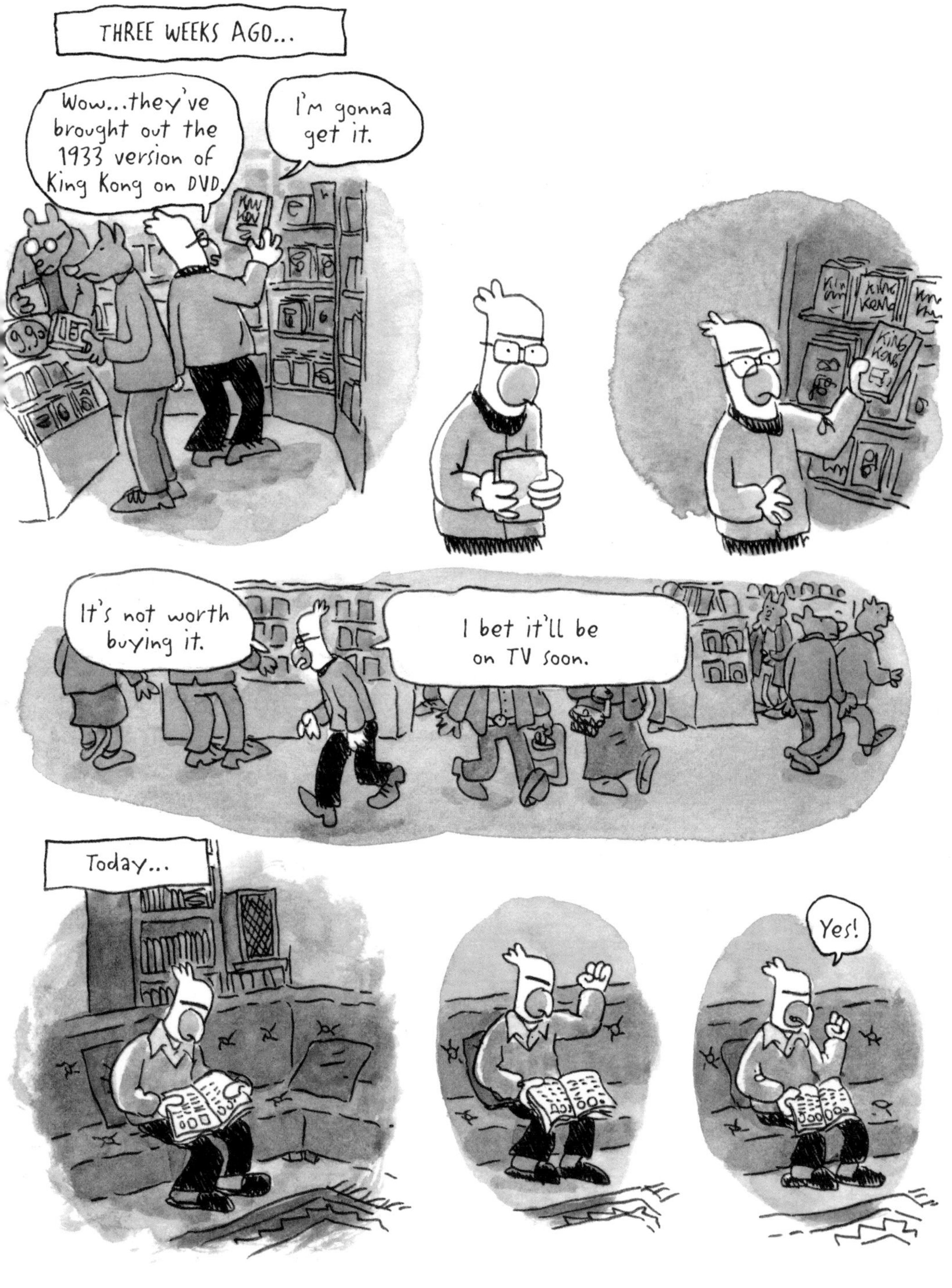
THREE WEEKS AGO...
Wow...they've brought out the 1933 version of King Kong on DVD.
I'm gonna get it.
It's not worth buying it.
I bet it'll be on TV soon.
Today...
Yes!

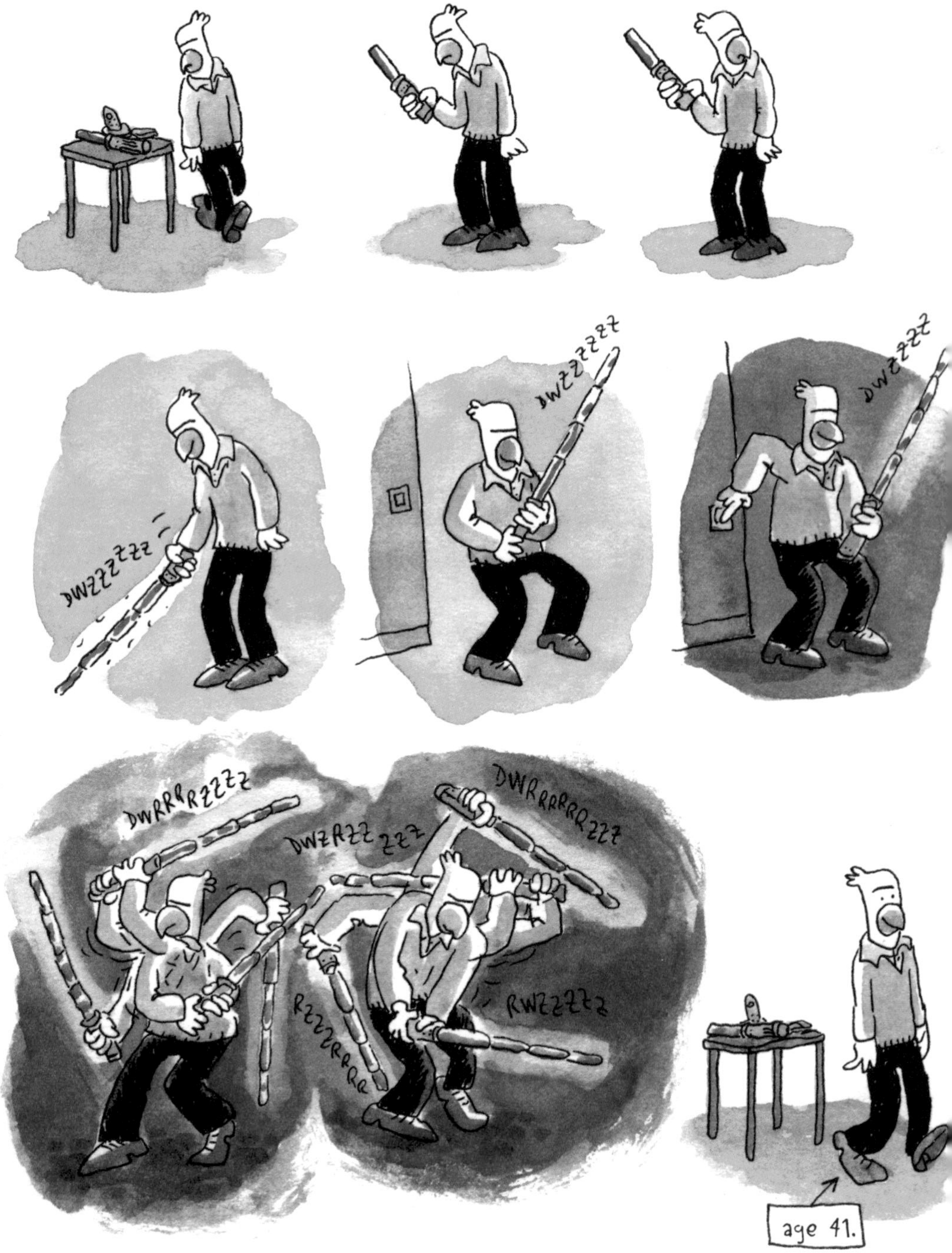
DWZZZZZZ
DWZZZZZZZ
DWZZZZ
DWRRRRZZZZ
DWZRZZZZZ
DWRRRRRRRZZZ
RZZZZRRRR
RWZZZZZ
age 41.

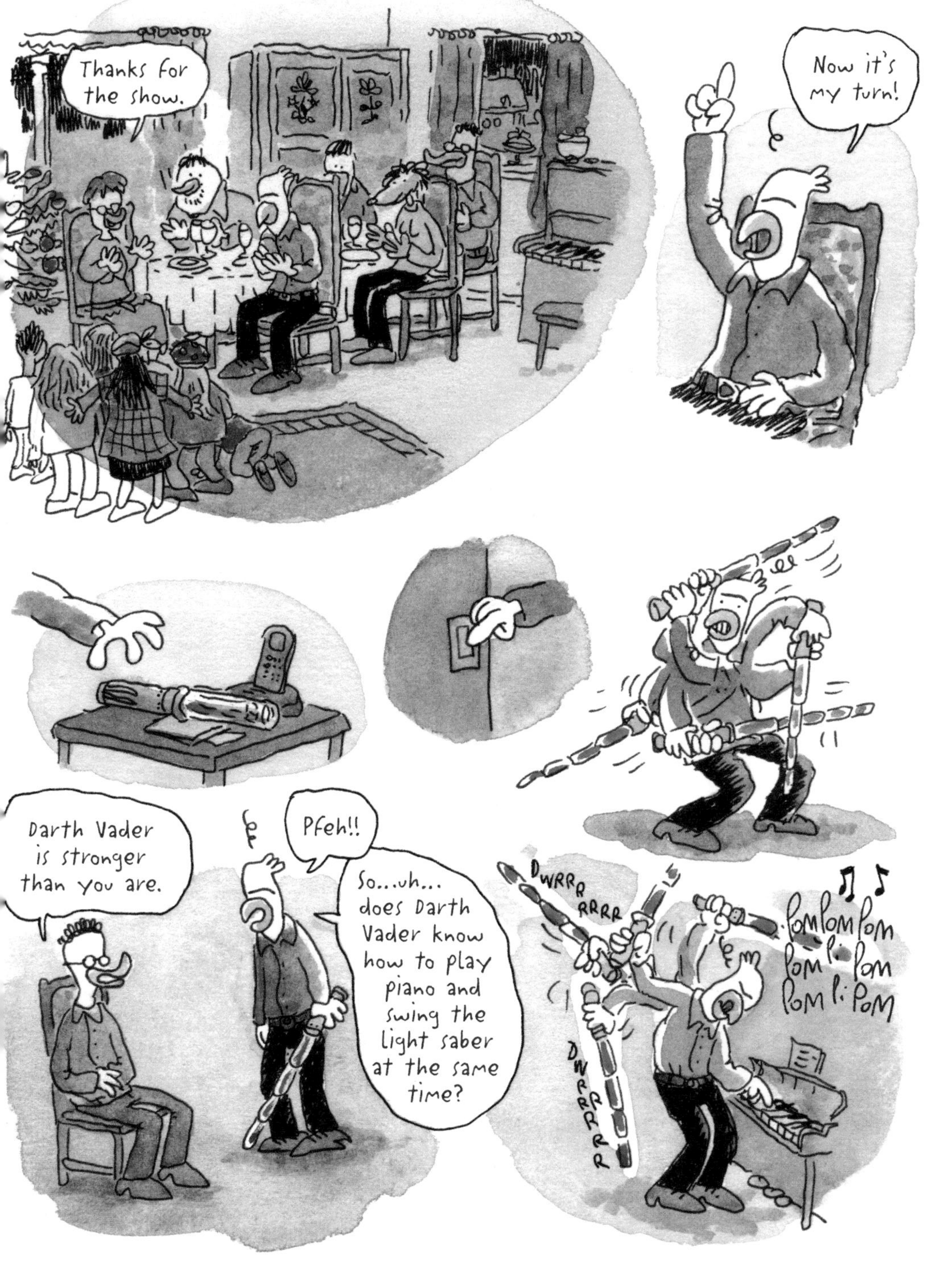
Thanks for the show.
Now it's my turn!
Darth Vader is stronger than you are.
Pfeh!!
So...uh... does Darth Vader know how to play piano and swing the light saber at the same time?
DWRRR RRRR
DWRRRRRRR
PomPomPom Pom Pi Pom Pom Pi Pom

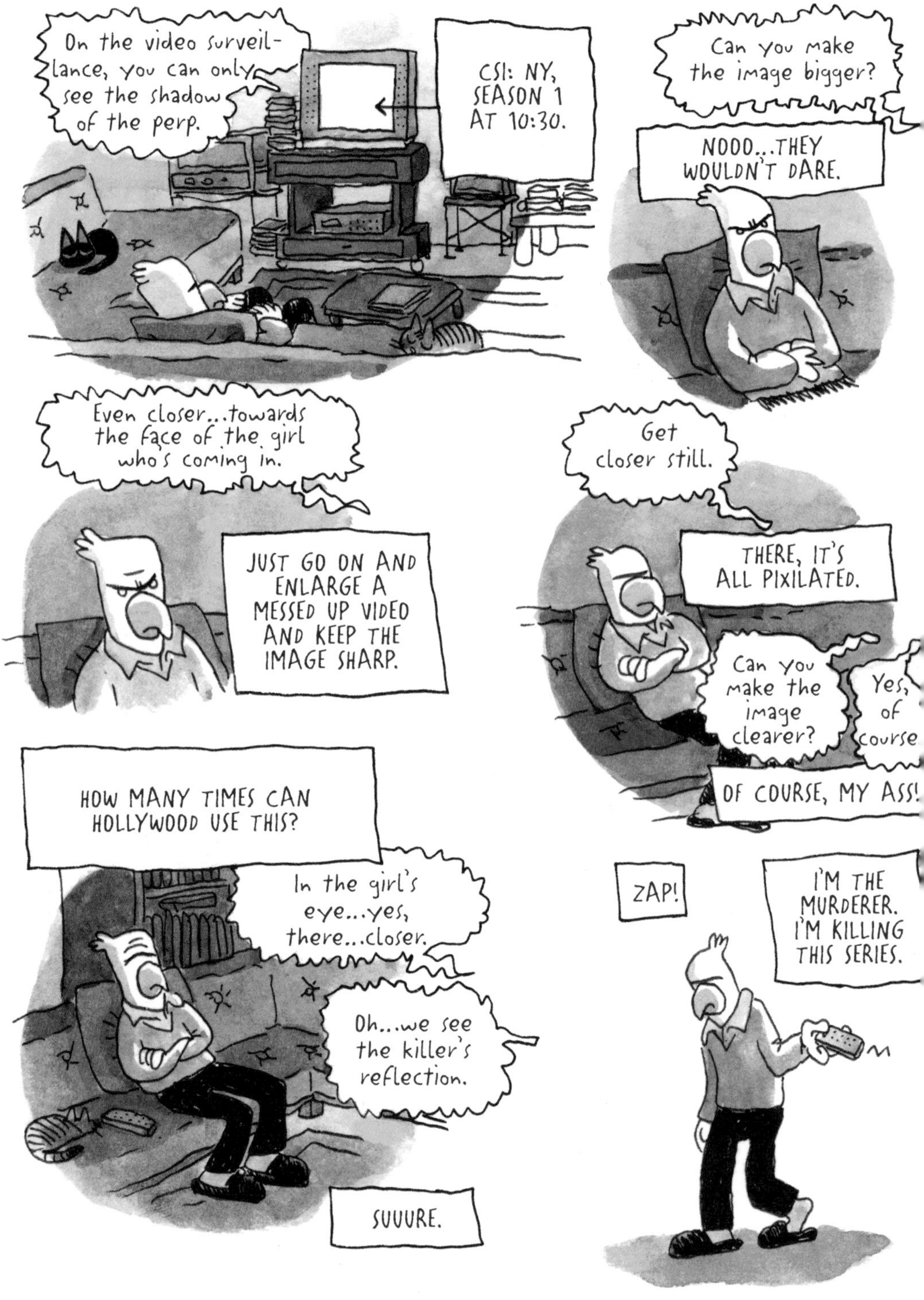
On the video surveil-lance, you can only see the shadow of the perp.
CSI: NY, SEASON 1 AT 10:30.
Can you make the image bigger?
NOOO...THEY WOULDN'T DARE.
Even closer...towards the face of the girl who's coming in.
JUST GO ON AND ENLARGE A MESSED UP VIDEO AND KEEP THE IMAGE SHARP.
Get closer still.
THERE, IT'S ALL PIXILATED.
Can you make the image clearer?
Yes, of course
OF COURSE, MY ASS!
HOW MANY TIMES CAN HOLLYWOOD USE THIS?
In the girl's eye...yes, there...closer.
Oh...we see the killer's reflection.
SUUURE.
ZAP!
I'M THE MURDERER. I'M KILLING THIS SERIES.

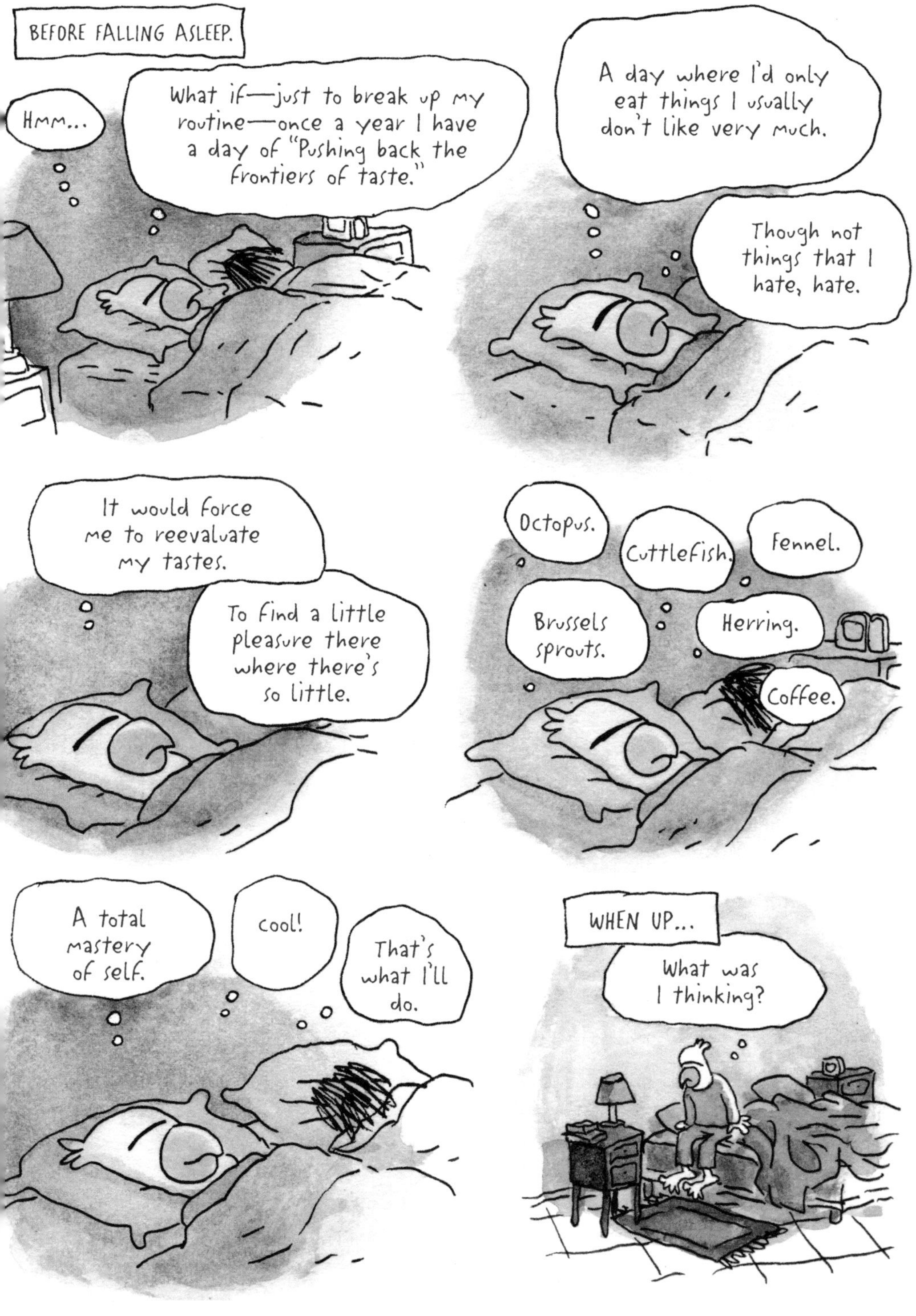
BEFORE FALLING ASLEEP.
Hmm...
What if—just to break up my routine—once a year I have a day of "Pushing back the frontiers of taste."
A day where I'd only eat things I usually don't like very much.
Though not things that I hate, hate.
It would force me to reevaluate my tastes.
To find a little pleasure there where there's so little.
Octopus.
Cuttlefish.
Fennel.
Brussels sprouts.
Herring.
Coffee.
A total mastery of self.
Cool!
That's what I'll do.
WHEN UP...
What was I thinking?

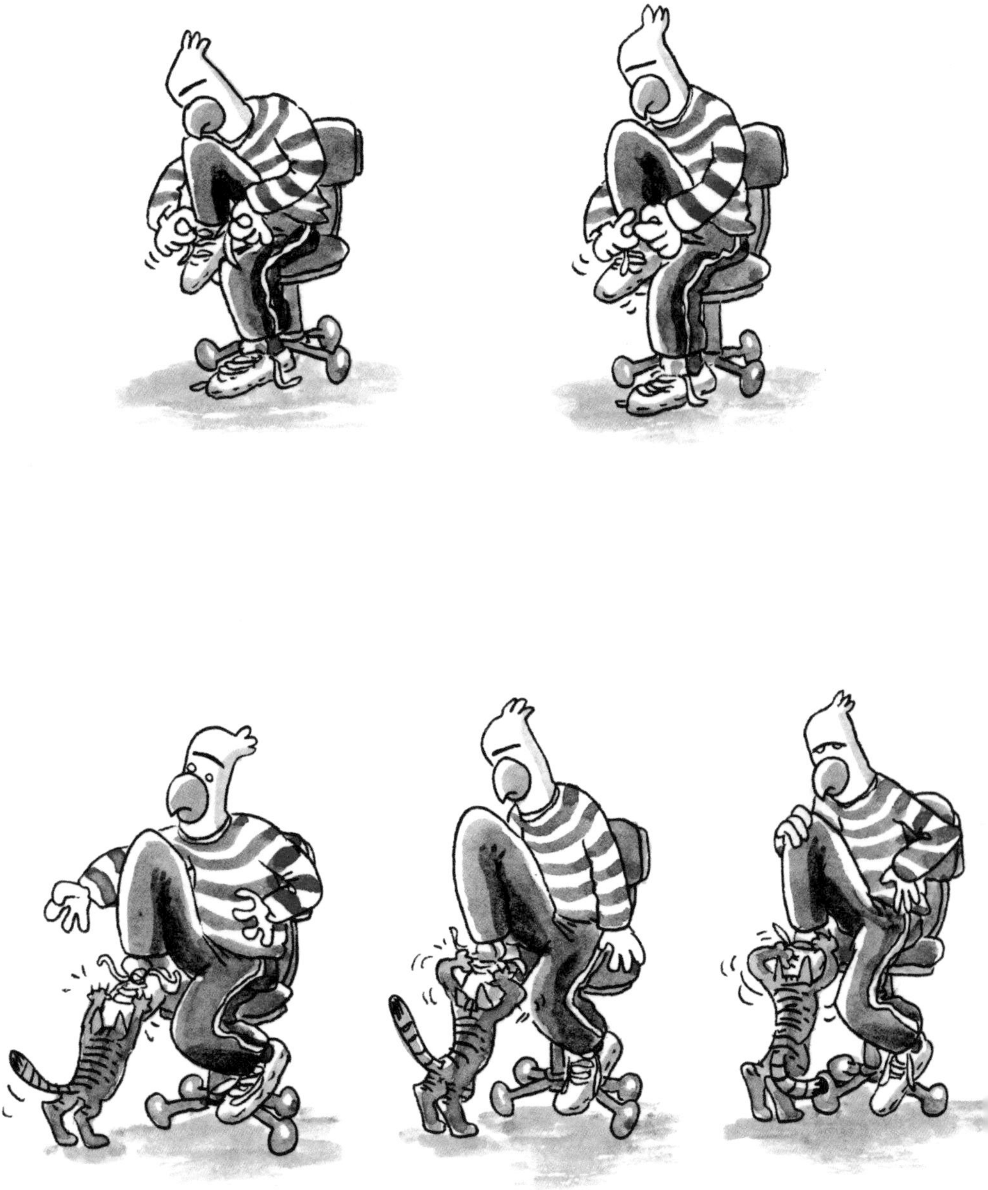

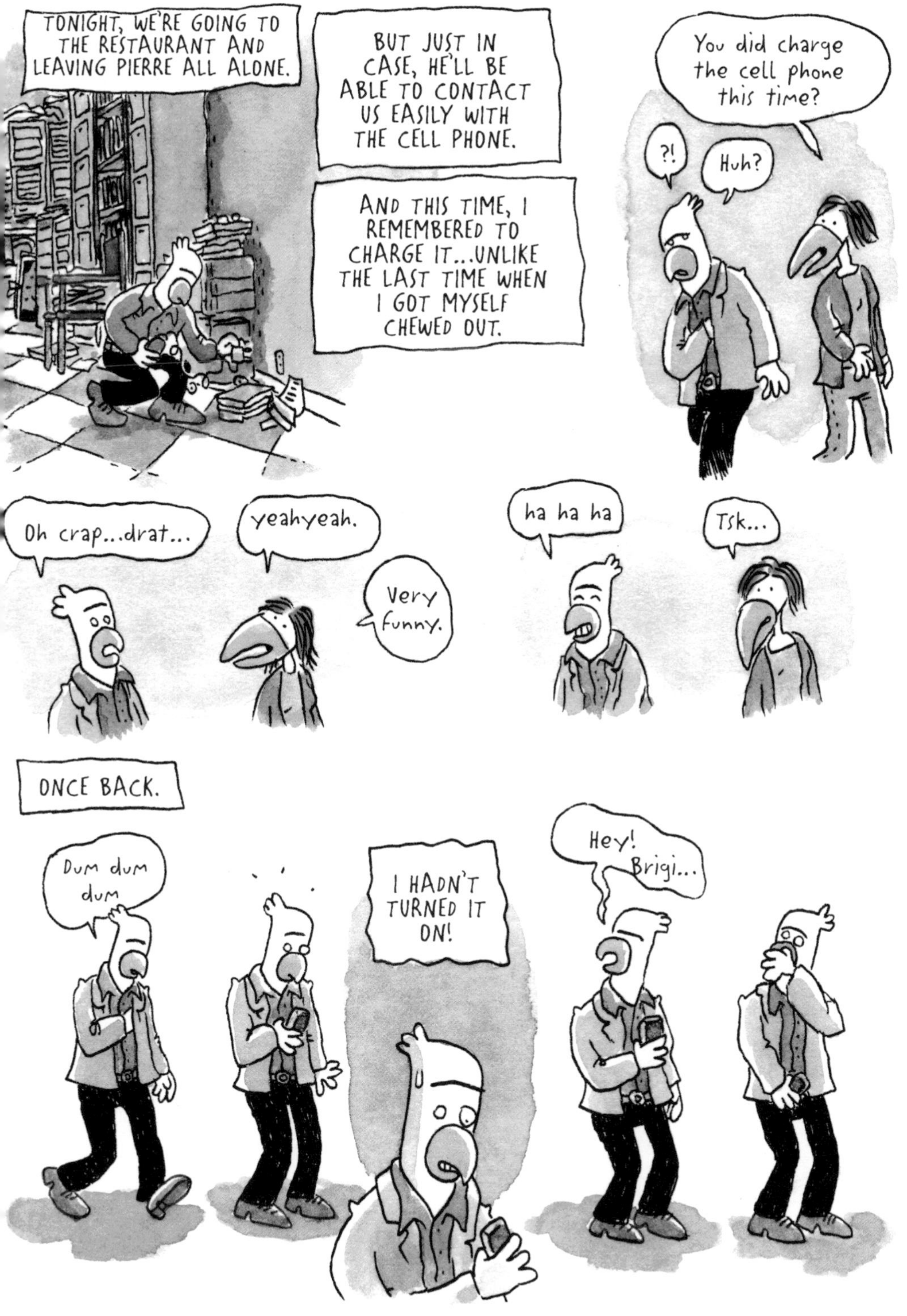

TONIGHT, WE'RE GOING TO THE RESTAURANT AND LEAVING PIERRE ALL ALONE.
BUT JUST IN CASE, HE'LL BE ABLE TO CONTACT US EASILY WITH THE CELL PHONE.
AND THIS TIME, I REMEMBERED TO CHARGE IT...UNLIKE THE LAST TIME WHEN I GOT MYSELF CHEWED OUT.
You did charge the cell phone this time?
?!
Huh?
Oh crap...drat...
yeahyeah.
Very funny.
ha ha ha
Tsk...
ONCE BACK.
Dum dum dum
I HADN'T TURNED IT ON!
Hey! Brigi...

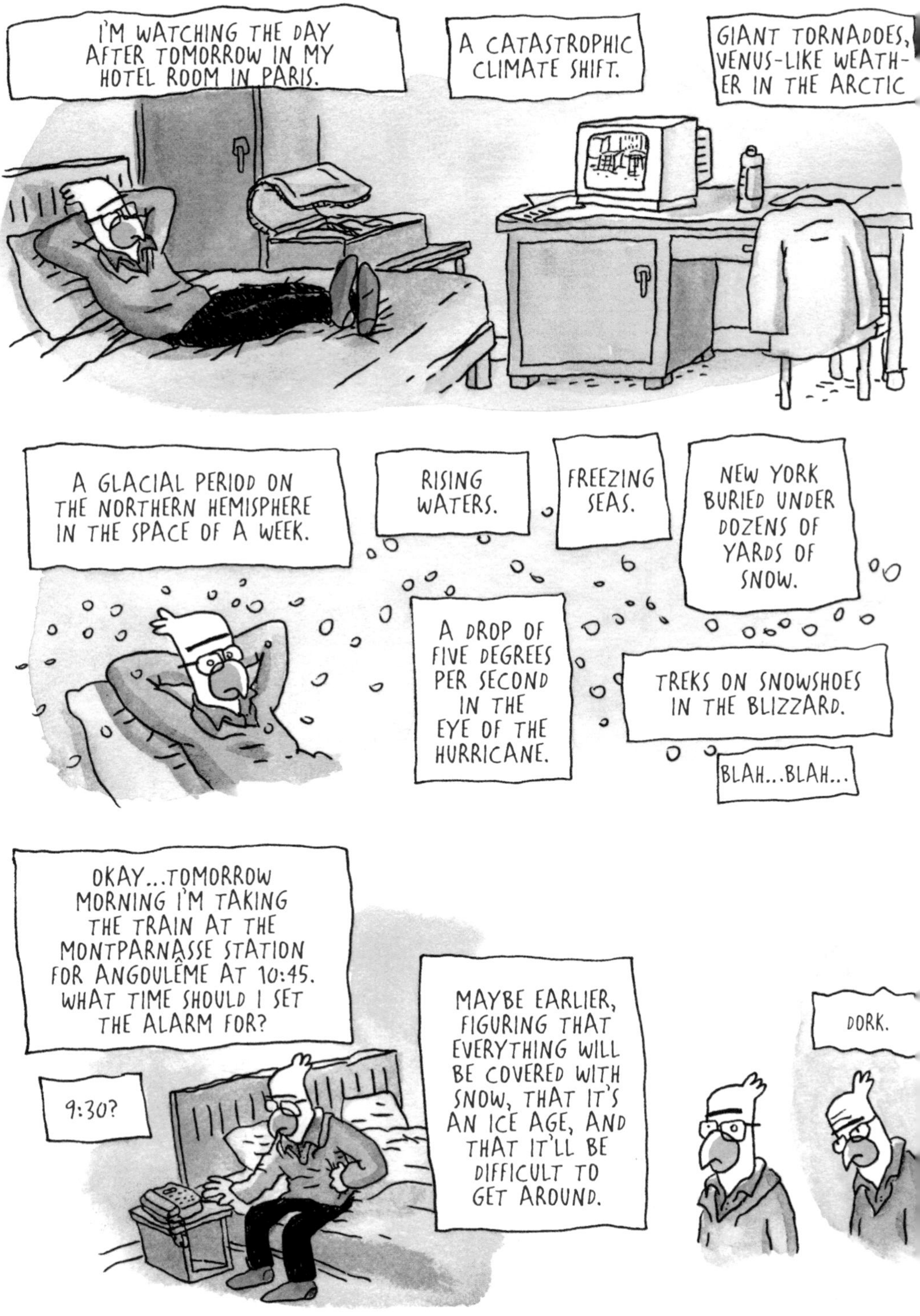
I'M WATCHING THE DAY AFTER TOMORROW IN MY HOTEL ROOM IN PARIS.
A CATASTROPHIC CLIMATE SHIFT.
GIANT TORNADOES, VENUS-LIKE WEATHER IN THE ARCTIC
A GLACIAL PERIOD ON THE NORTHERN HEMISPHERE IN THE SPACE OF A WEEK.
RISING WATERS.
FREEZING SEAS.
NEW YORK BURIED UNDER DOZENS OF YARDS OF SNOW.
A DROP OF FIVE DEGREES PER SECOND IN THE EYE OF THE HURRICANE.
TREKS ON SNOWSHOES IN THE BLIZZARD.
BLAH...BLAH...
OKAY...TOMORROW MORNING I'M TAKING THE TRAIN AT THE MONTPARNASSE STATION FOR ANGOULÊME AT 10:45. WHAT TIME SHOULD I SET THE ALARM FOR?
9:30?
MAYBE EARLIER, FIGURING THAT EVERYTHING WILL BE COVERED WITH SNOW, THAT IT'S AN ICE AGE, AND THAT IT'LL BE DIFFICULT TO GET AROUND.
DORK.

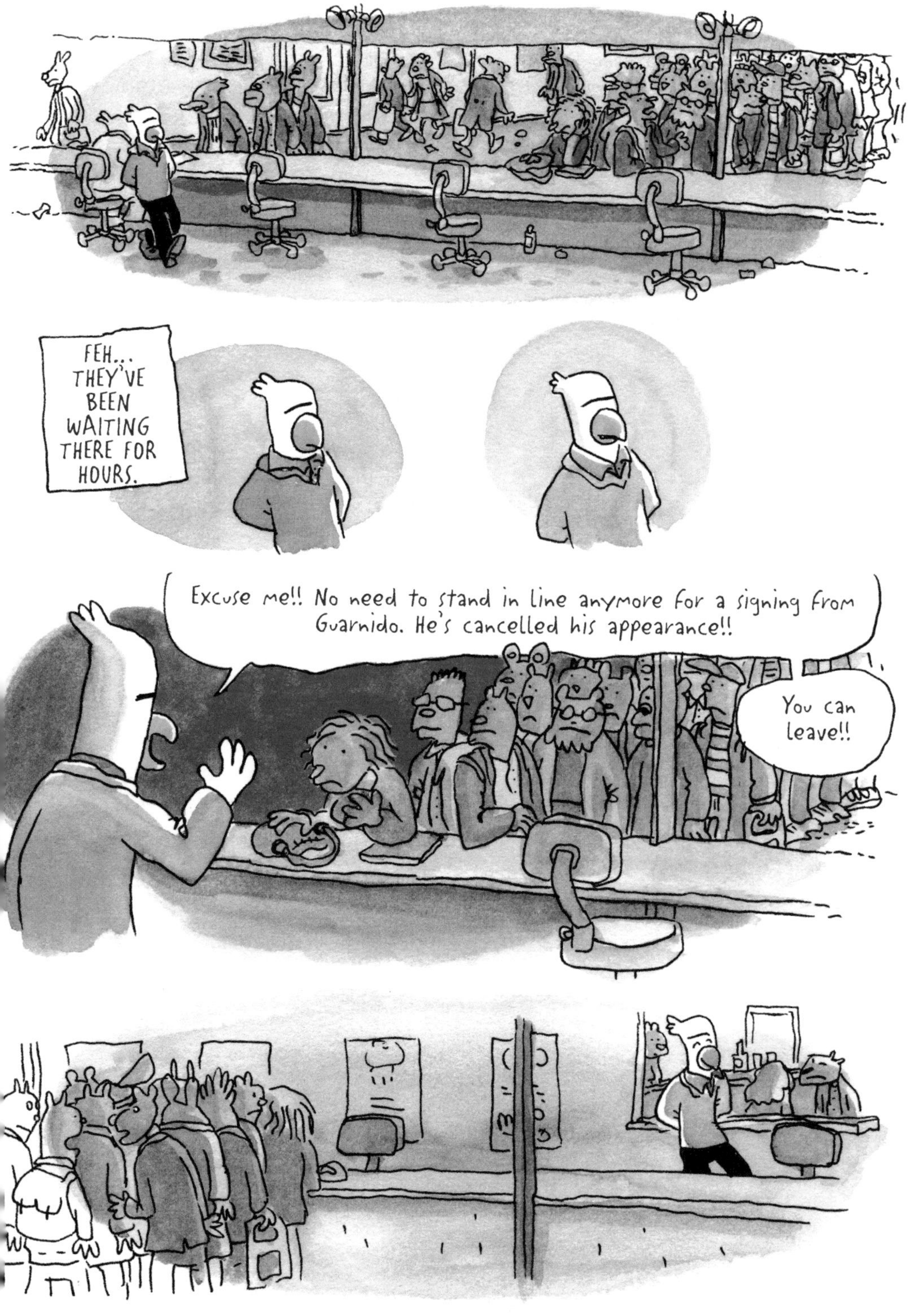
FEH... THEY'VE BEEN WAITING THERE FOR HOURS.
Excuse me!! No need to stand in line anymore for a signing from Guarnido. He's cancelled his appearance!!
You can leave!!

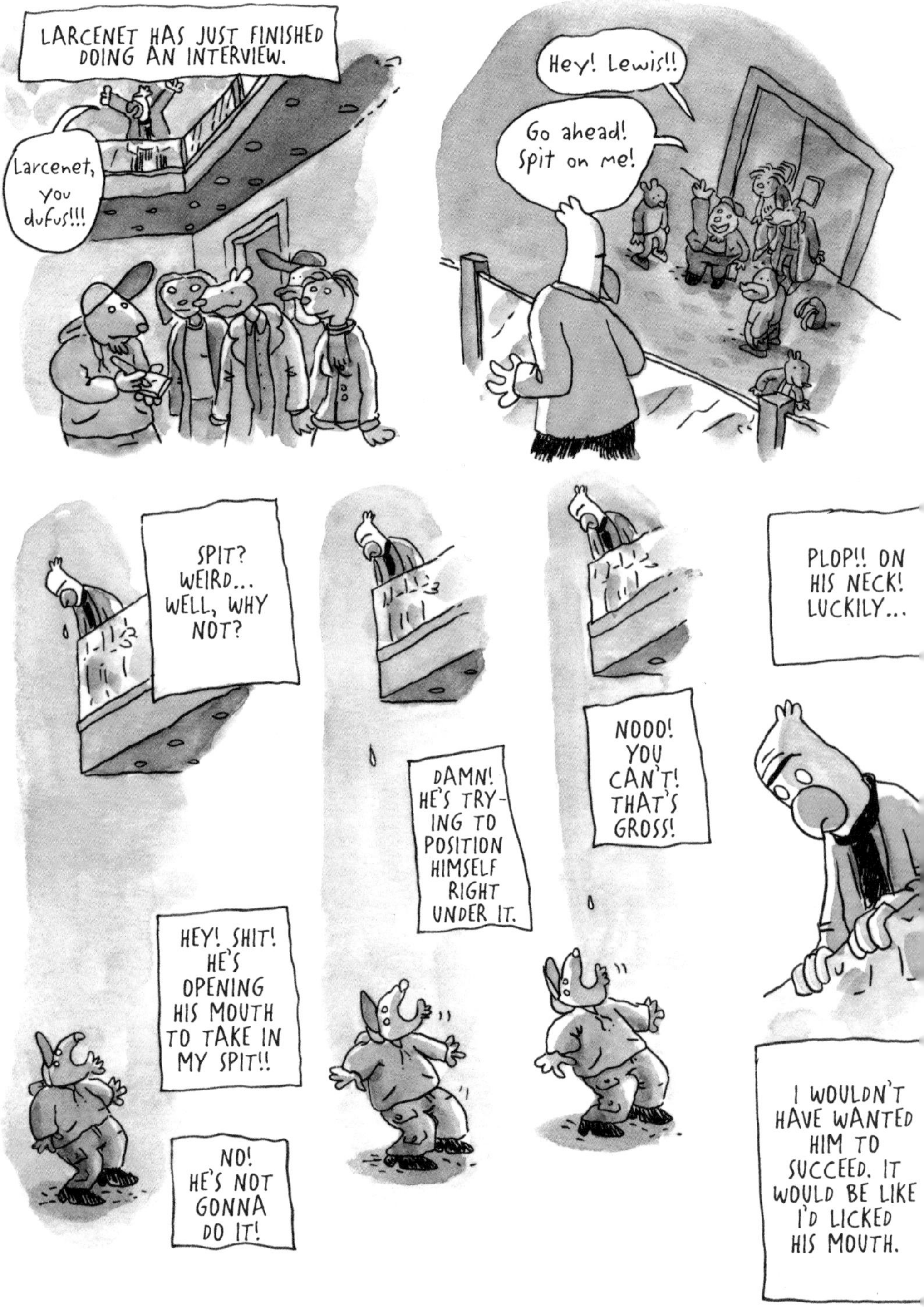
LARCENET HAS JUST FINISHED DOING AN INTERVIEW.
Larcenet, you dufus!!!
Hey! Lewis!!
Go ahead! Spit on me!
SPIT? WEIRD... WELL, WHY NOT?
HEY! SHIT! HE'S OPENING HIS MOUTH TO TAKE IN MY SPIT!!
NO! HE'S NOT GONNA DO IT!
DAMN! HE'S TRY-ING TO POSITION HIMSELF RIGHT UNDER IT.
NOOO! YOU CAN'T! THAT'S GROSS!
PLOP!! ON HIS NECK! LUCKILY...
I WOULDN'T HAVE WANTED HIM TO SUCCEED. IT WOULD BE LIKE I'D LICKED HIS MOUTH.

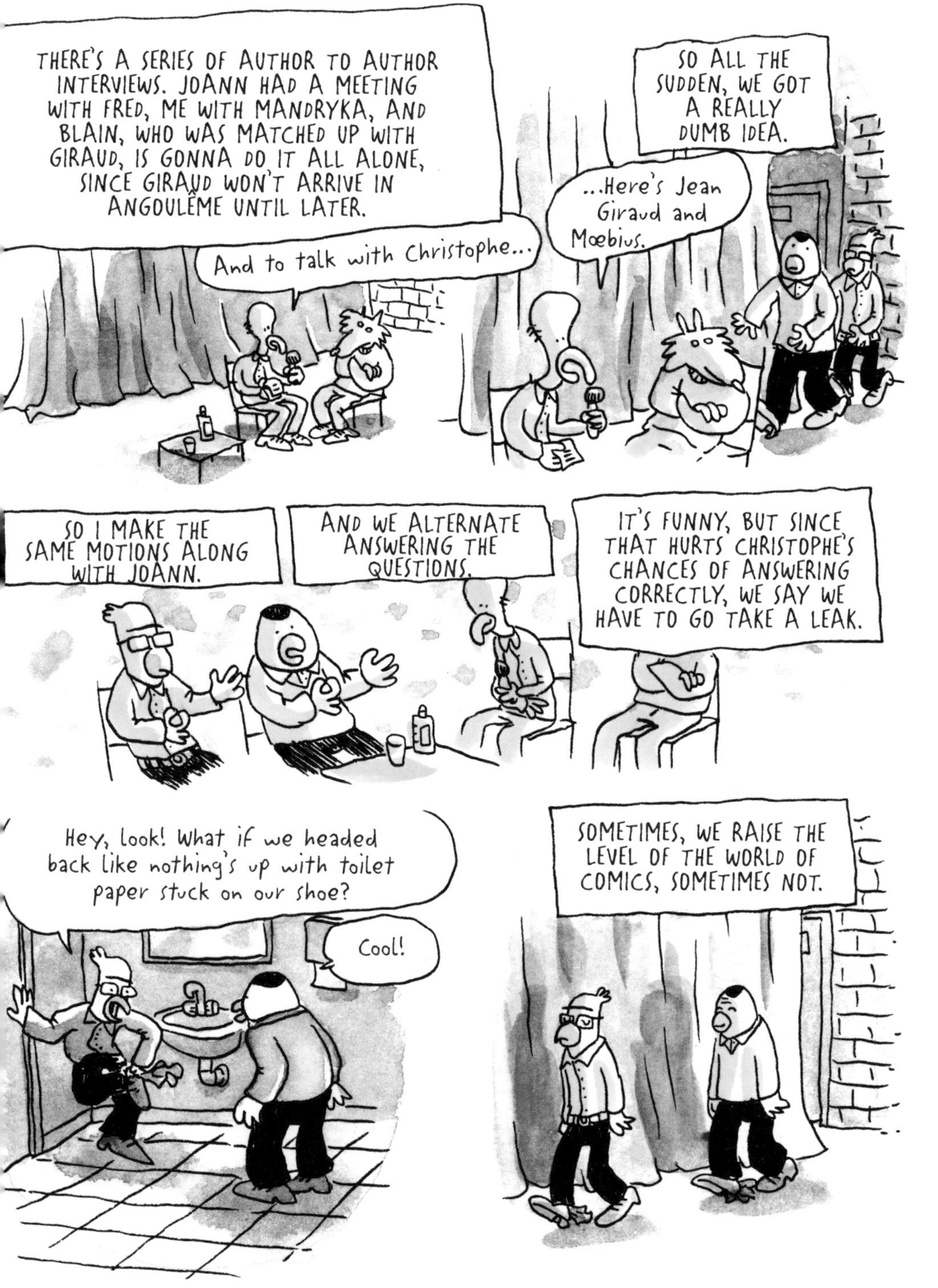

THERE'S A SERIES OF AUTHOR TO AUTHOR INTERVIEWS. JOANN HAD A MEETING WITH FRED, ME WITH MANDRYKA, AND BLAIN, WHO WAS MATCHED UP WITH GIRAUD, IS GONNA DO IT ALL ALONE, SINCE GIRAUD WON'T ARRIVE IN ANGOULÊME UNTIL LATER.
And to talk with Christophe...
SO ALL THE SUDDEN, WE GOT A REALLY DUMB IDEA.
...Here's Jean Giraud and Mœbius.
SO I MAKE THE SAME MOTIONS ALONG WITH JOANN.
AND WE ALTERNATE ANSWERING THE QUESTIONS.
IT'S FUNNY, BUT SINCE THAT HURTS CHRISTOPHE'S CHANCES OF ANSWERING CORRECTLY, WE SAY WE HAVE TO GO TAKE A LEAK.
Hey, look! What if we headed back like nothing's up with toilet paper stuck on our shoe?
Cool!
SOMETIMES, WE RAISE THE LEVEL OF THE WORLD OF COMICS, SOMETIMES NOT.

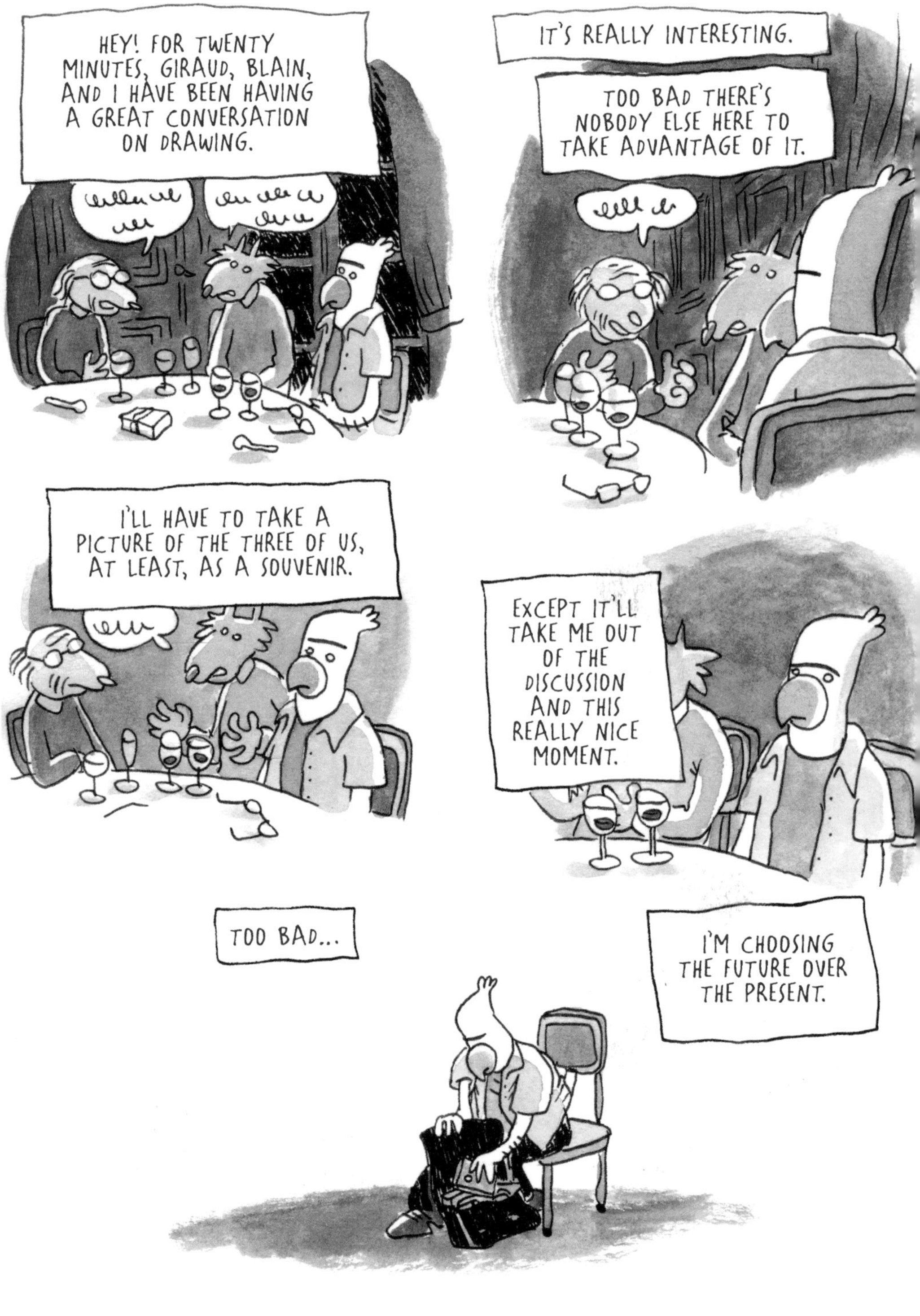
HEY! FOR TWENTY MINUTES, GIRAUD, BLAIN, AND I HAVE BEEN HAVING A GREAT CONVERSATION ON DRAWING.
IT'S REALLY INTERESTING.
TOO BAD THERE'S NOBODY ELSE HERE TO TAKE ADVANTAGE OF IT.
I'LL HAVE TO TAKE A PICTURE OF THE THREE OF US, AT LEAST, AS A SOUVENIR.
EXCEPT IT'LL TAKE ME OUT OF THE DISCUSSION AND THIS REALLY NICE MOMENT.
TOO BAD...
I'M CHOOSING THE FUTURE OVER THE PRESENT.

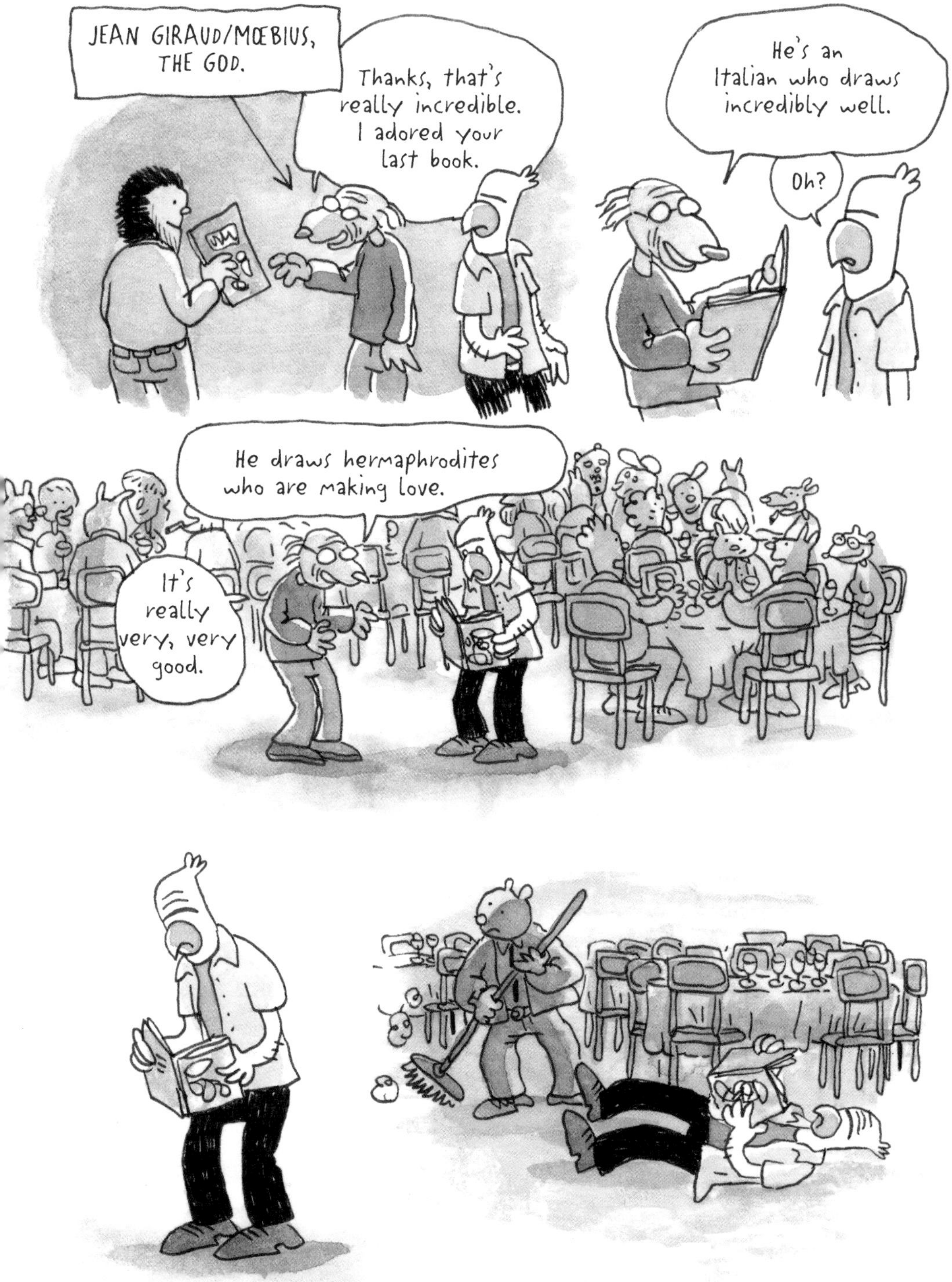
JEAN GIRAUD/MŒBIUS, THE GOD.
Thanks, that's really incredible. I adored your last book.
He's an Italian who draws incredibly well.
Oh?
He draws hermaphrodites who are making love.
It's really very, very good.

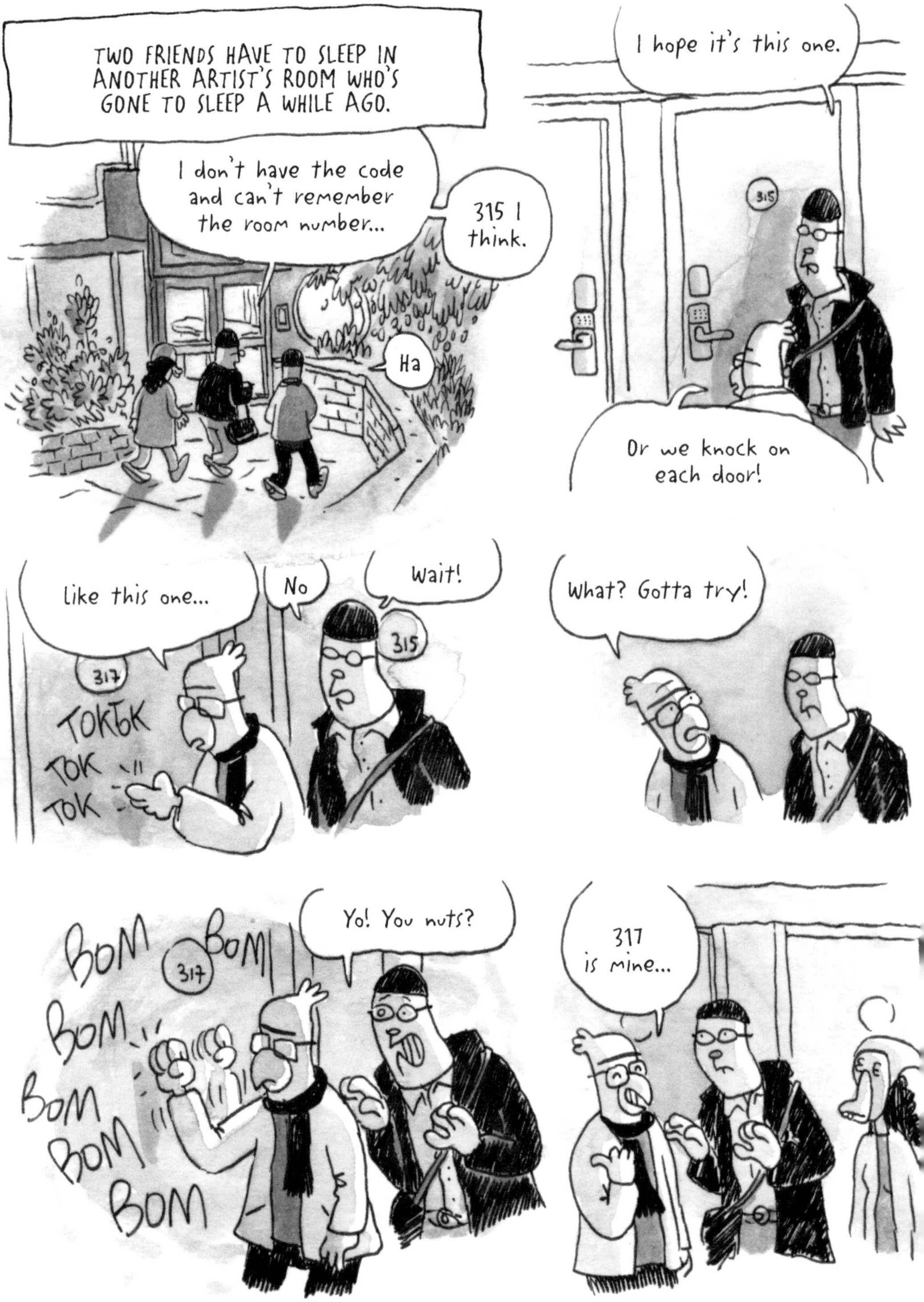
TWO FRIENDS HAVE TO SLEEP IN ANOTHER ARTIST'S ROOM WHO'S GONE TO SLEEP A WHILE AGO.
I don't have the code and can't remember the room number...
315 I think.
Ha
I hope it's this one.
315
Or we knock on each door!
Like this one...
No
Wait!
315
317
TOKTOK
TOK
TOK
What? Gotta try!
Yo! You nuts?
BOM BOM
317
BOM
BOM
BOM
BOM
317 is mine...

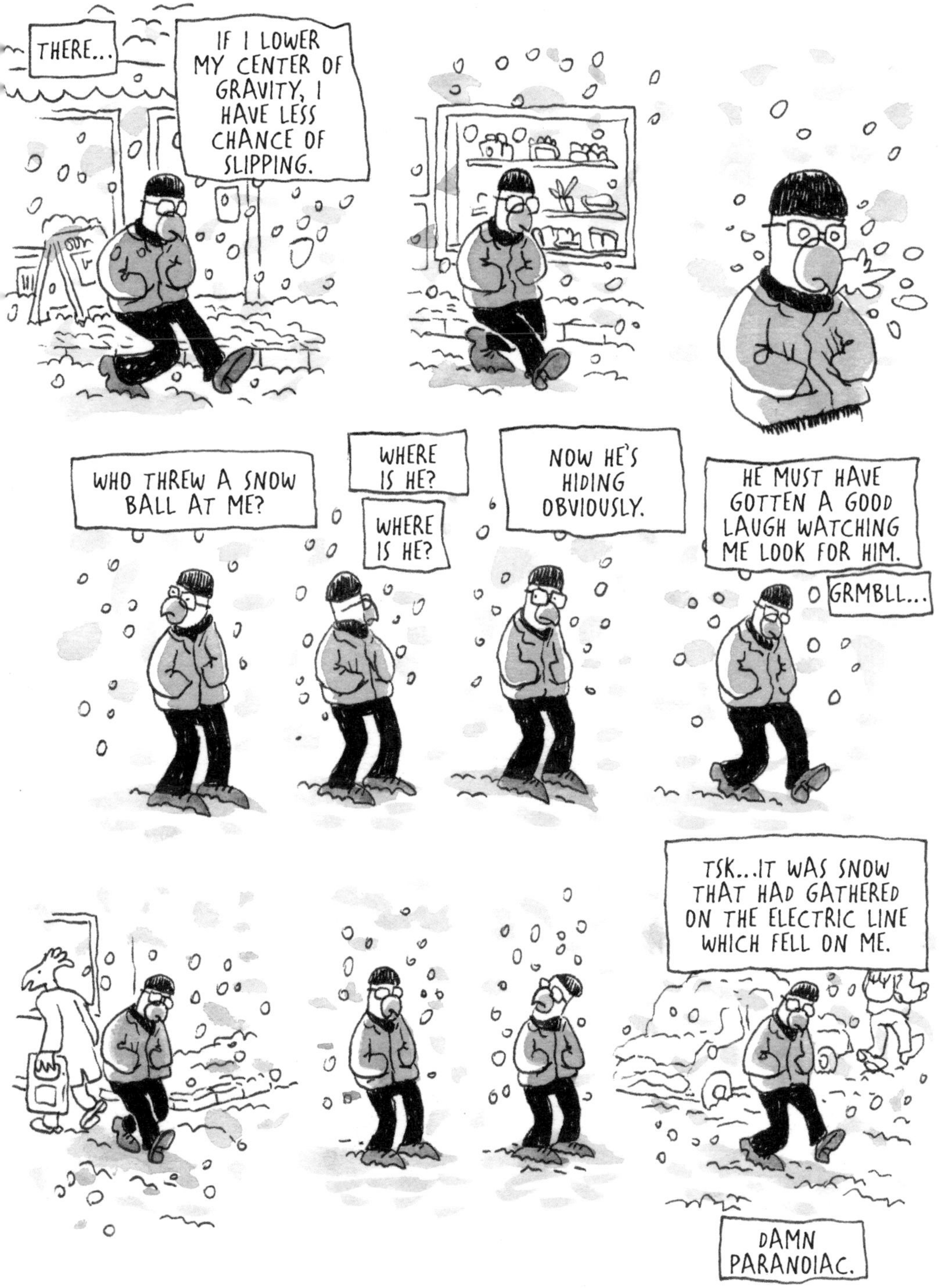
THERE...
IF I LOWER MY CENTER OF GRAVITY, I HAVE LESS CHANCE OF SLIPPING.
WHO THREW A SNOW BALL AT ME?
WHERE IS HE?
WHERE IS HE?
NOW HE'S HIDING OBVIOUSLY.
HE MUST HAVE GOTTEN A GOOD LAUGH WATCHING ME LOOK FOR HIM.
GRMBLL...
TSK...IT WAS SNOW THAT HAD GATHERED ON THE ELECTRIC LINE WHICH FELL ON ME.
DAMN PARANOIAC.

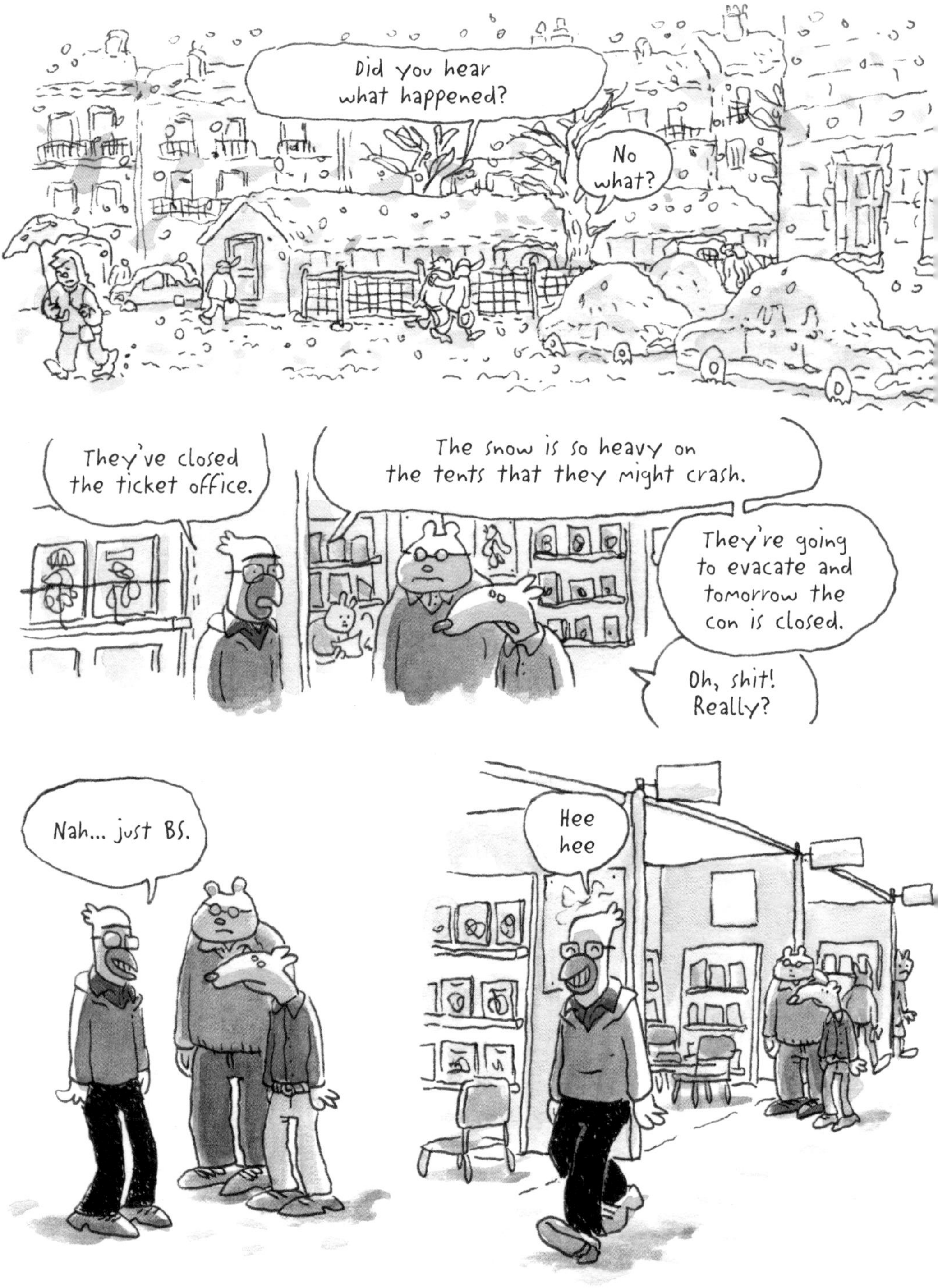
Did you hear what happened?
No what?
They've closed the ticket office.
The snow is so heavy on the tents that they might crash.
They're going to evacate and tomorrow the con is closed.
Oh, shit! Really?
Nah... just BS.
Hee hee

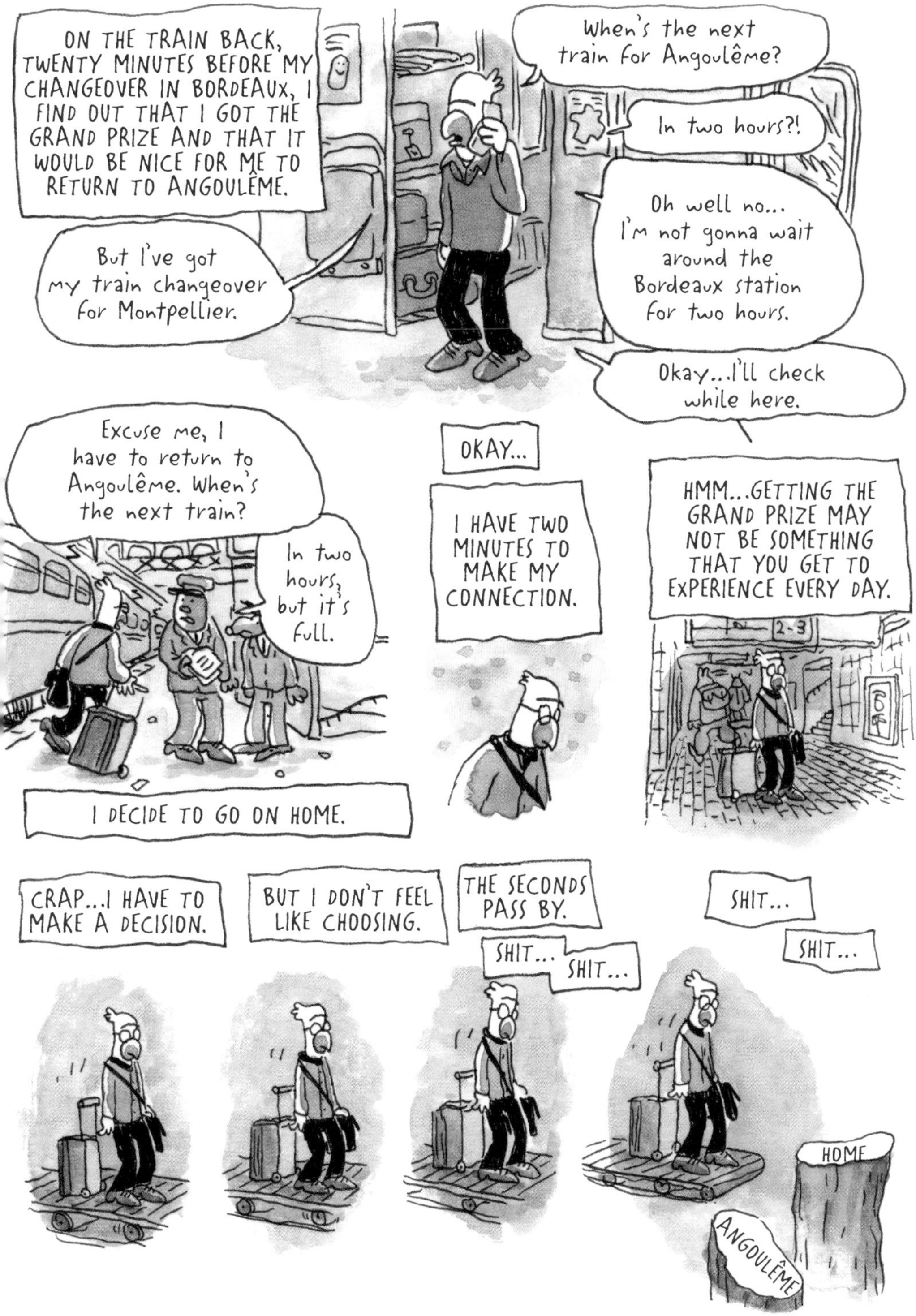
ON THE TRAIN BACK, TWENTY MINUTES BEFORE MY CHANGEOVER IN BORDEAUX, I FIND OUT THAT I GOT THE GRAND PRIZE AND THAT IT WOULD BE NICE FOR ME TO RETURN TO ANGOULÊME.
But I've got my train changeover for Montpellier.
When's the next train for Angoulême?
In two hours?!
Oh well no... I'm not gonna wait around the Bordeaux station for two hours.
Okay...I'll check while here.
Excuse me, I have to return to Angoulême. When's the next train?
In two hours, but it's full.
I DECIDE TO GO ON HOME.
OKAY...
I HAVE TWO MINUTES TO MAKE MY CONNECTION.
HMM...GETTING THE GRAND PRIZE MAY NOT BE SOMETHING THAT YOU GET TO EXPERIENCE EVERY DAY.
2-3
CRAP...I HAVE TO MAKE A DECISION.
BUT I DON'T FEEL LIKE CHOOSING.
THE SECONDS PASS BY.
SHIT...
SHIT...
SHIT...
SHIT...
HOME
ANGOULÊME

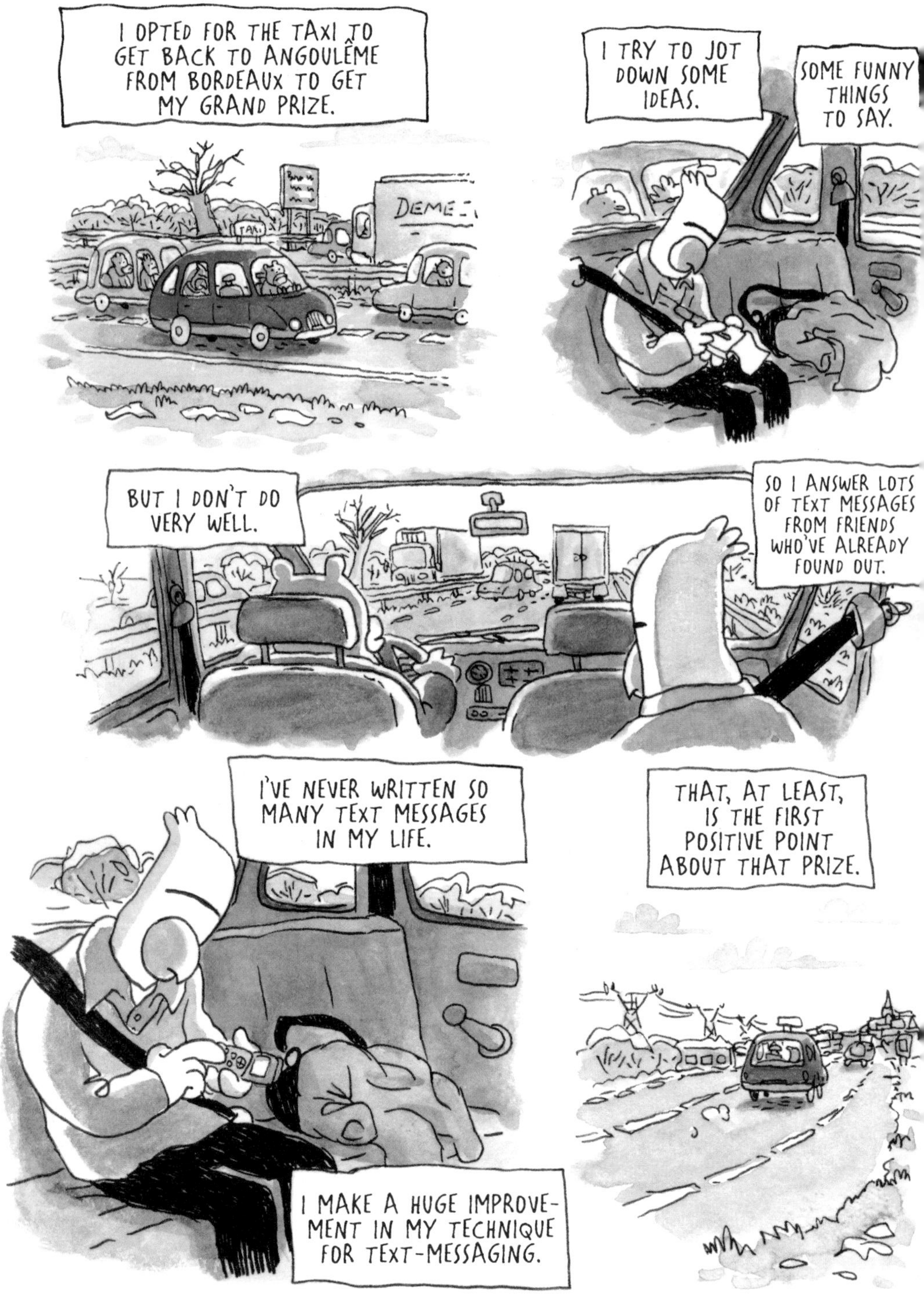
I OPTED FOR THE TAXI TO GET BACK TO ANGOULÊME FROM BORDEAUX TO GET MY GRAND PRIZE.
TAXI
DEME
I TRY TO JOT DOWN SOME IDEAS.
SOME FUNNY THINGS TO SAY.
BUT I DON'T DO VERY WELL.
SO I ANSWER LOTS OF TEXT MESSAGES FROM FRIENDS WHO'VE ALREADY FOUND OUT.
I'VE NEVER WRITTEN SO MANY TEXT MESSAGES IN MY LIFE.
I MAKE A HUGE IMPROVEMENT IN MY TECHNIQUE FOR TEXT-MESSAGING.
THAT, AT LEAST, IS THE FIRST POSITIVE POINT ABOUT THAT PRIZE.

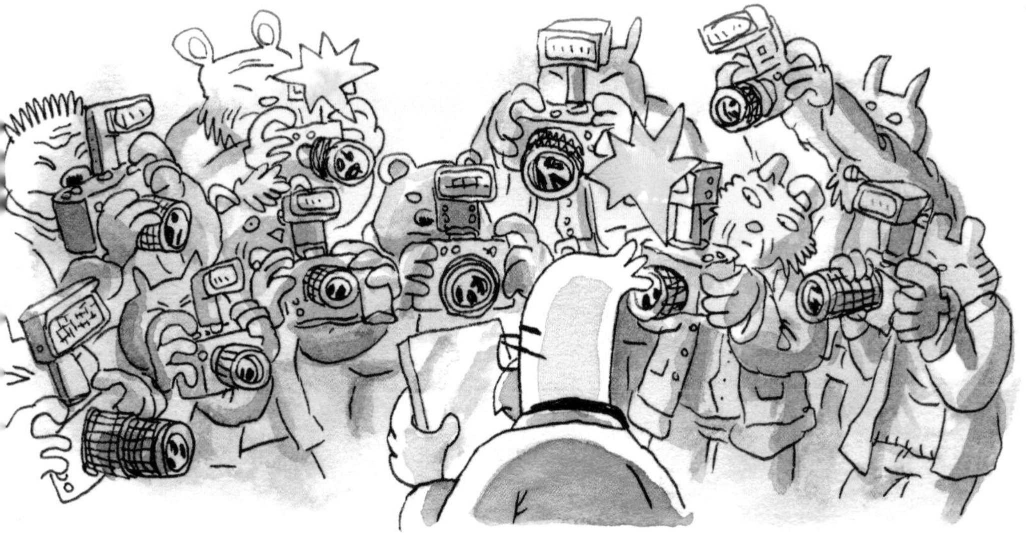

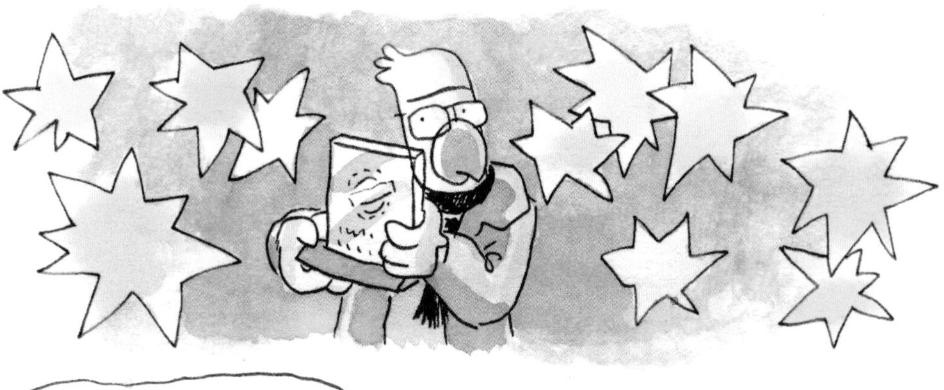

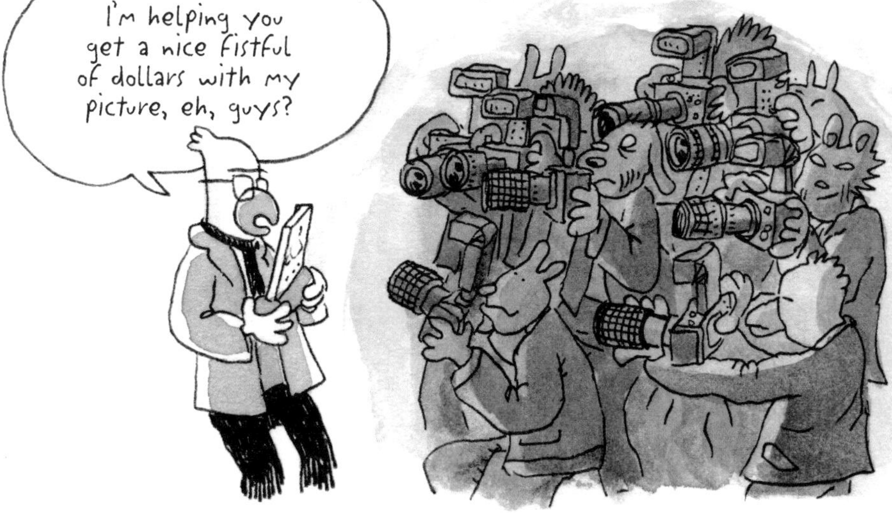
I'm helping you get a nice fistful of dollars with my picture, eh, guys?

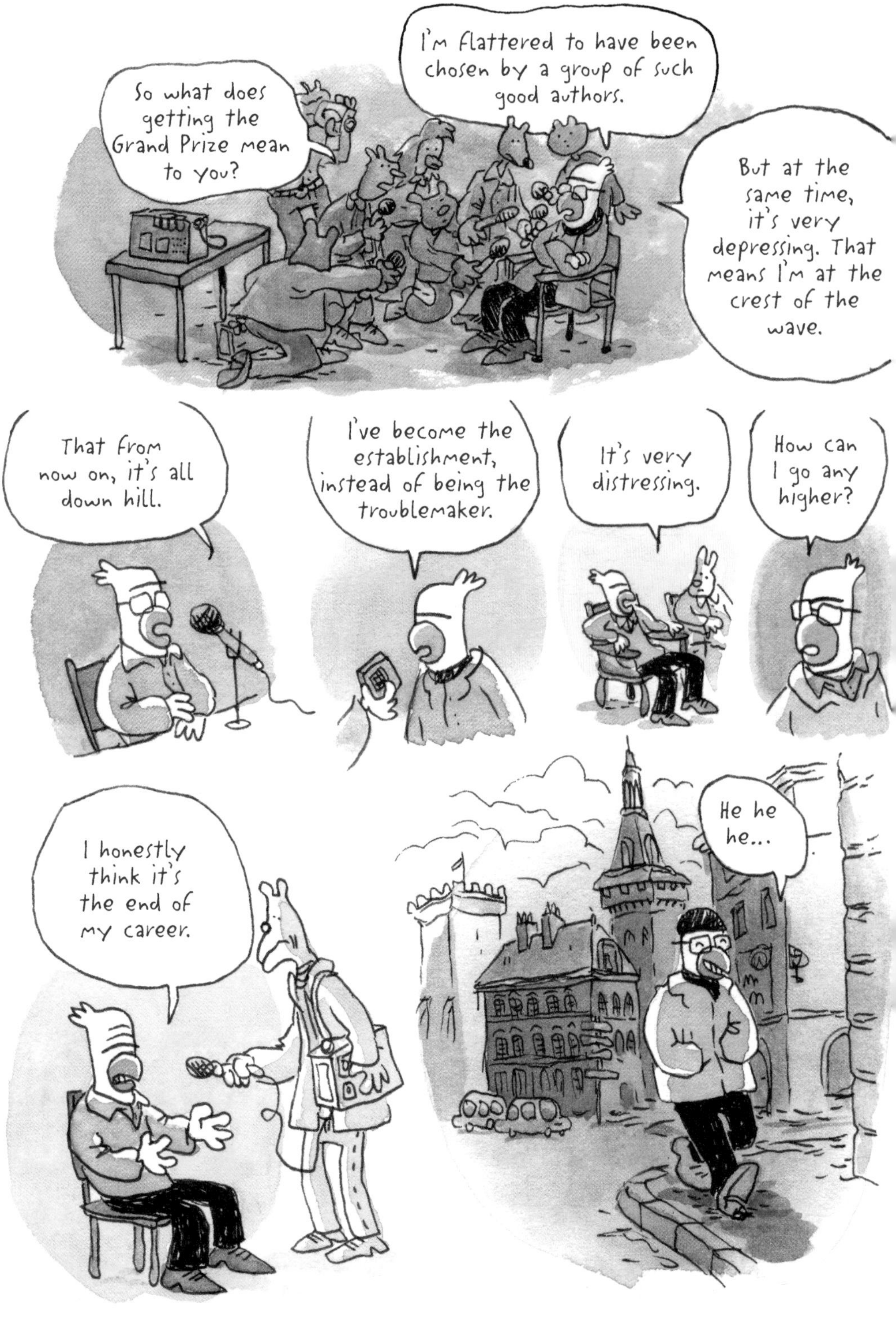
So what does getting the Grand Prize mean to you?
I'm flattered to have been chosen by a group of such good authors.
But at the same time, it's very depressing. That means I'm at the crest of the wave.
That from now on, it's all down hill.
I've become the establishment, instead of being the troublemaker.
It's very distressing.
How can I go any higher?
I honestly think it's the end of my career.
He he he...

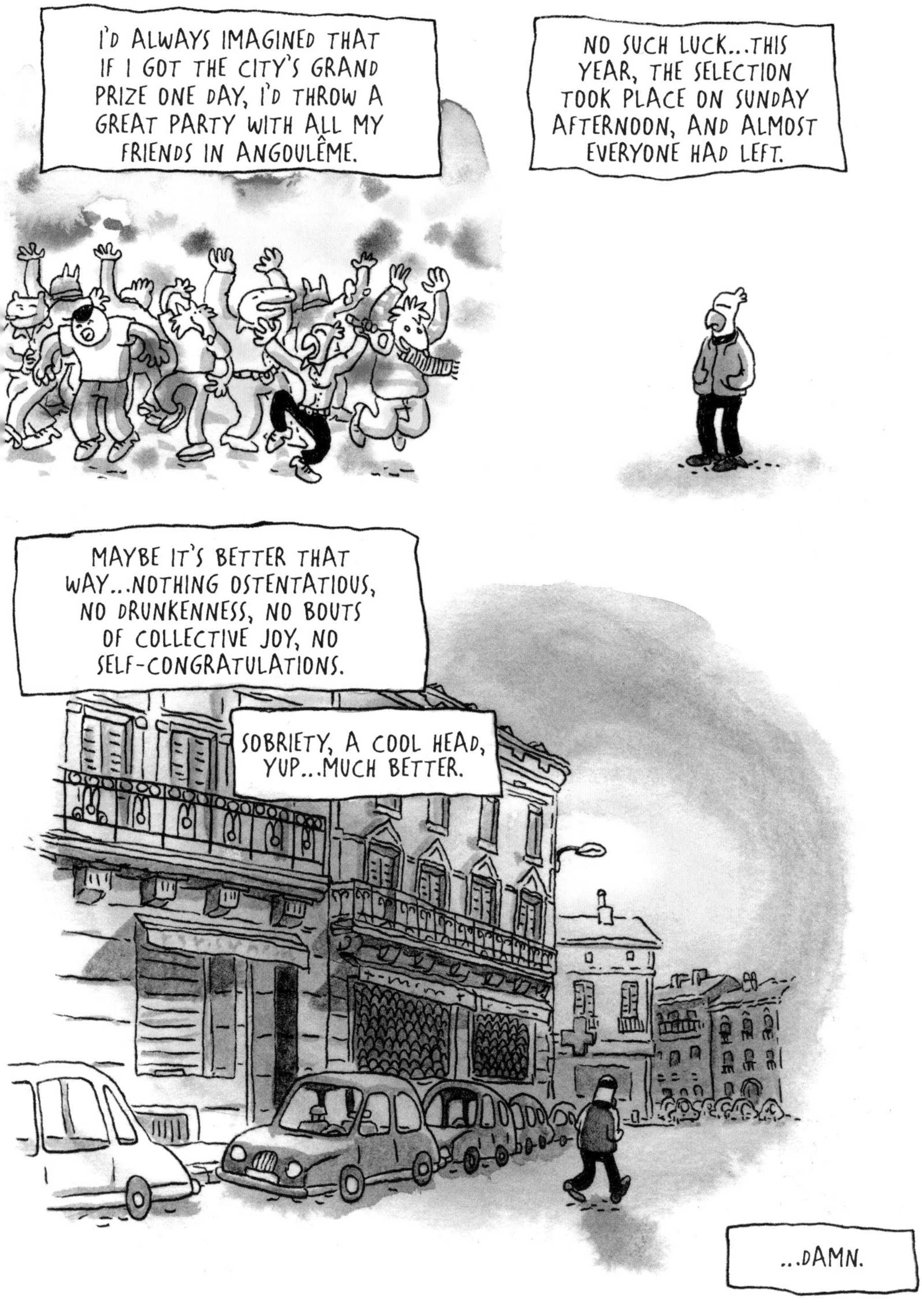
I'D ALWAYS IMAGINED THAT IF I GOT THE CITY'S GRAND PRIZE ONE DAY, I'D THROW A GREAT PARTY WITH ALL MY FRIENDS IN ANGOULÊME.
NO SUCH LUCK...THIS YEAR, THE SELECTION TOOK PLACE ON SUNDAY AFTERNOON, AND ALMOST EVERYONE HAD LEFT.
MAYBE IT'S BETTER THAT WAY...NOTHING OSTENTATIOUS, NO DRUNKENNESS, NO BOUTS OF COLLECTIVE JOY, NO SELF-CONGRATULATIONS.
SOBRIETY, A COOL HEAD, YUP...MUCH BETTER.
...DAMN.

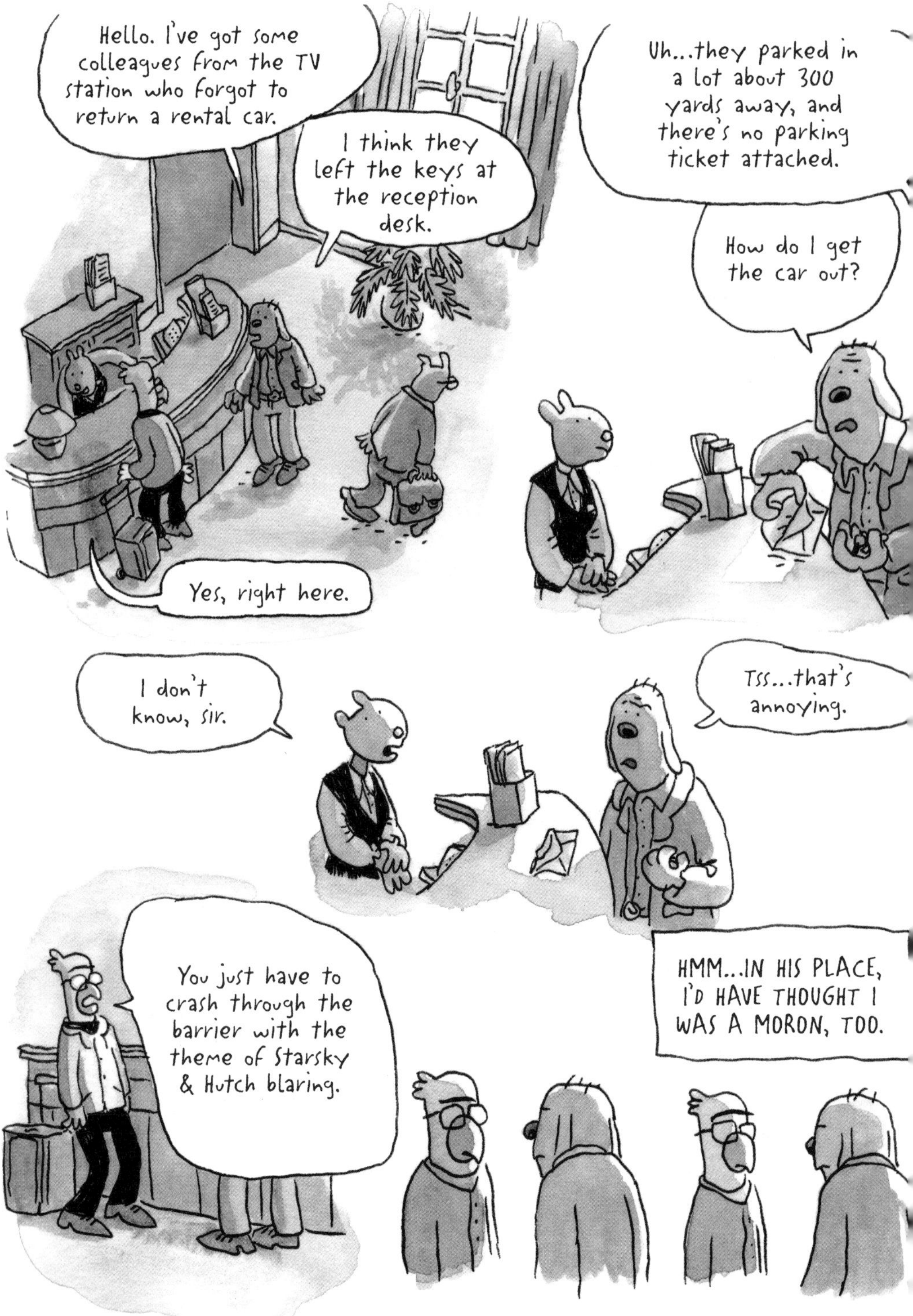

Hello. I've got some colleagues from the TV station who forgot to return a rental car.
I think they left the keys at the reception desk.
Yes, right here.
Uh...they parked in a lot about 300 yards away, and there's no parking ticket attached.
How do I get the car out?
I don't know, sir.
Tss...that's annoying.
You just have to crash through the barrier with the theme of Starsky & Hutch blaring.
HMM...IN HIS PLACE, I'D HAVE THOUGHT I WAS A MORON, TOO.

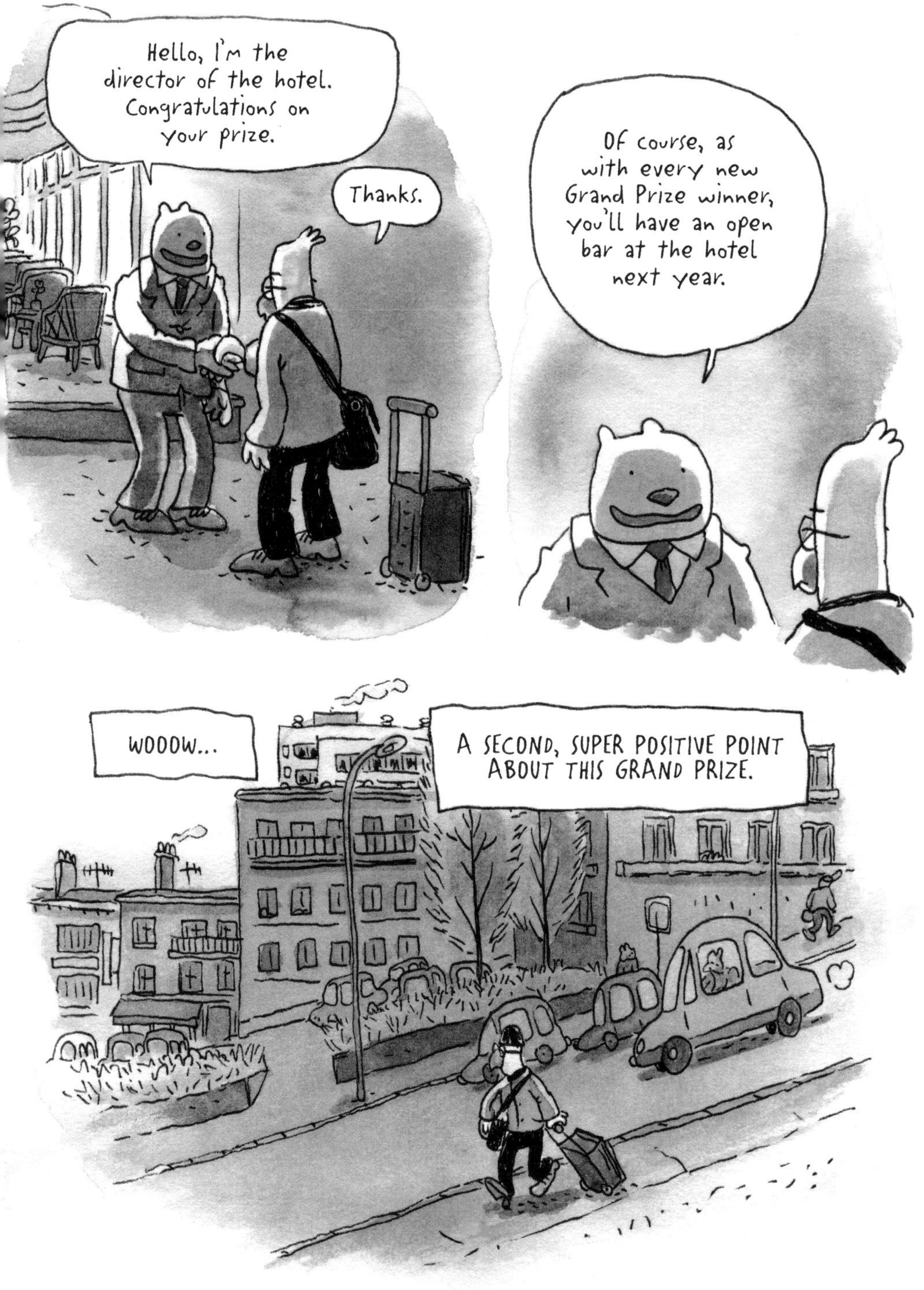
Hello, I'm the director of the hotel. Congratulations on your prize.
Thanks.
Of course, as with every new Grand Prize winner, you'll have an open bar at the hotel next year.
WOOOW...
A SECOND, SUPER POSITIVE POINT ABOUT THIS GRAND PRIZE.

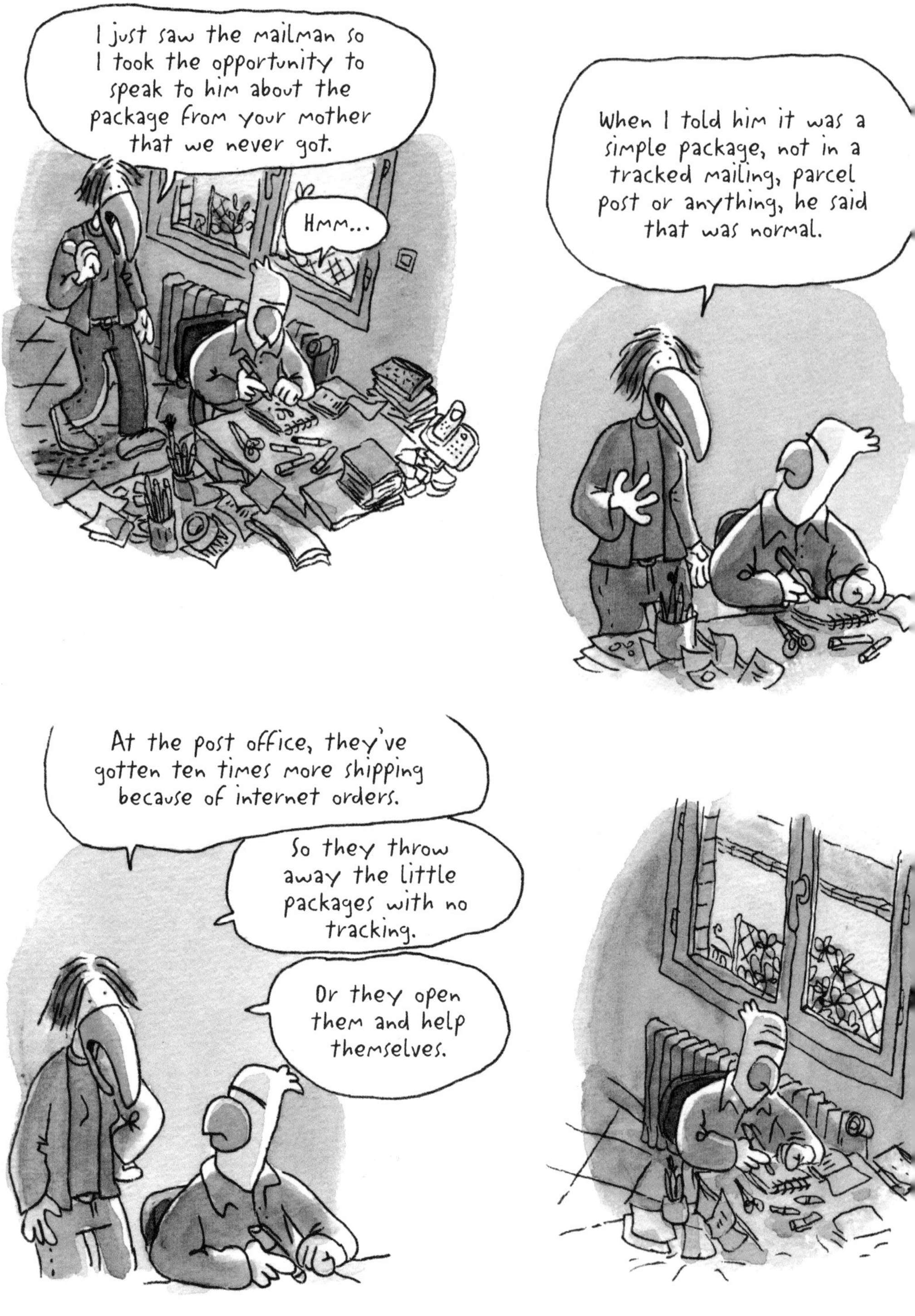

I just saw the mailman so I took the opportunity to speak to him about the package from your mother that we never got.
Hmm...
When I told him it was a simple package, not in a tracked mailing, parcel post or anything, he said that was normal.
At the post office, they've gotten ten times more shipping because of internet orders.
So they throw away the little packages with no tracking.
Or they open them and help themselves.

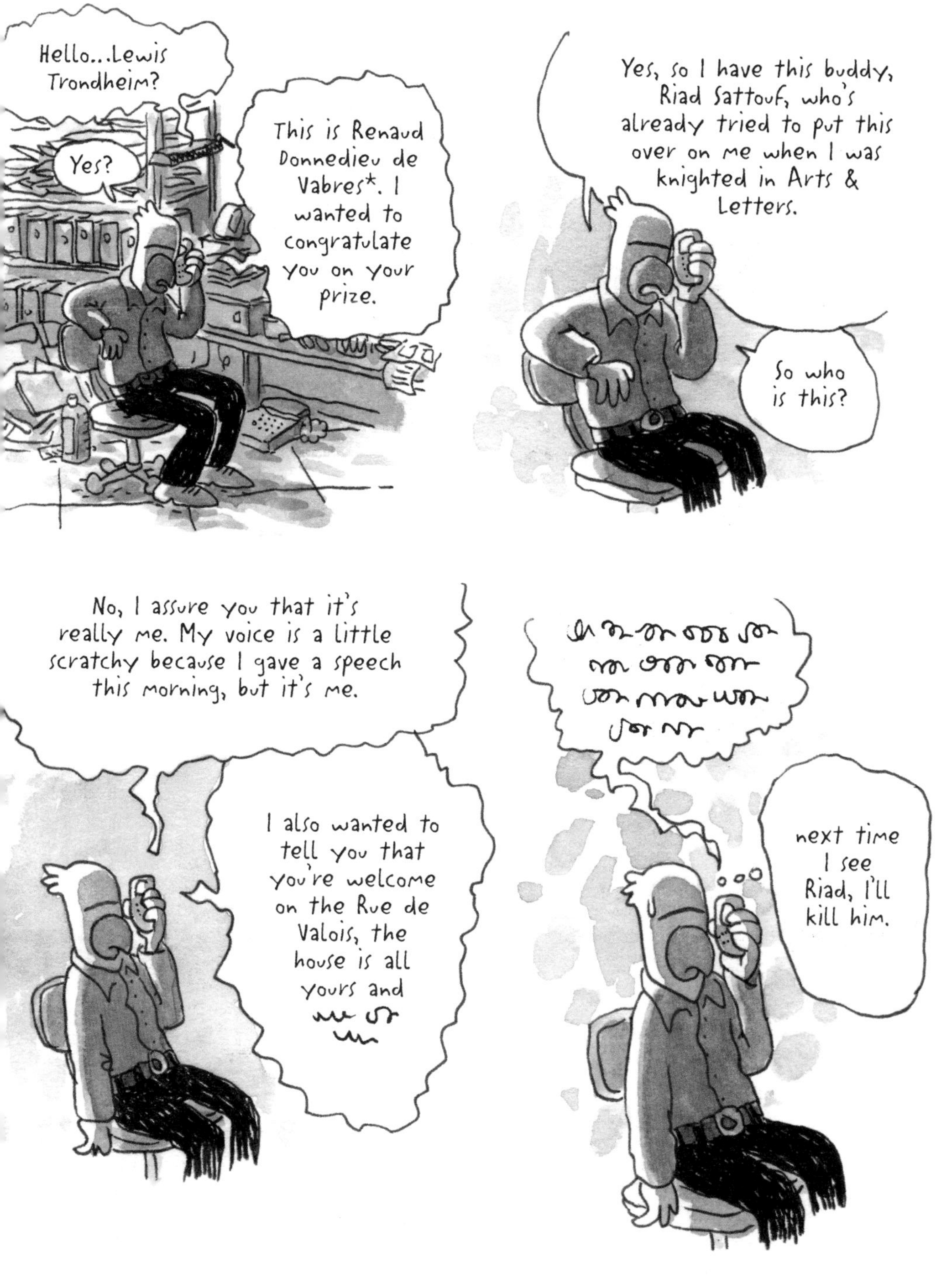
Hello...Lewis Trondheim?
Yes?
This is Renaud Donnedieu de Vabres*. I wanted to congratulate you on your prize.
Yes, so I have this buddy, Riad Sattouf, who's already tried to put this over on me when I was knighted in Arts & Letters.
So who is this?
No, I assure you that it's really me. My voice is a little scratchy because I gave a speech this morning, but it's me.
I also wanted to tell you that you're welcome on the Rue de Valois, the house is all yours and
next time I see Riad, I'll kill him.

* Minister of Culture.

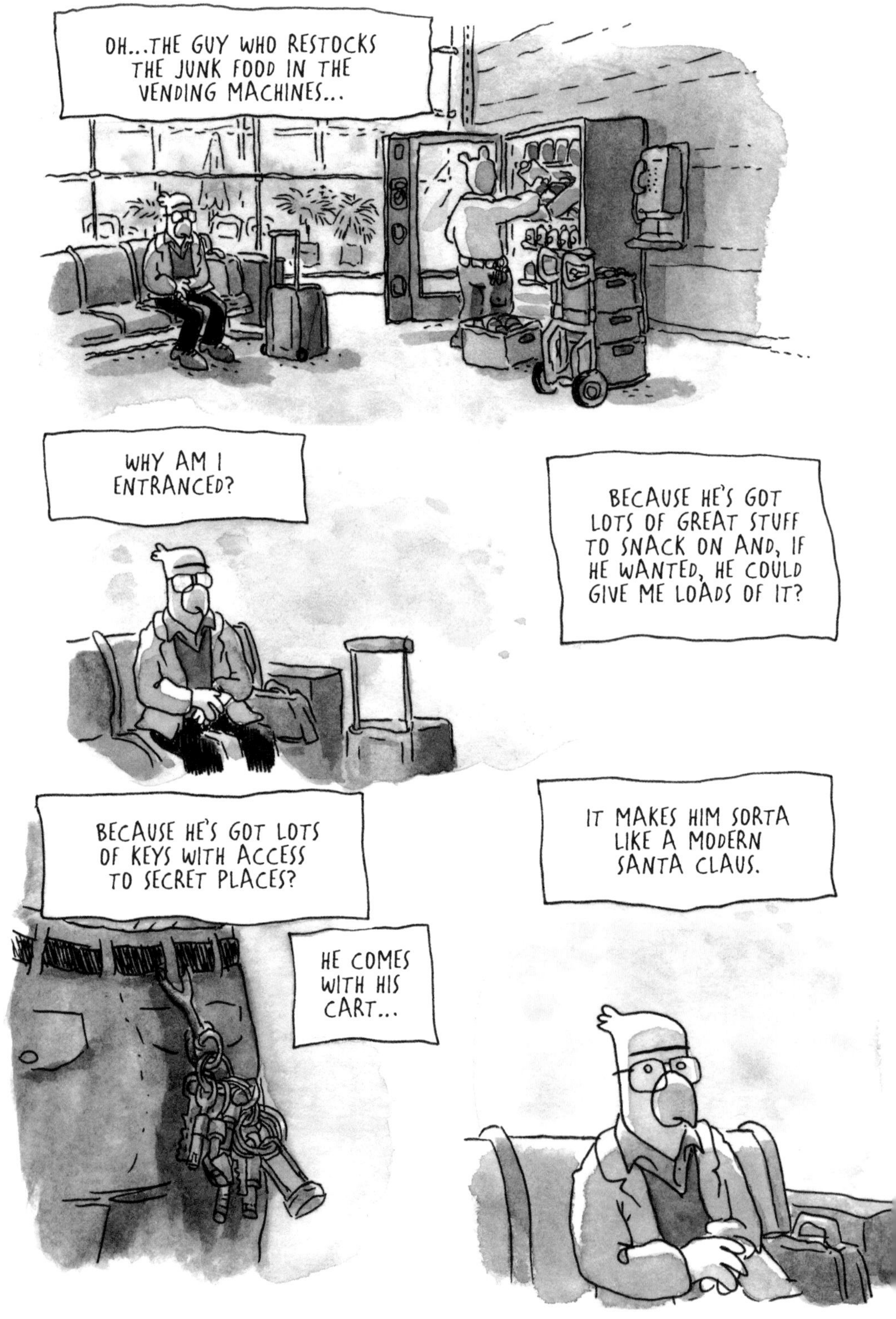
OH...THE GUY WHO RESTOCKS THE JUNK FOOD IN THE VENDING MACHINES...
WHY AM I ENTRANCED?
BECAUSE HE'S GOT LOTS OF GREAT STUFF TO SNACK ON AND, IF HE WANTED, HE COULD GIVE ME LOADS OF IT?
BECAUSE HE'S GOT LOTS OF KEYS WITH ACCESS TO SECRET PLACES?
HE COMES WITH HIS CART...
IT MAKES HIM SORTA LIKE A MODERN SANTA CLAUS.

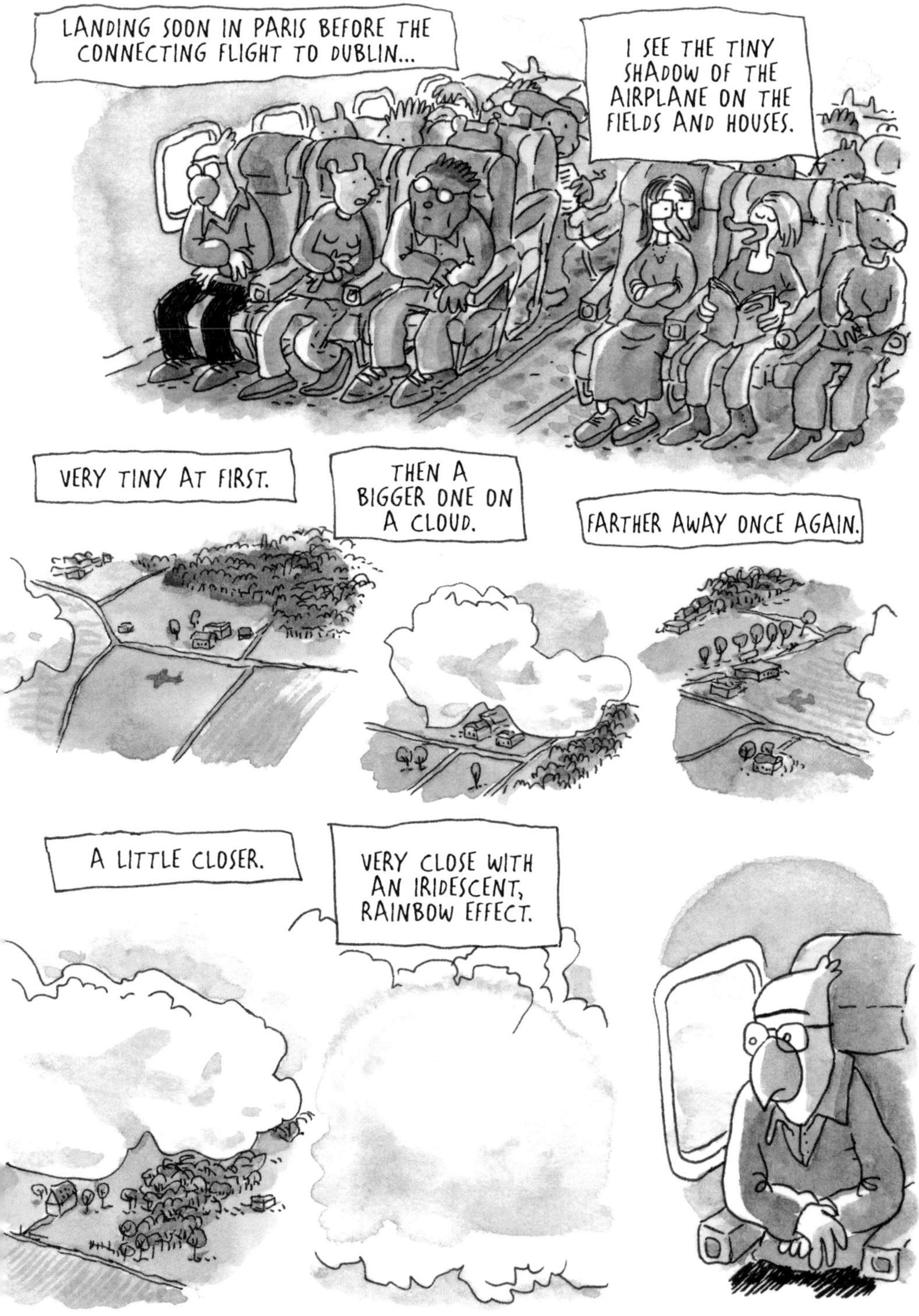
LANDING SOON IN PARIS BEFORE THE CONNECTING FLIGHT TO DUBLIN...
I SEE THE TINY SHADOW OF THE AIRPLANE ON THE FIELDS AND HOUSES.
VERY TINY AT FIRST.
THEN A BIGGER ONE ON A CLOUD.
FARTHER AWAY ONCE AGAIN.
A LITTLE CLOSER.
VERY CLOSE WITH AN IRIDESCENT, RAINBOW EFFECT.

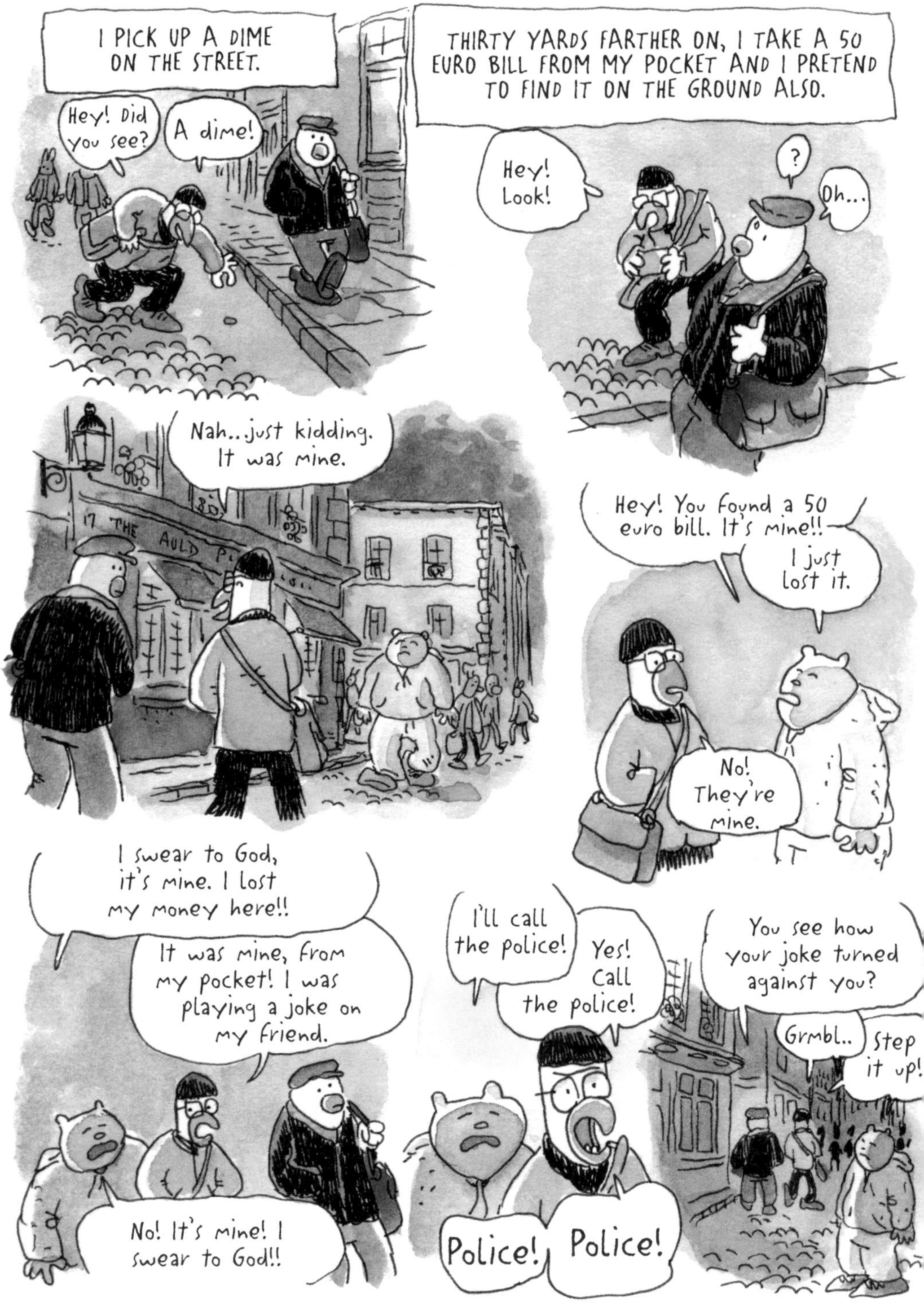
I PICK UP A DIME ON THE STREET.
Hey! Did you see?
A dime!
THIRTY YARDS FARTHER ON, I TAKE A 50 EURO BILL FROM MY POCKET AND I PRETEND TO FIND IT ON THE GROUND ALSO.
Hey! Look!
?
Oh...
Nah... just kidding. It was mine.
Hey! You found a 50 euro bill. It's mine!!
I just lost it.
No! They're mine.
I swear to God, it's mine. I lost my money here!!
It was mine, from my pocket! I was playing a joke on my friend.
No! It's mine! I swear to God!!
I'll call the police!
Yes! Call the police!
Police!
Police!
You see how your joke turned against you?
Grmbl..
Step it up!

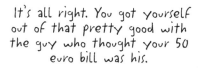

It's all right. You got yourself out of that pretty good with the guy who thought your 50 euro bill was his.

Mmm...

Still, let's take a left right away just in case he decides to look for us.

I would have just given it to him.

And I'll also take off my cap. He won't look for a bald man from a distance.

You take off your hat, too, you never know.

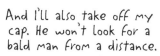

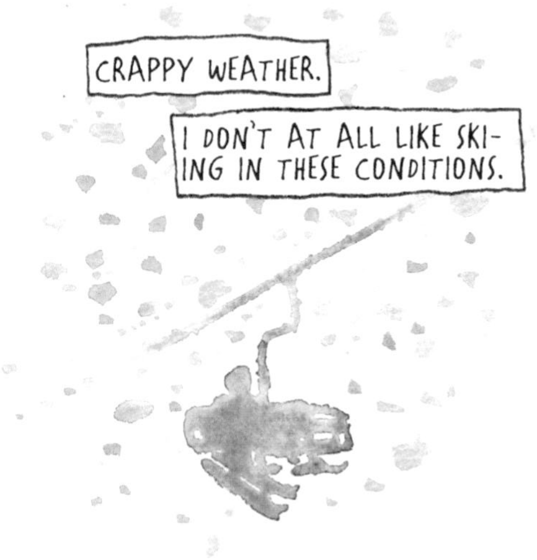
CRAPPY WEATHER.
I DON'T AT ALL LIKE SKI-ING IN THESE CONDITIONS.

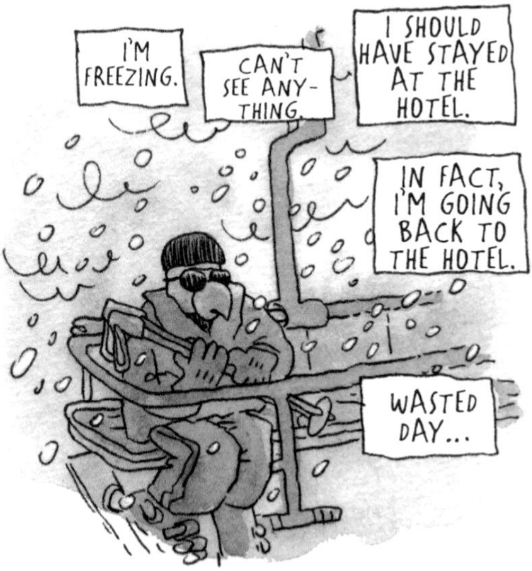
I'M FREEZING.
CAN'T SEE ANY-THING.
I SHOULD HAVE STAYED AT THE HOTEL.
IN FACT, I'M GOING BACK TO THE HOTEL.
WASTED DAY...

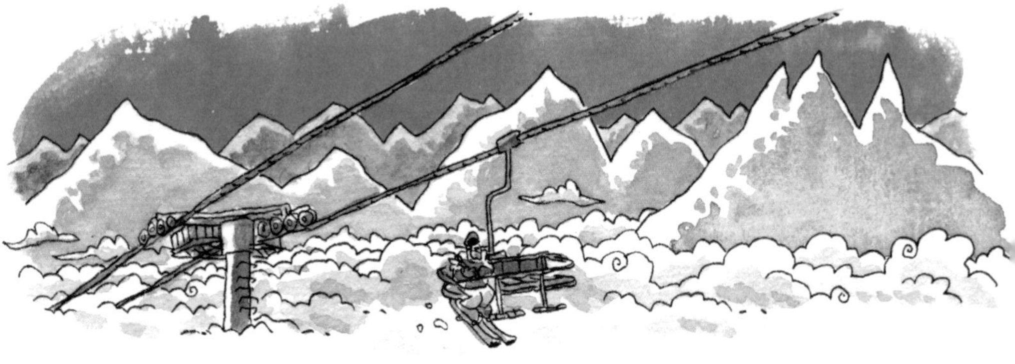

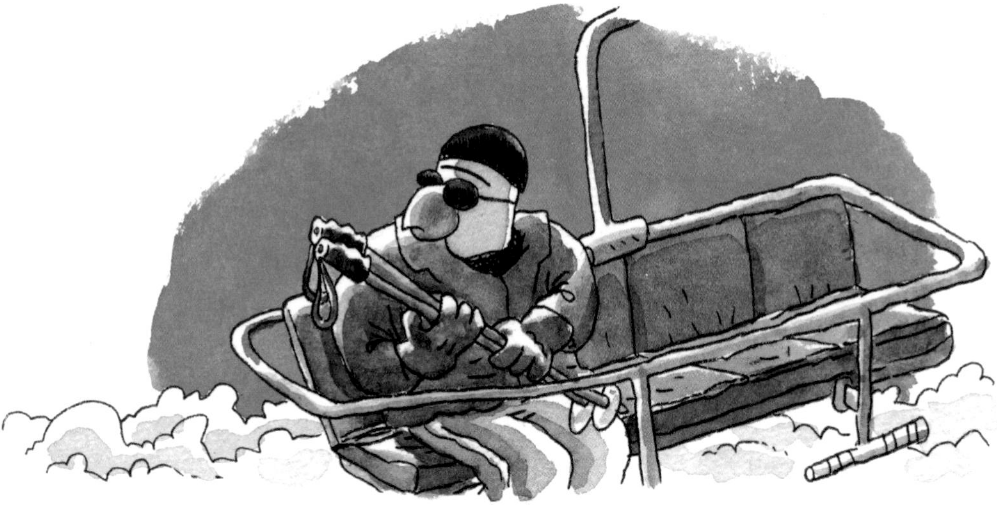

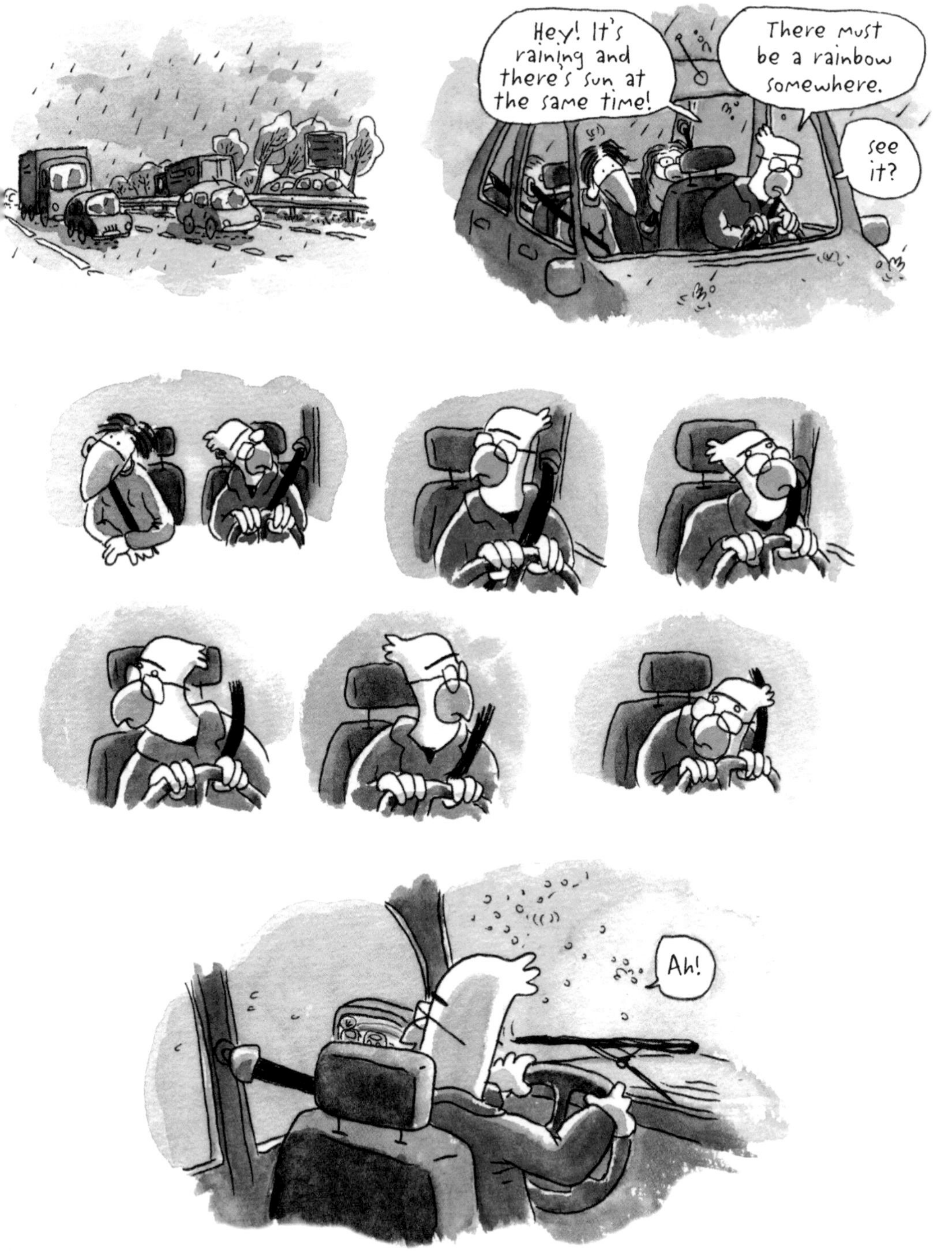
Hey! It's raining and there's sun at the same time!
There must be a rainbow somewhere.
see it?
Ah!

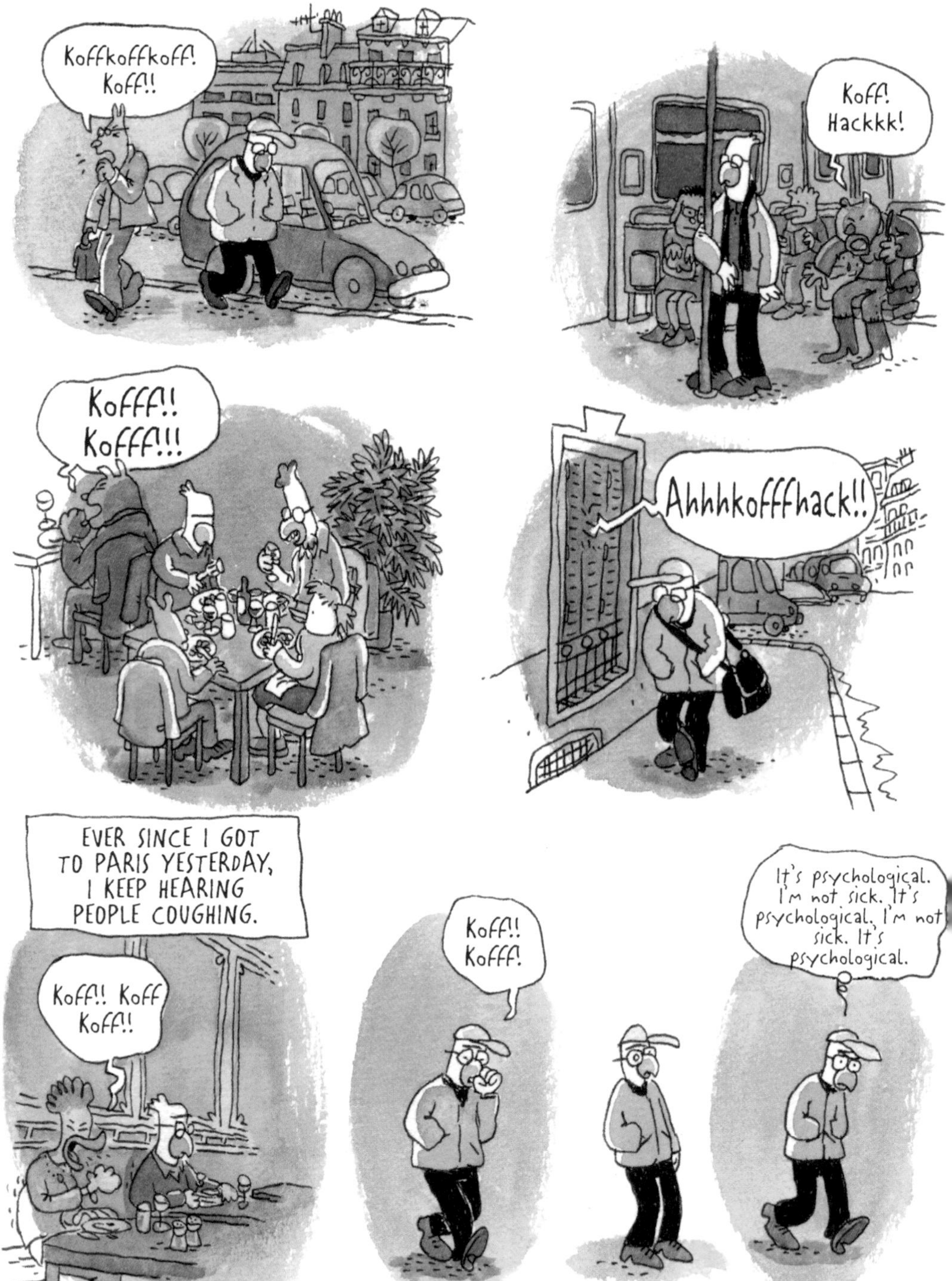
Koffkoffkoff! Koff!!
Koff! Hackkk!
Kofff!! Kofff!!!
Ahhhkofffhack!!
EVER SINCE I GOT TO PARIS YESTERDAY, I KEEP HEARING PEOPLE COUGHING.
Koff!! Koff Koff!!
Koff!! Kofff!
It's psychological. I'm not sick. It's psychological. I'm not sick. It's psychological.

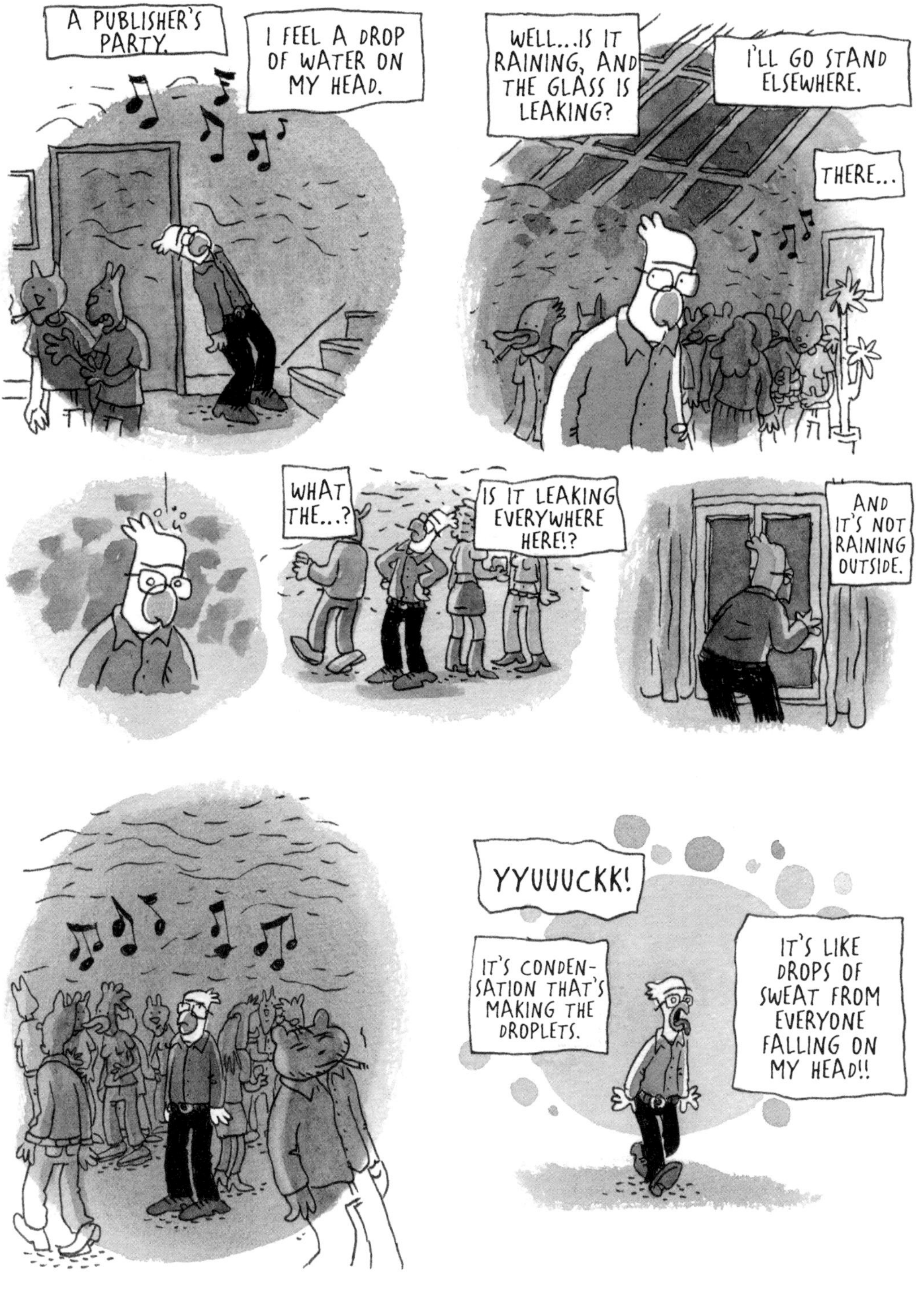
A PUBLISHER'S PARTY.
I FEEL A DROP OF WATER ON MY HEAD.
WELL...IS IT RAINING, AND THE GLASS IS LEAKING?
I'LL GO STAND ELSEWHERE.
THERE...
WHAT THE...?
IS IT LEAKING EVERYWHERE HERE!?
AND IT'S NOT RAINING OUTSIDE.
YYUUUCKK!
IT'S CONDEN-SATION THAT'S MAKING THE DROPLETS.
IT'S LIKE DROPS OF SWEAT FROM EVERYONE FALLING ON MY HEAD!!

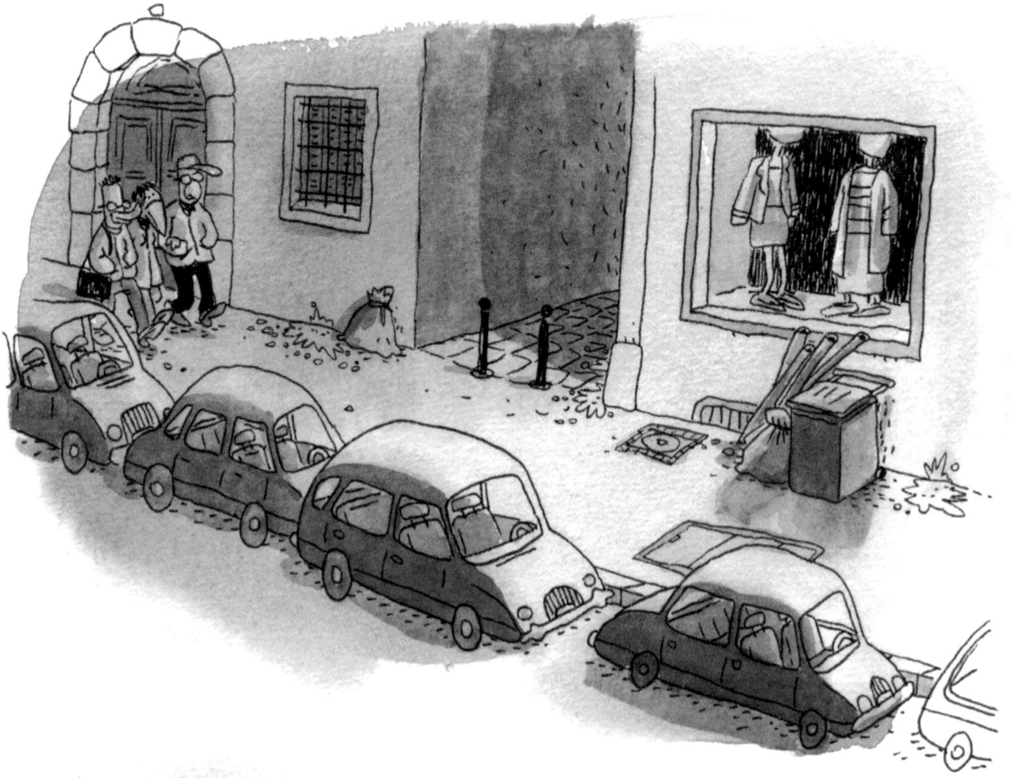

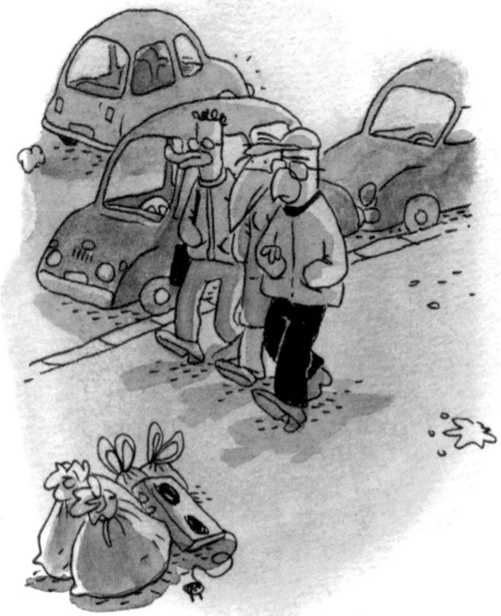

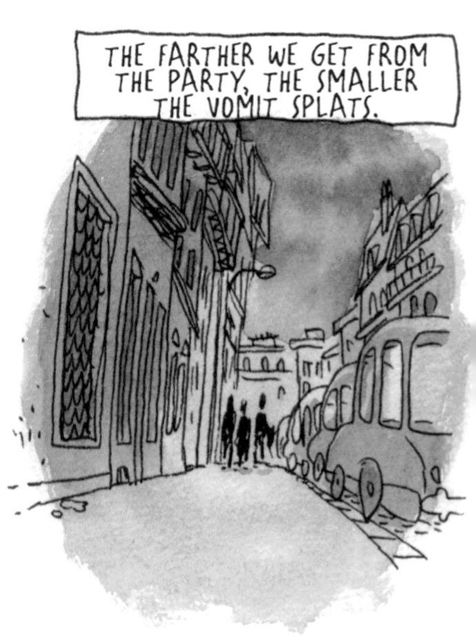
THE FARTHER WE GET FROM THE PARTY, THE SMALLER THE VOMIT SPLATS.

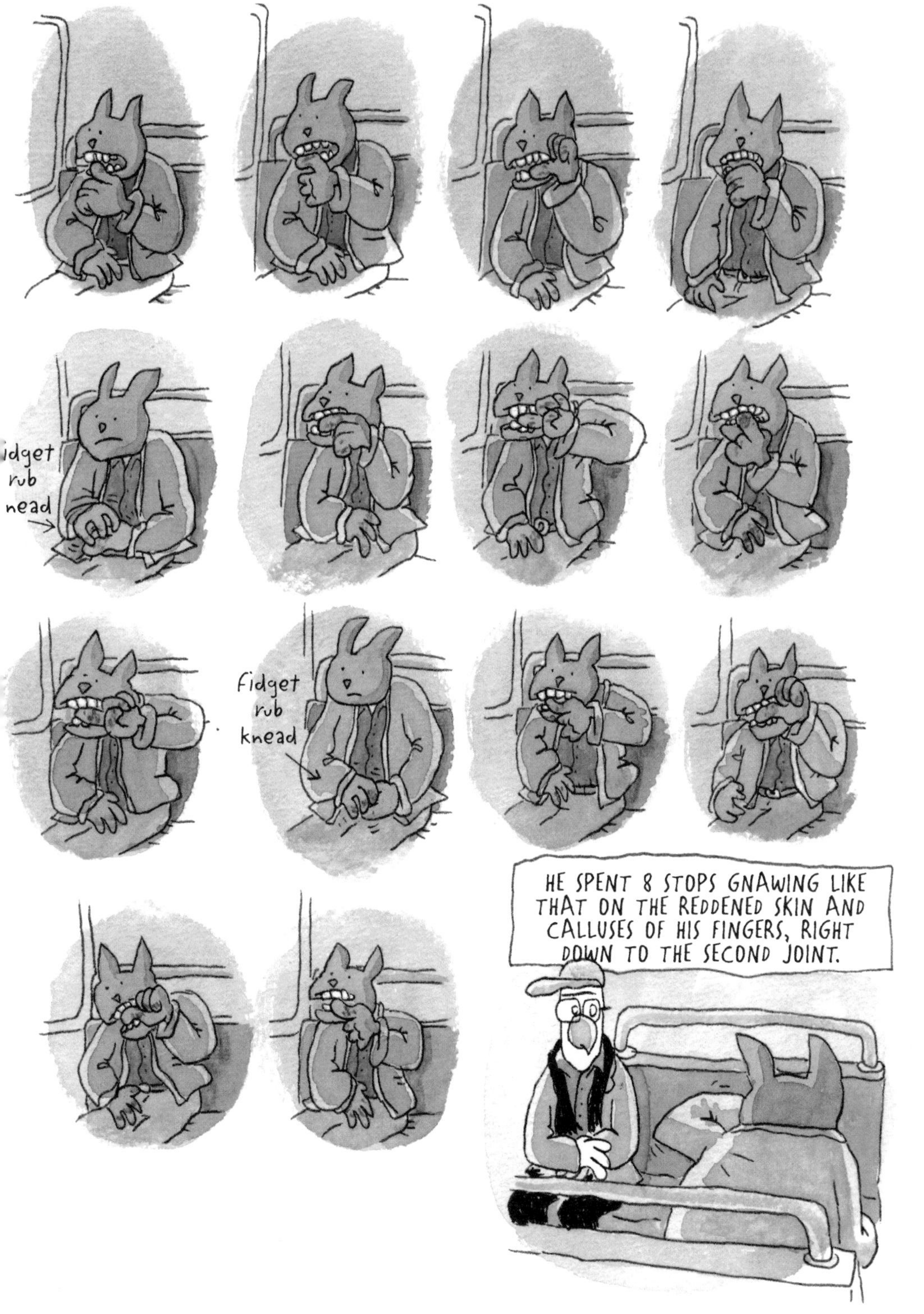
idget
rub
nead
fidget
rub
knead
HE SPENT 8 STOPS GNAWING LIKE THAT ON THE REDDENED SKIN AND CALLUSES OF HIS FINGERS, RIGHT DOWN TO THE SECOND JOINT.

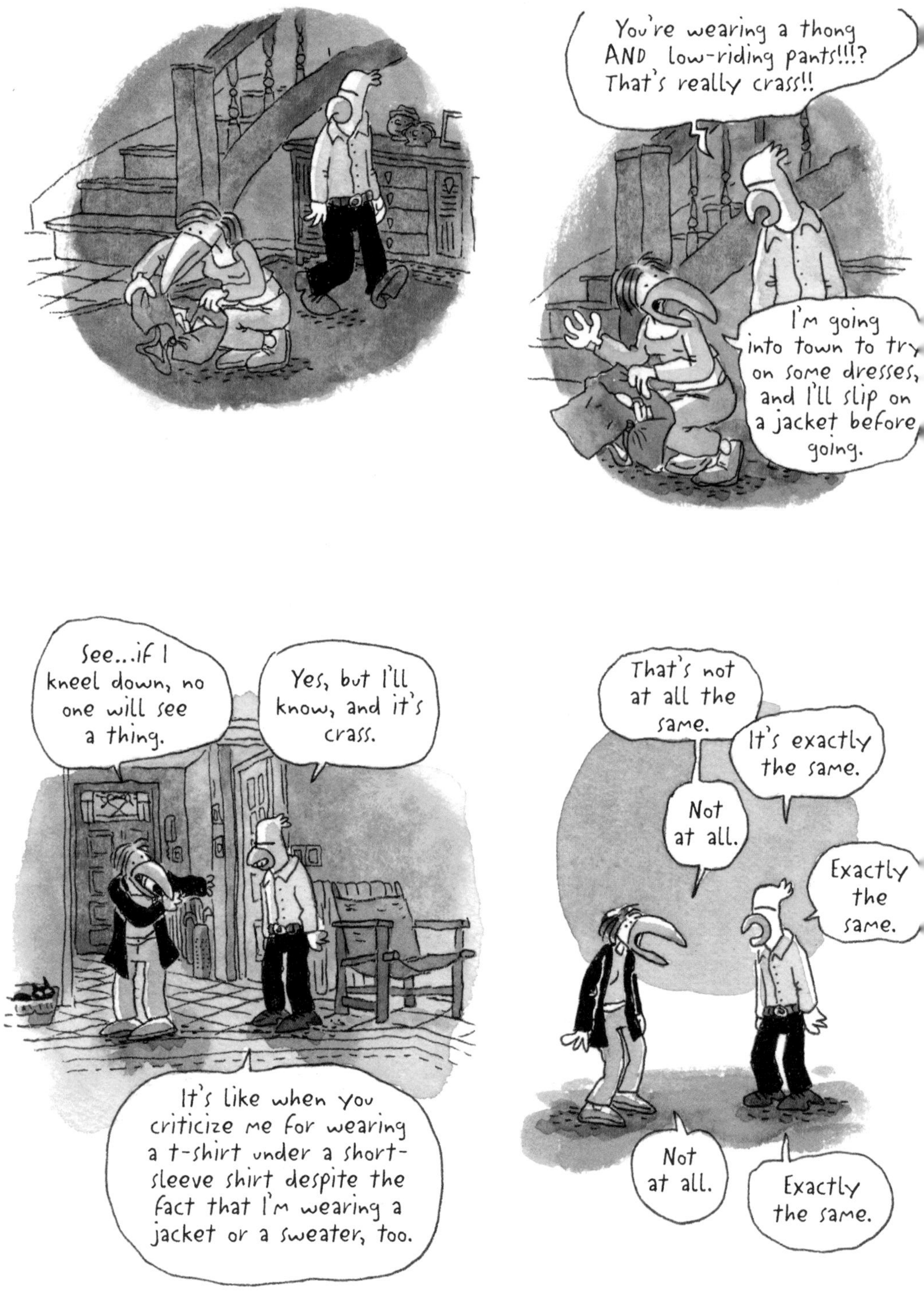

You're wearing a thong AND low-riding pants!!!? That's really crass!!
I'm going into town to try on some dresses, and I'll slip on a jacket before going.
See...if I kneel down, no one will see a thing.
Yes, but I'll know, and it's crass.
It's like when you criticize me for wearing a t-shirt under a short-sleeve shirt despite the fact that I'm wearing a jacket or a sweater, too.
That's not at all the same.
It's exactly the same.
Not at all.
Exactly the same.
Not at all.
Exactly the same.

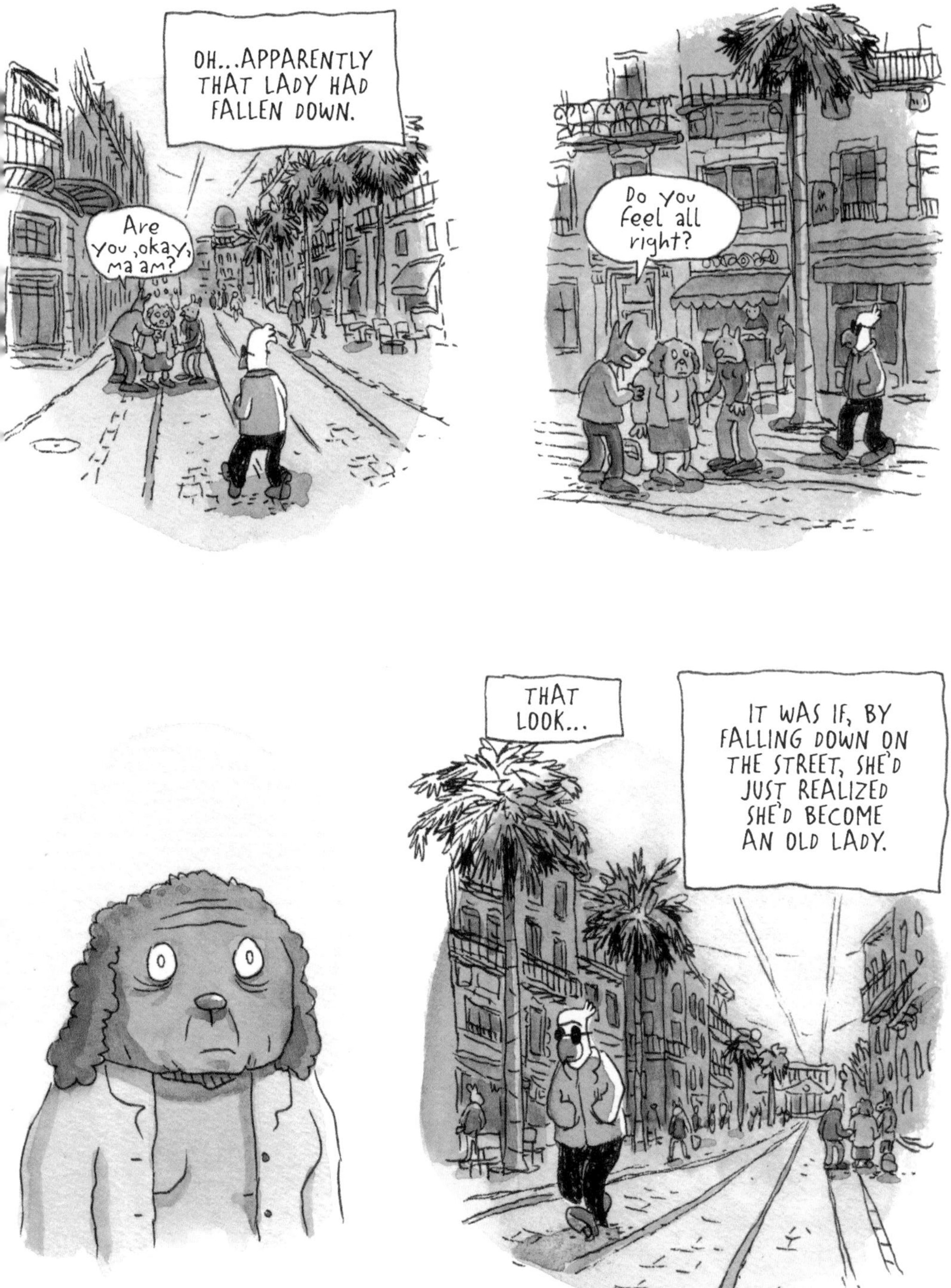
OH...APPARENTLY THAT LADY HAD FALLEN DOWN.
Are you, okay, ma'am?
Do you feel all right?
THAT LOOK...
IT WAS IF, BY FALLING DOWN ON THE STREET, SHE'D JUST REALIZED SHE'D BECOME AN OLD LADY.

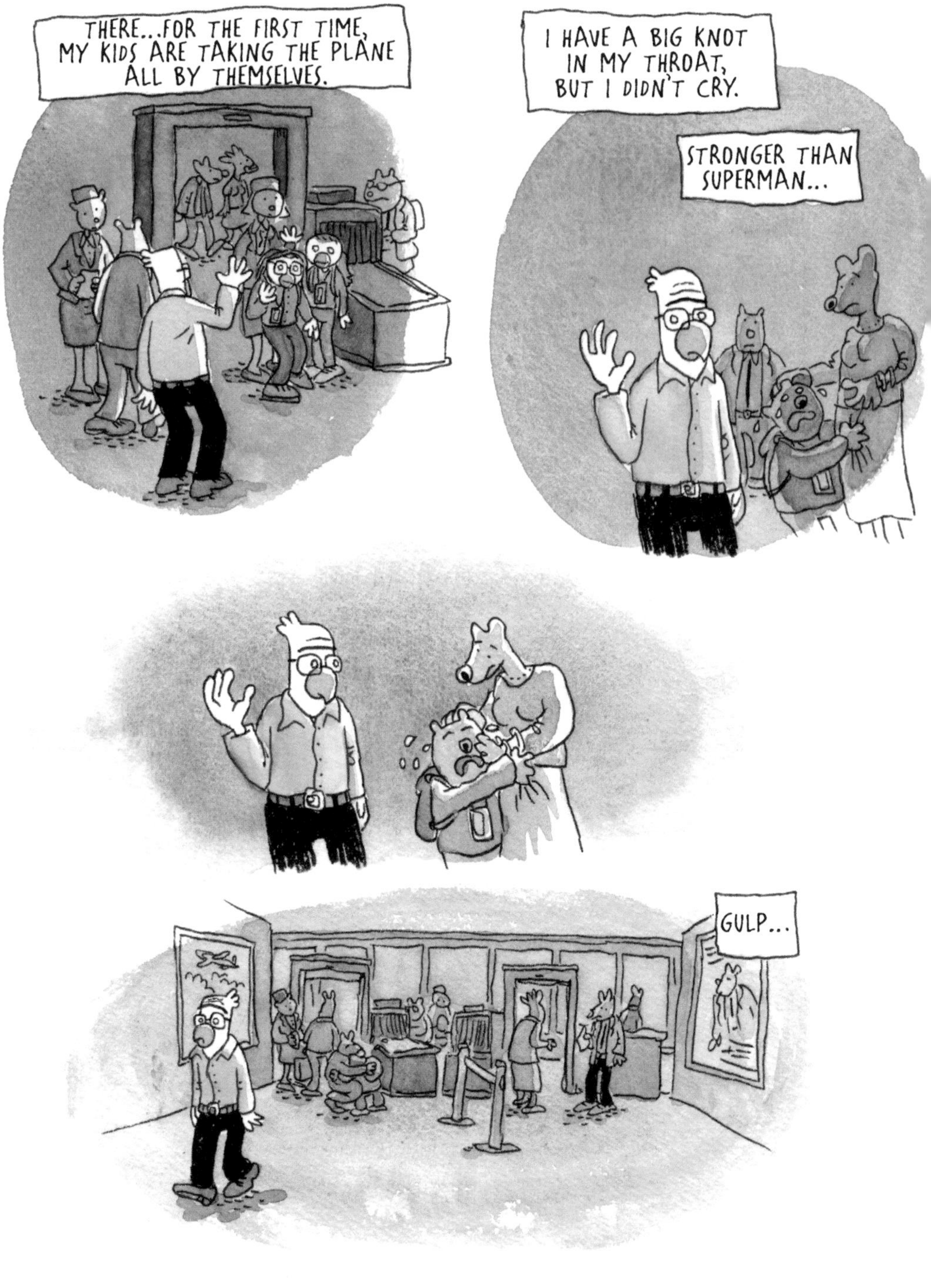

THERE...FOR THE FIRST TIME, MY KIDS ARE TAKING THE PLANE ALL BY THEMSELVES.
I HAVE A BIG KNOT IN MY THROAT, BUT I DIDN'T CRY.
STRONGER THAN SUPERMAN...
GULP...

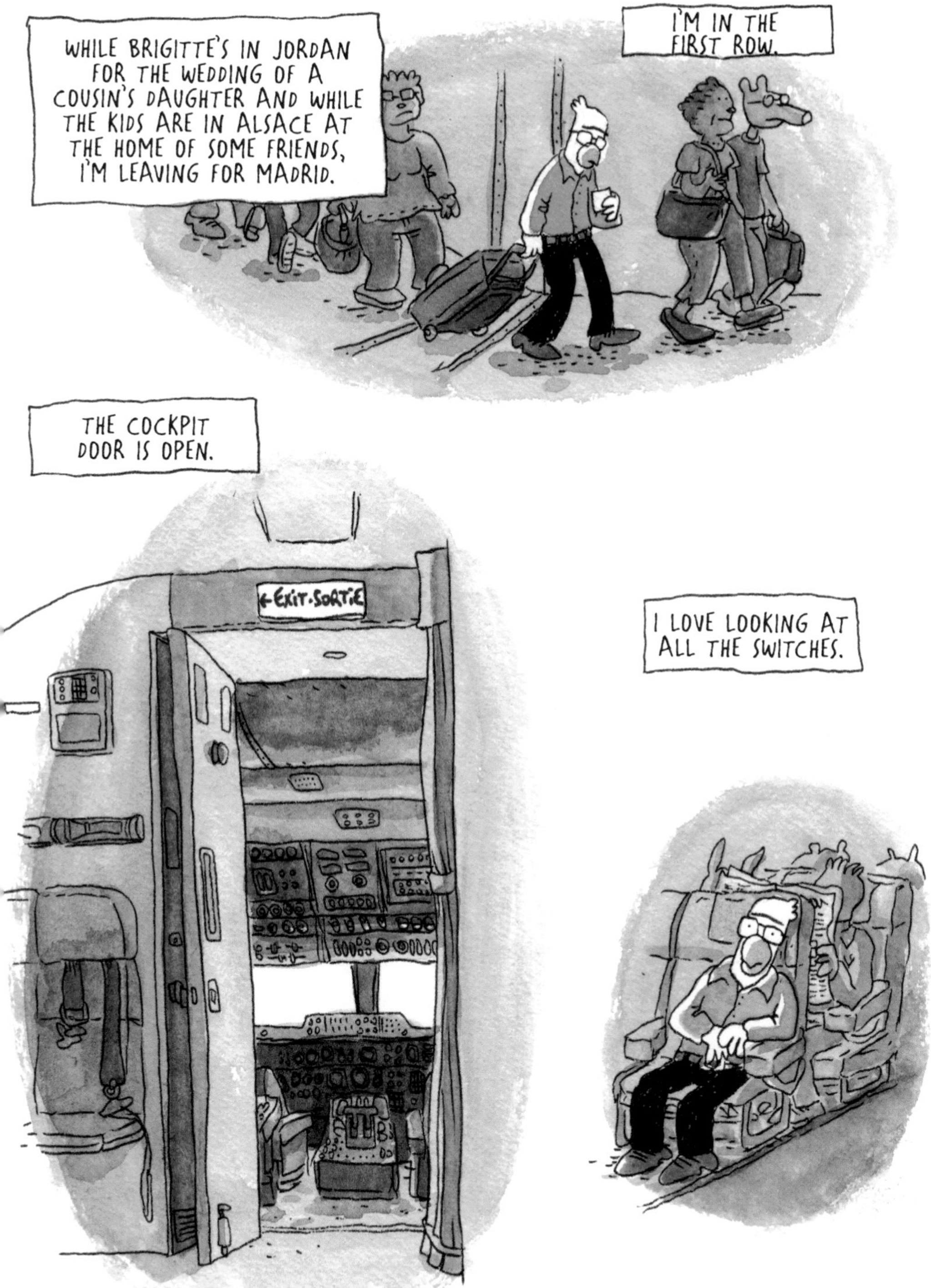
WHILE BRIGITTE'S IN JORDAN FOR THE WEDDING OF A COUSIN'S DAUGHTER AND WHILE THE KIDS ARE IN ALSACE AT THE HOME OF SOME FRIENDS, I'M LEAVING FOR MADRID.
I'M IN THE FIRST ROW.
THE COCKPIT DOOR IS OPEN.
←EXIT·SORTIE
I LOVE LOOKING AT ALL THE SWITCHES.

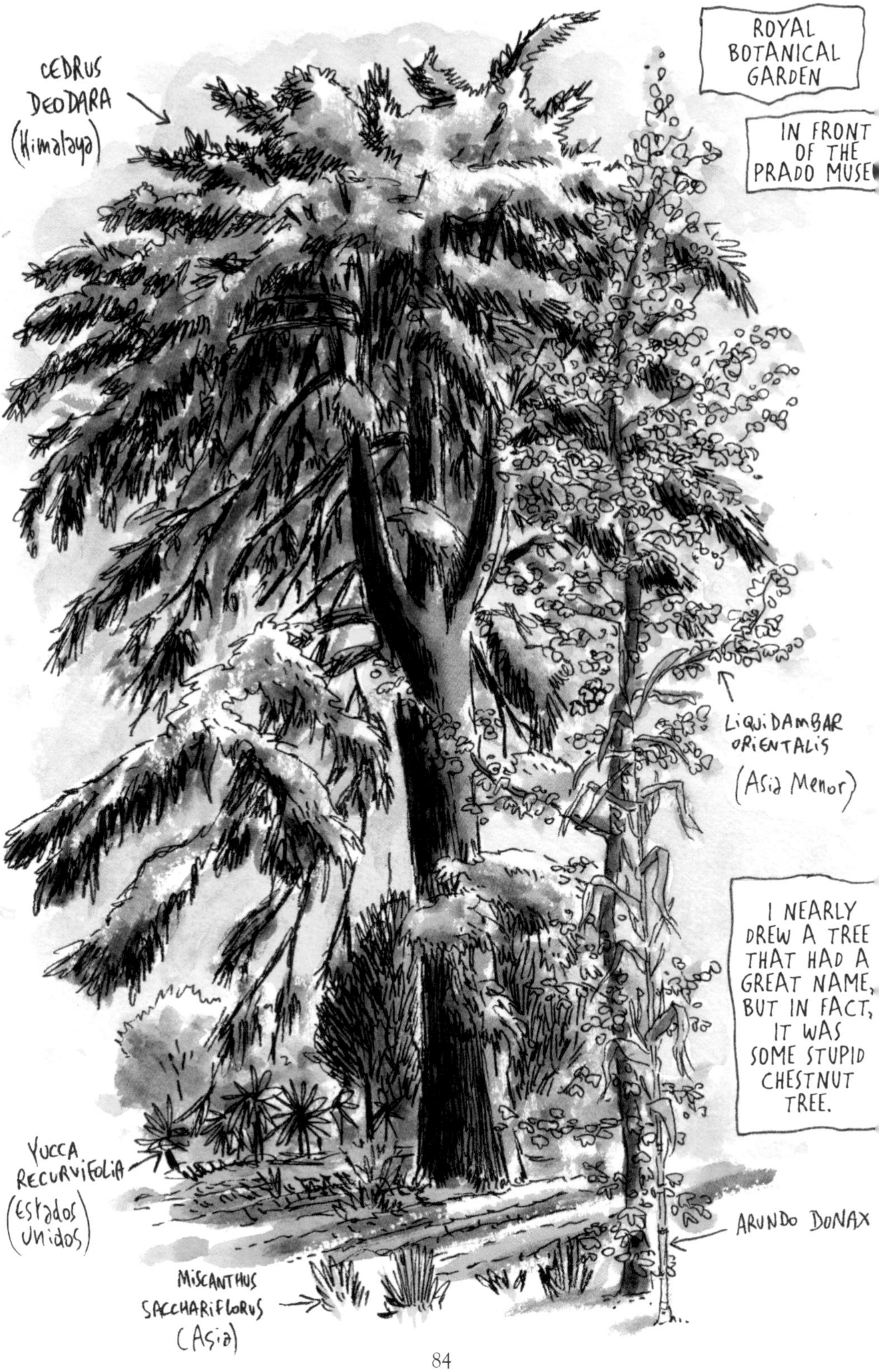
ROYAL BOTANICAL GARDEN
IN FRONT OF THE PRADO MUSE
CEDRUS DEODARA (Himalaya)
LIQUIDAMBAR ORIENTALIS (Asia Menor)
I NEARLY DREW A TREE THAT HAD A GREAT NAME, BUT IN FACT, IT WAS SOME STUPID CHESTNUT TREE.
YUCCA RECURVIFOLIA (Estados Unidos)
ARUNDO DONAX
MISCANTHUS SACCHARIFLORUS (Asia)

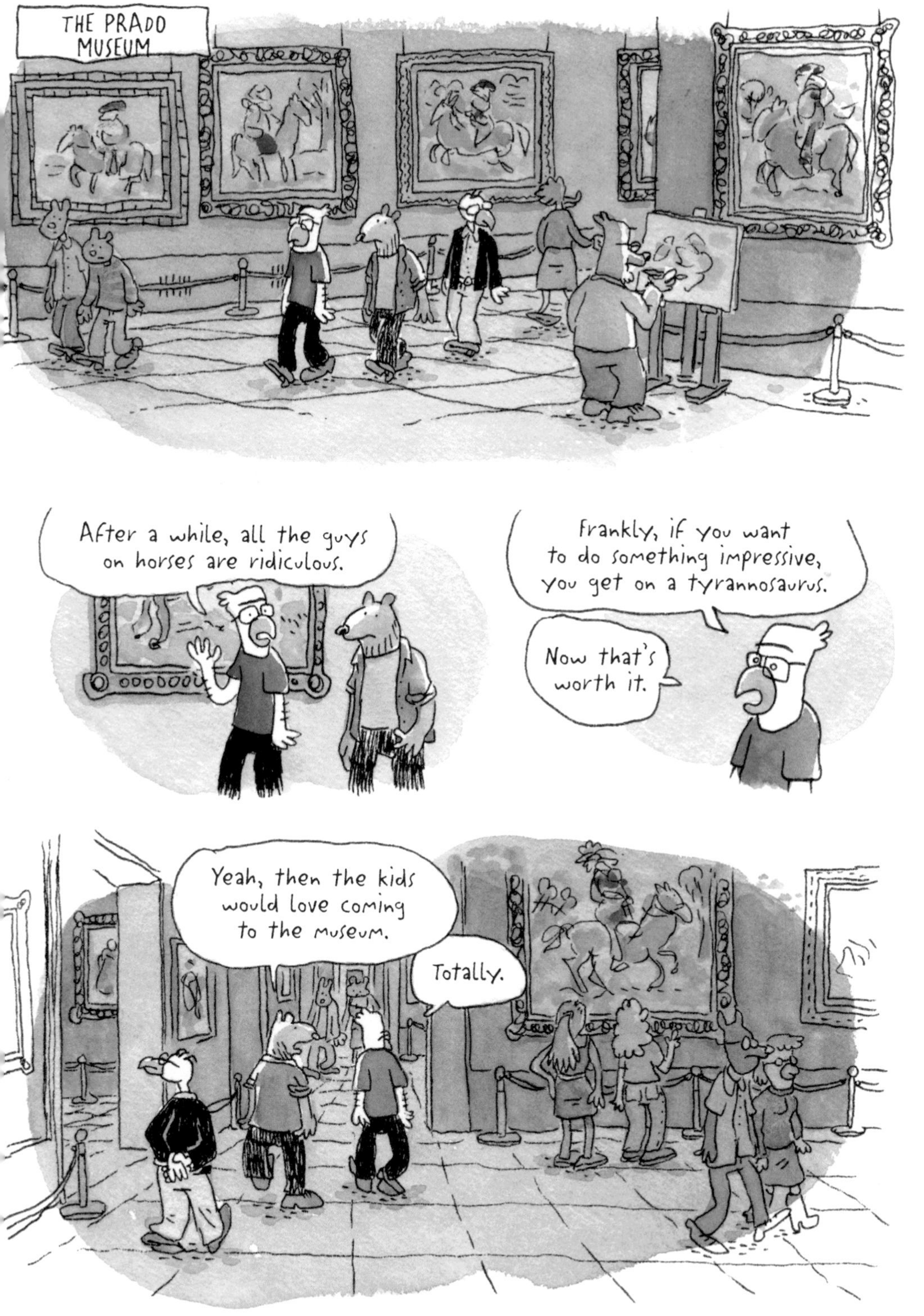
THE PRADO MUSEUM
After a while, all the guys on horses are ridiculous.
Frankly, if you want to do something impressive, you get on a tyrannosaurus.
Now that's worth it.
Yeah, then the kids would love coming to the museum.
Totally.

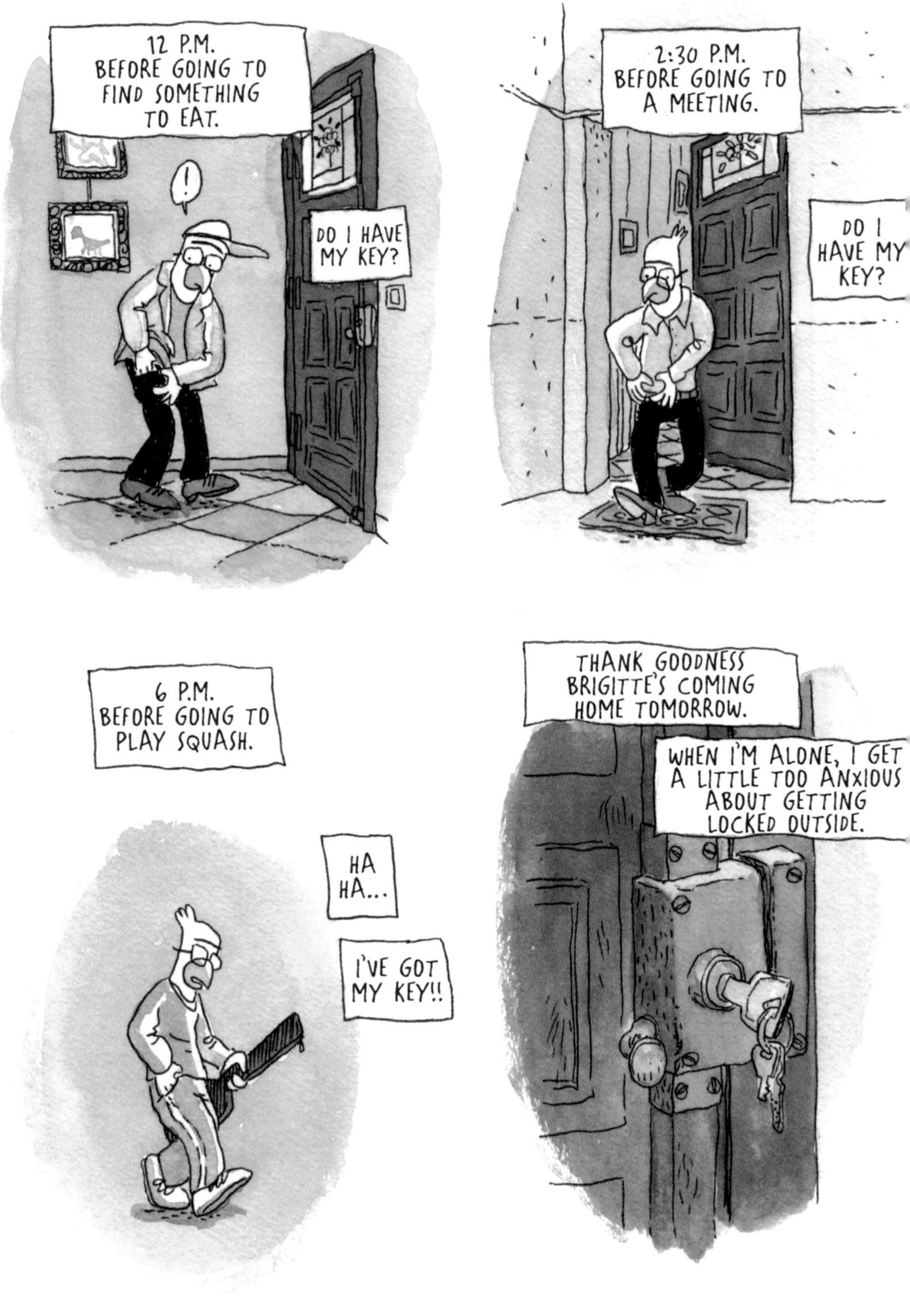

12 P.M.
BEFORE GOING TO FIND SOMETHING TO EAT.
!
DO I HAVE MY KEY?
2:30 P.M.
BEFORE GOING TO A MEETING.
DO I HAVE MY KEY?
6 P.M.
BEFORE GOING TO PLAY SQUASH.
HA HA...
I'VE GOT MY KEY!!
THANK GOODNESS BRIGITTE'S COMING HOME TOMORROW.
WHEN I'M ALONE, I GET A LITTLE TOO ANXIOUS ABOUT GETTING LOCKED OUTSIDE.

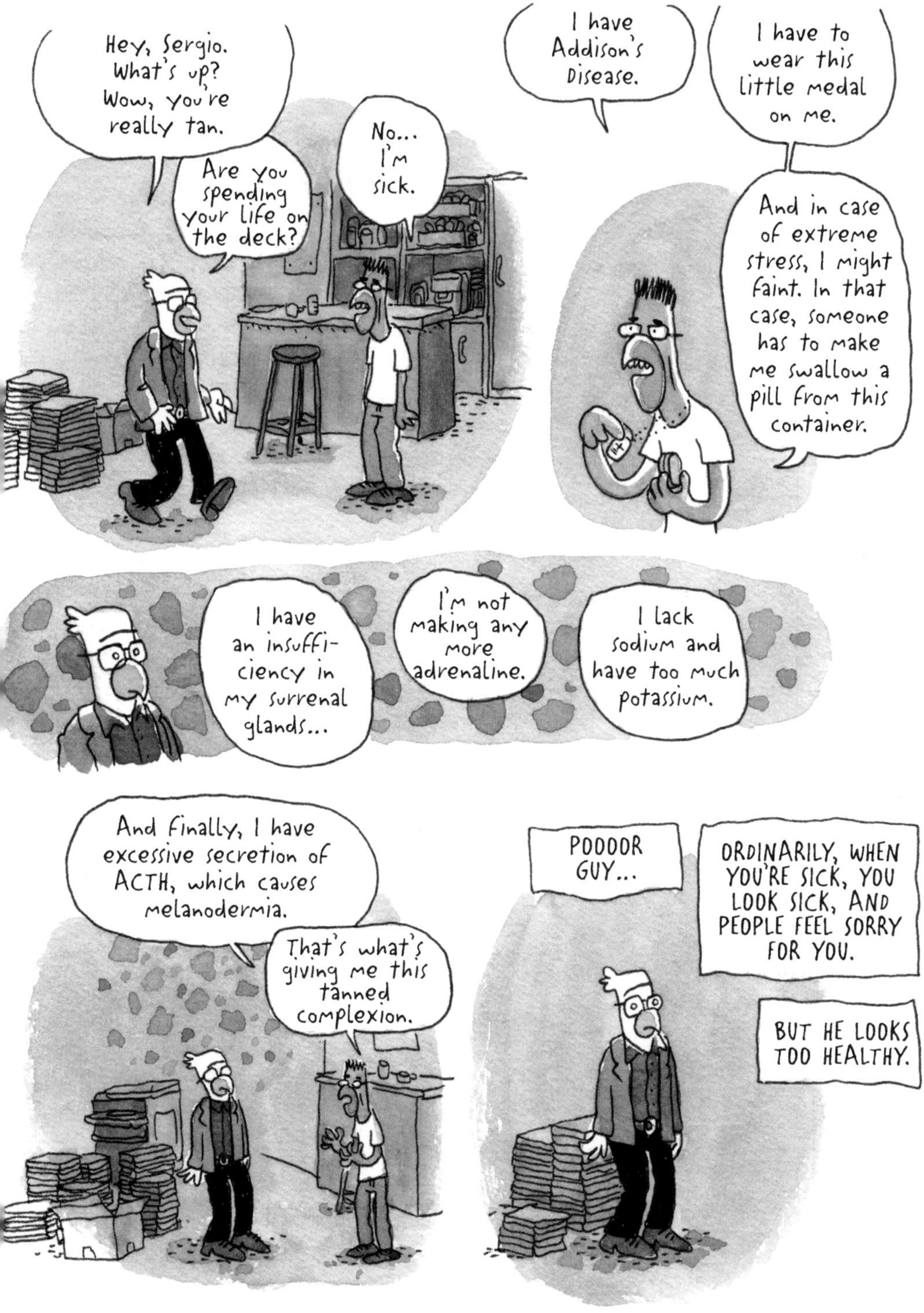
Hey, Sergio. What's up? Wow, you're really tan.
Are you spending your life on the deck?
No... I'm sick.
I have Addison's Disease.
I have to wear this little medal on me.
And in case of extreme stress, I might faint. In that case, someone has to make me swallow a pill from this container.
I have an insuffi-ciency in my surrenal glands...
I'm not making any more adrenaline.
I lack sodium and have too much potassium.
And finally, I have excessive secretion of ACTH, which causes melanodermia.
That's what's giving me this tanned complexion.
POOOOR GUY...
ORDINARILY, WHEN YOU'RE SICK, YOU LOOK SICK, AND PEOPLE FEEL SORRY FOR YOU.
BUT HE LOOKS TOO HEALTHY.

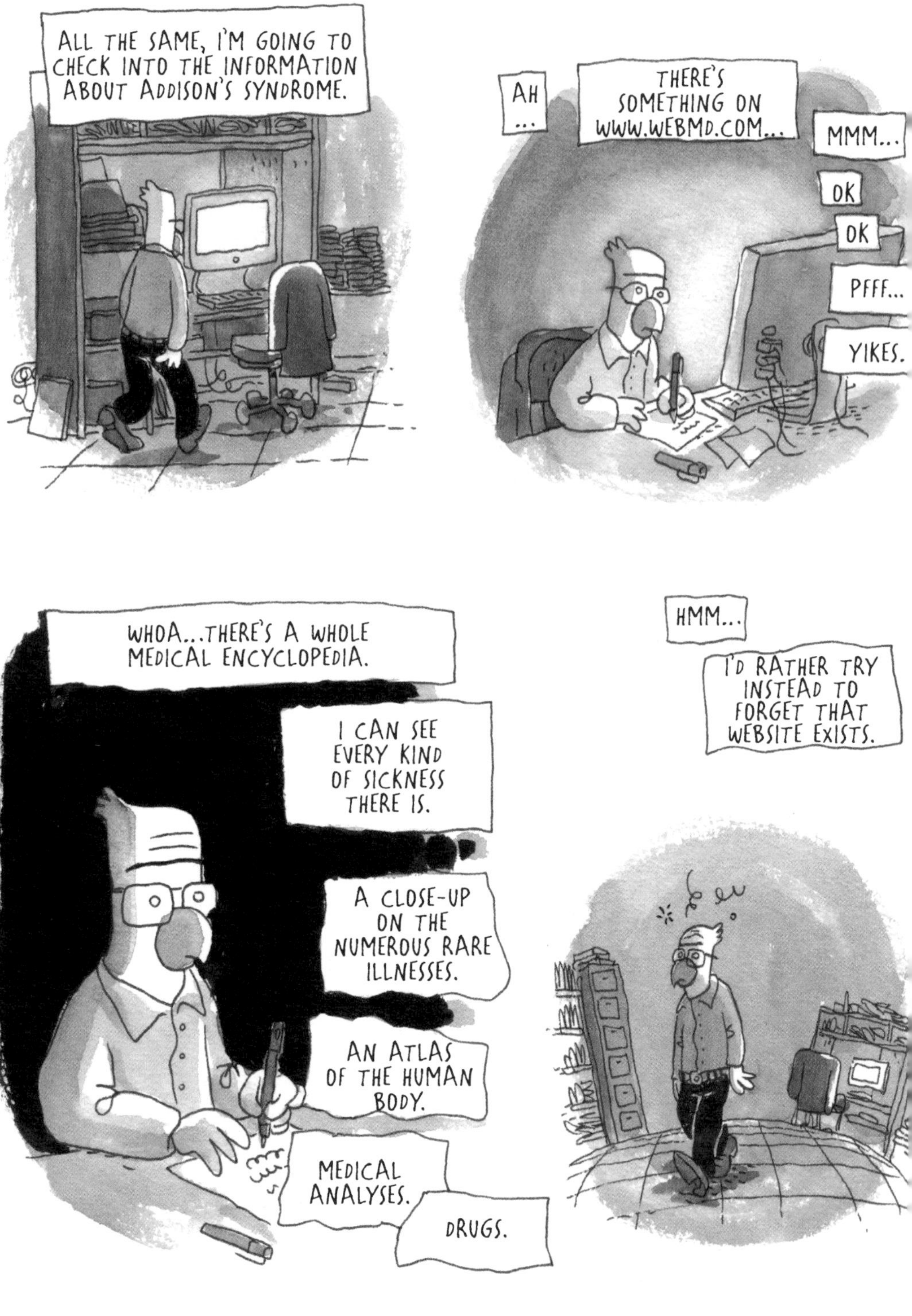
ALL THE SAME, I'M GOING TO CHECK INTO THE INFORMATION ABOUT ADDISON'S SYNDROME.
AH ...
THERE'S SOMETHING ON WWW.WEBMD.COM...
MMM...
OK
OK
PFFF...
YIKES.
WHOA...THERE'S A WHOLE MEDICAL ENCYCLOPEDIA.
I CAN SEE EVERY KIND OF SICKNESS THERE IS.
A CLOSE-UP ON THE NUMEROUS RARE ILLNESSES.
AN ATLAS OF THE HUMAN BODY.
MEDICAL ANALYSES.
DRUGS.
HMM...
I'D RATHER TRY INSTEAD TO FORGET THAT WEBSITE EXISTS.

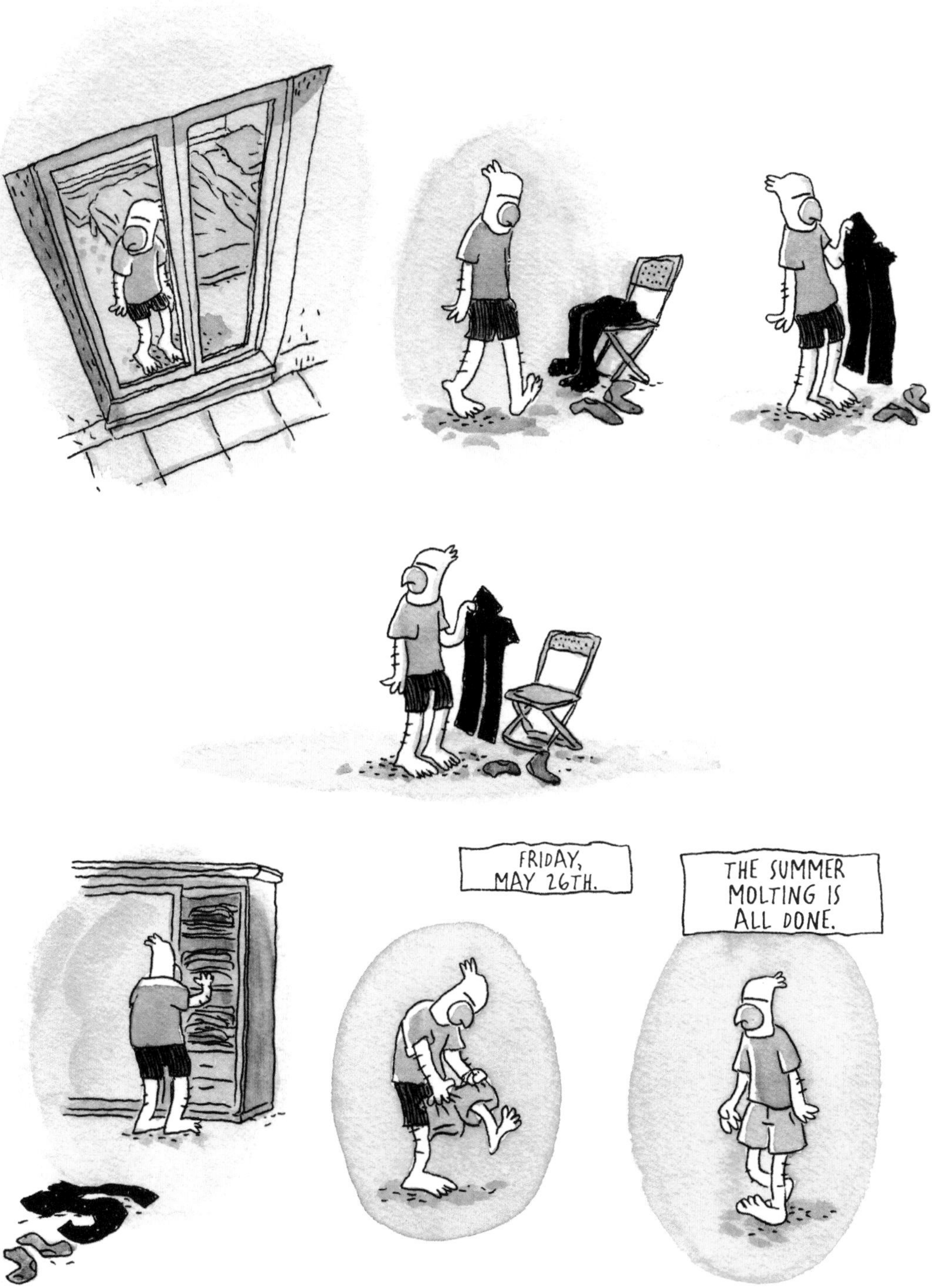
FRIDAY, MAY 26TH.
THE SUMMER MOLTING IS ALL DONE.

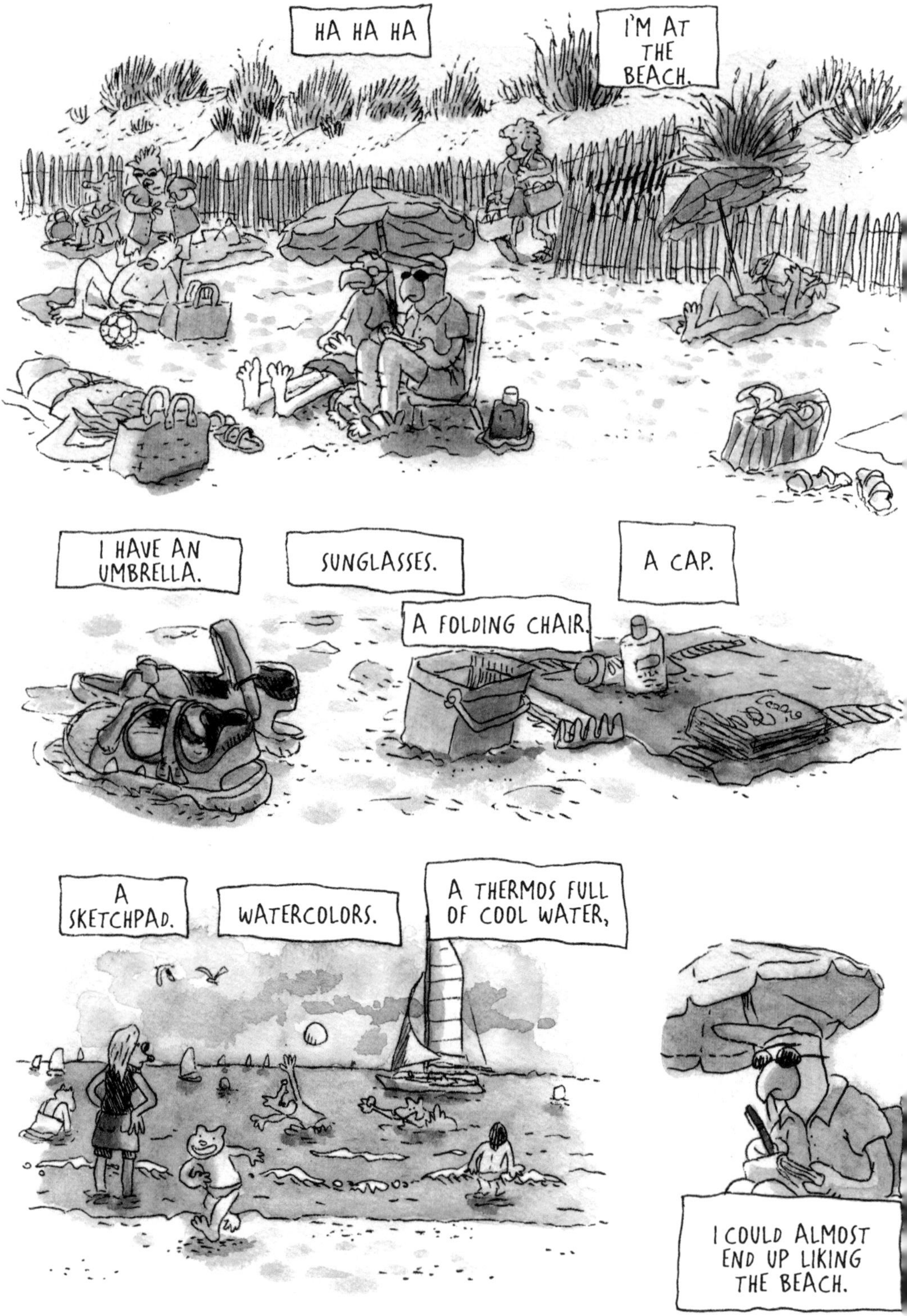
HA HA HA
I'M AT THE BEACH.
I HAVE AN UMBRELLA.
SUNGLASSES.
A CAP.
A FOLDING CHAIR.
A SKETCHPAD.
WATERCOLORS.
A THERMOS FULL OF COOL WATER,
I COULD ALMOST END UP LIKING THE BEACH.

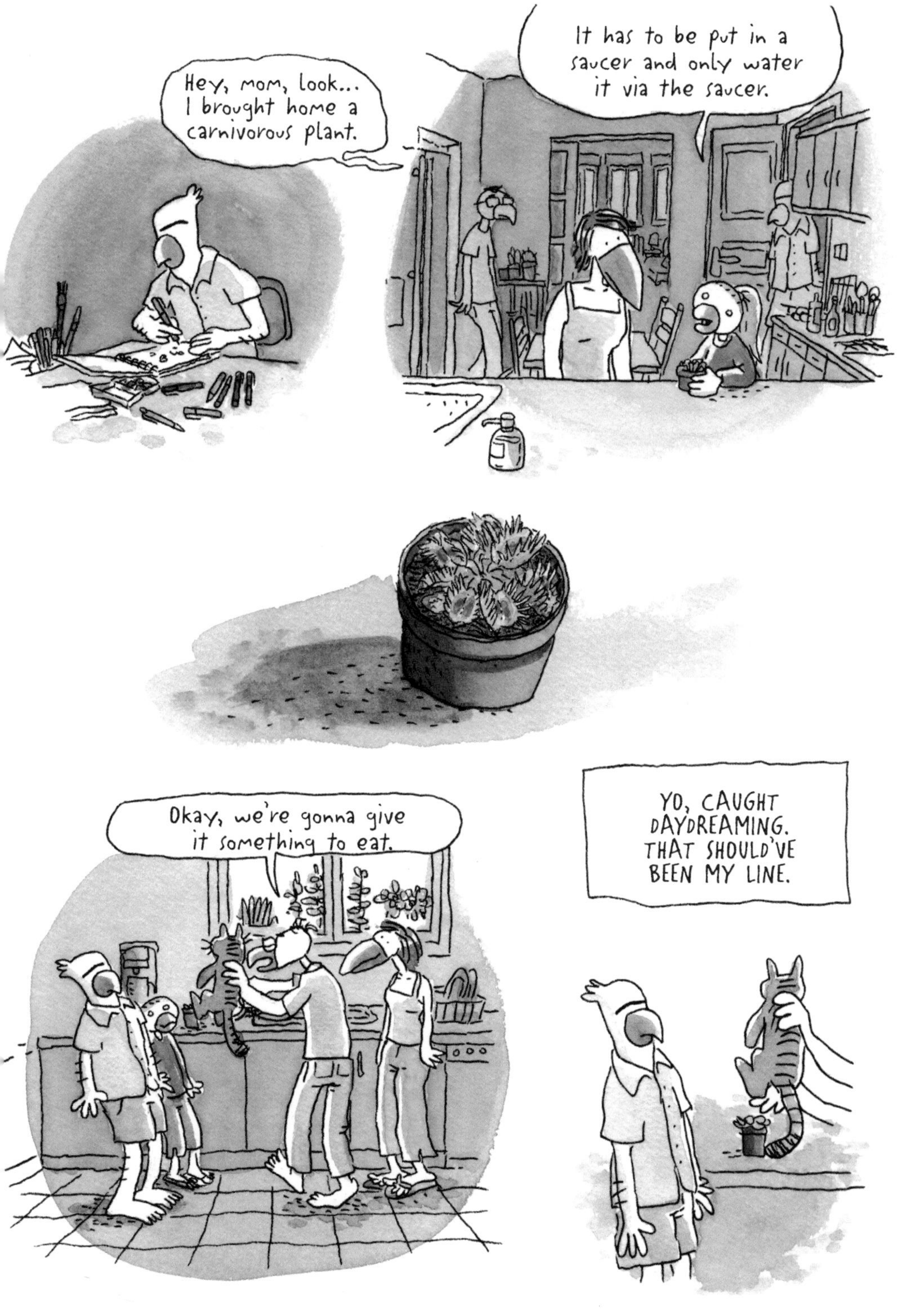
Hey, mom, look... I brought home a carnivorous plant.
It has to be put in a saucer and only water it via the saucer.
Okay, we're gonna give it something to eat.
YO, CAUGHT DAYDREAMING. THAT SHOULD'VE BEEN MY LINE.

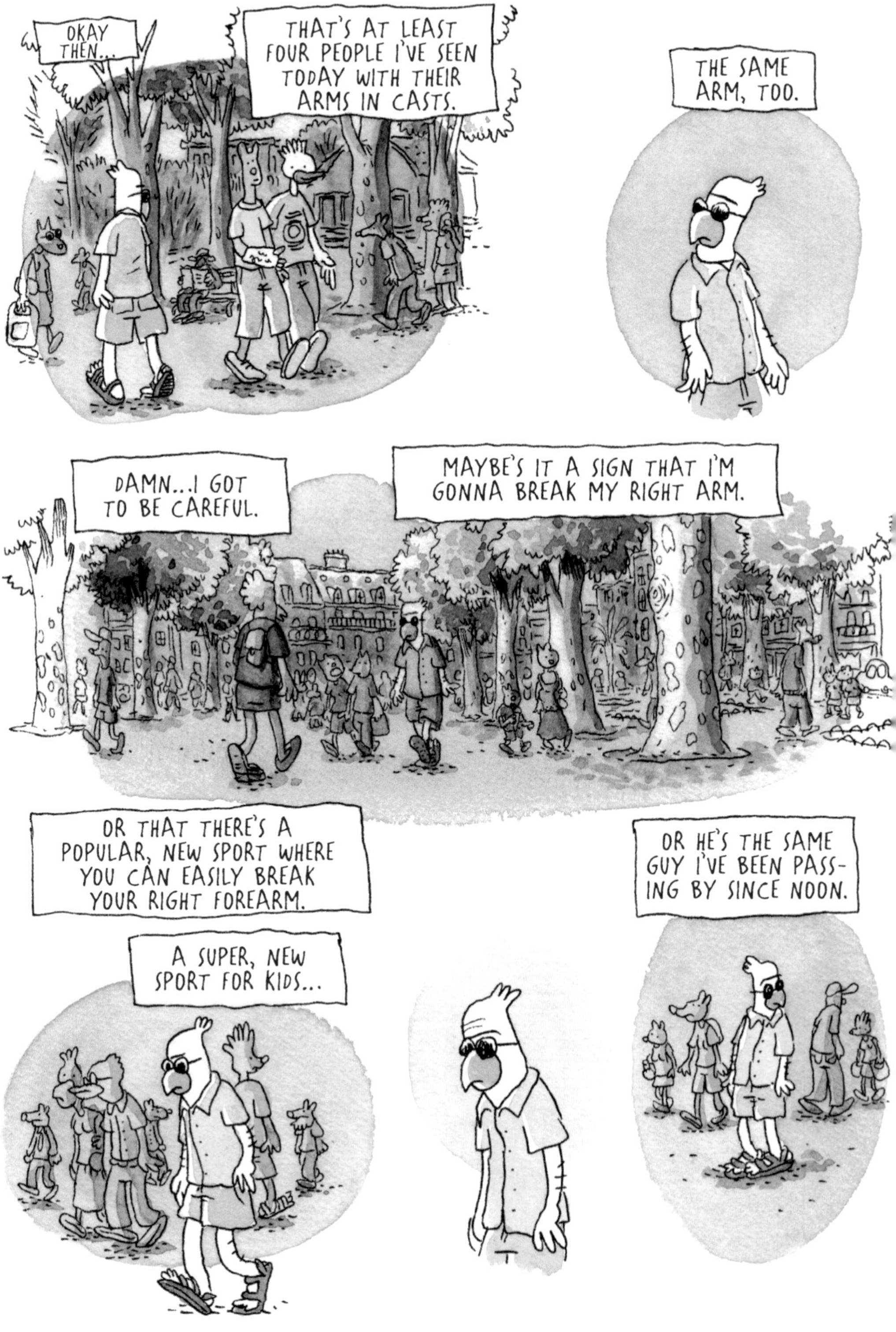
OKAY THEN...
THAT'S AT LEAST FOUR PEOPLE I'VE SEEN TODAY WITH THEIR ARMS IN CASTS.
THE SAME ARM, TOO.
DAMN...I GOT TO BE CAREFUL.
MAYBE'S IT A SIGN THAT I'M GONNA BREAK MY RIGHT ARM.
OR THAT THERE'S A POPULAR, NEW SPORT WHERE YOU CAN EASILY BREAK YOUR RIGHT FOREARM.
A SUPER, NEW SPORT FOR KIDS...
OR HE'S THE SAME GUY I'VE BEEN PASS-ING BY SINCE NOON.

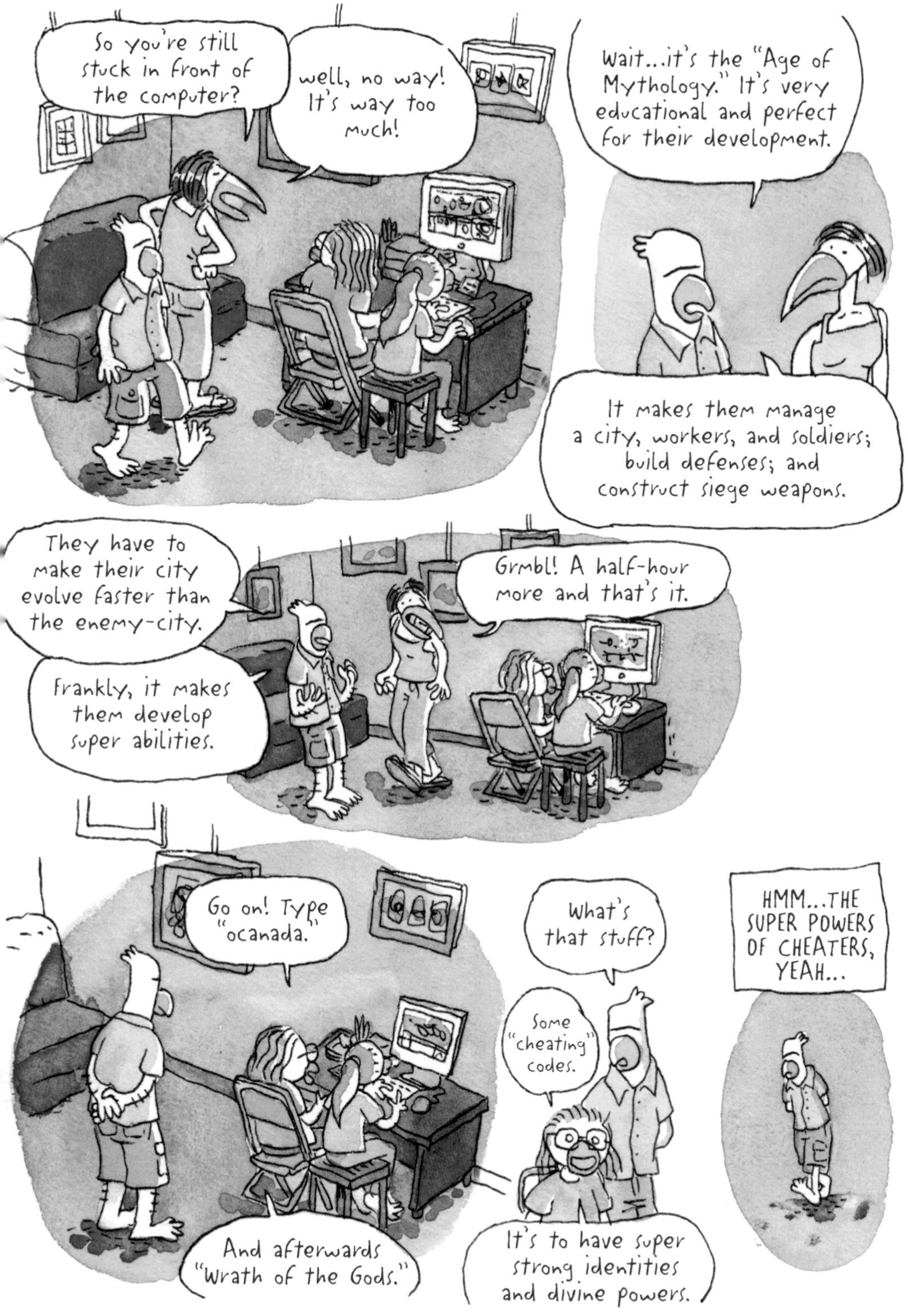
So you're still stuck in front of the computer?
well, no way! It's way too much!
Wait...it's the "Age of Mythology." It's very educational and perfect for their development.
It makes them manage a city, workers, and soldiers; build defenses; and construct siege weapons.
They have to make their city evolve faster than the enemy-city.
Frankly, it makes them develop super abilities.
Grmbl! A half-hour more and that's it.
Go on! Type "ocanada."
And afterwards "Wrath of the Gods."
What's that stuff?
Some "cheating" codes.
It's to have super strong identities and divine powers.
HMM...THE SUPER POWERS OF CHEATERS, YEAH...

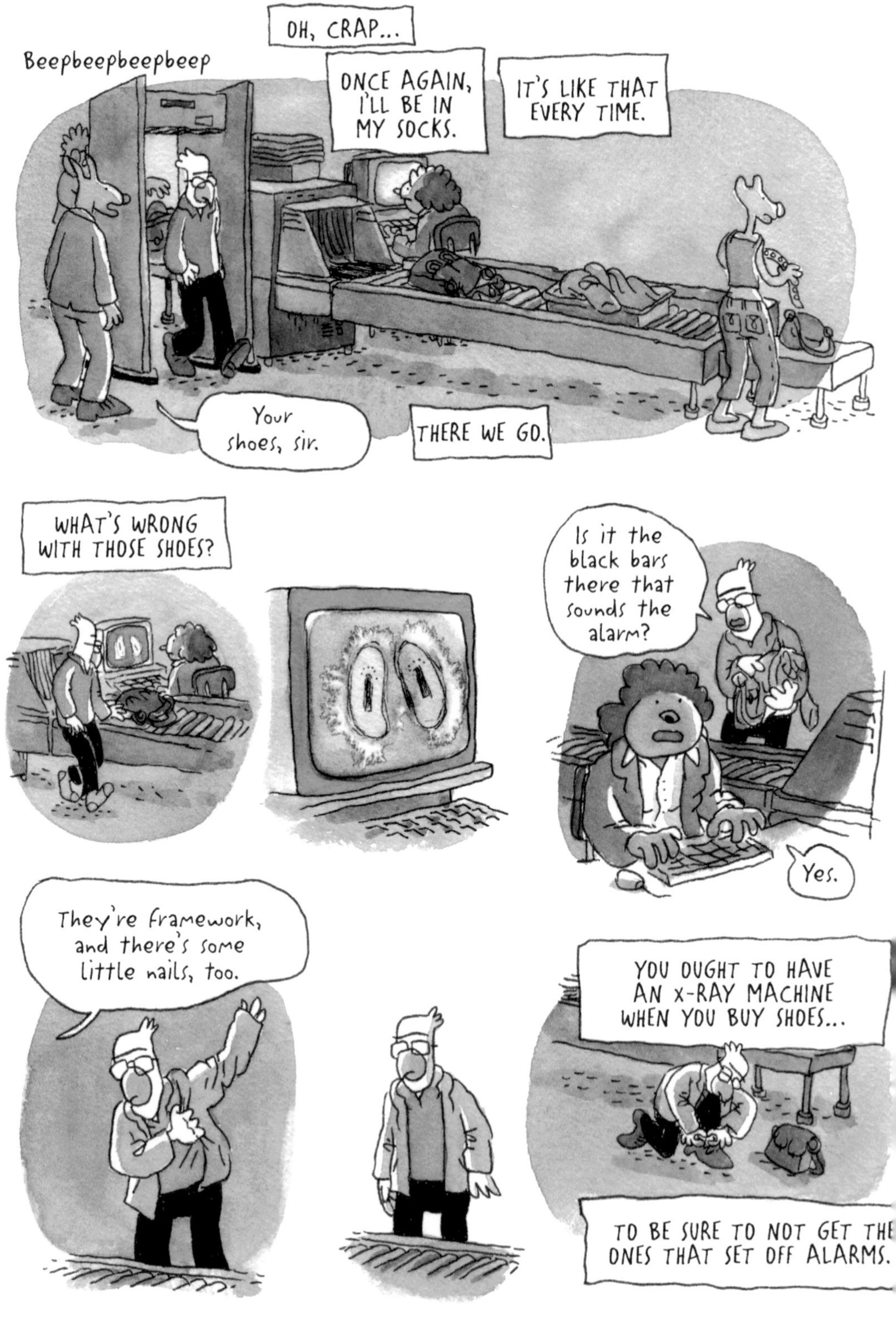
OH, CRAP...
Beepbeepbeepbeep
ONCE AGAIN, I'LL BE IN MY SOCKS.
IT'S LIKE THAT EVERY TIME.
Your shoes, sir.
THERE WE GO.
WHAT'S WRONG WITH THOSE SHOES?
Is it the black bars there that sounds the alarm?
Yes.
They're framework, and there's some little nails, too.
YOU OUGHT TO HAVE AN X-RAY MACHINE WHEN YOU BUY SHOES...
TO BE SURE TO NOT GET THE ONES THAT SET OFF ALARMS.

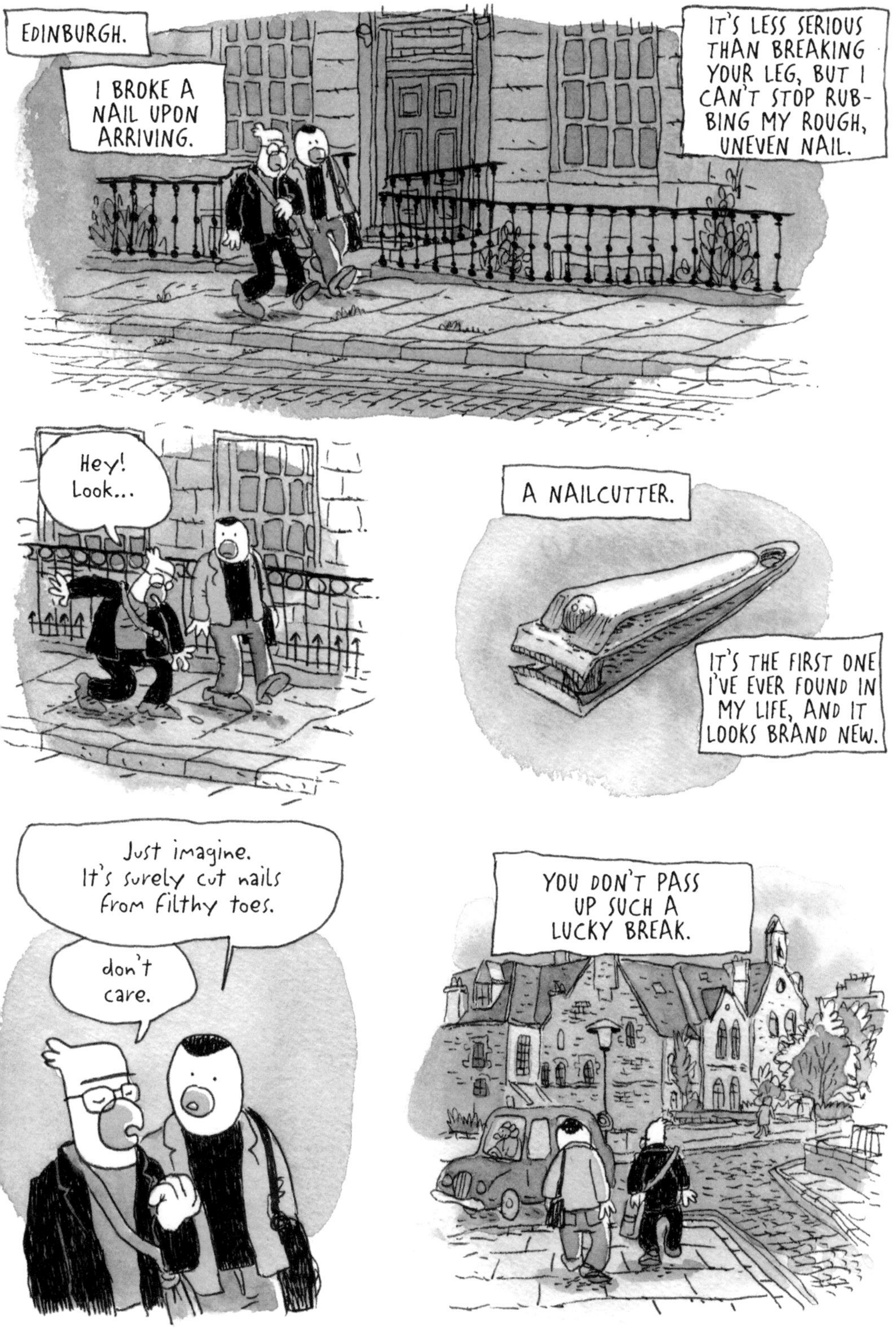
EDINBURGH.
I BROKE A NAIL UPON ARRIVING.
IT'S LESS SERIOUS THAN BREAKING YOUR LEG, BUT I CAN'T STOP RUBBING MY ROUGH, UNEVEN NAIL.
Hey! Look...
A NAILCUTTER.
IT'S THE FIRST ONE I'VE EVER FOUND IN MY LIFE, AND IT LOOKS BRAND NEW.
Just imagine. It's surely cut nails from filthy toes.
don't care.
YOU DON'T PASS UP SUCH A LUCKY BREAK.

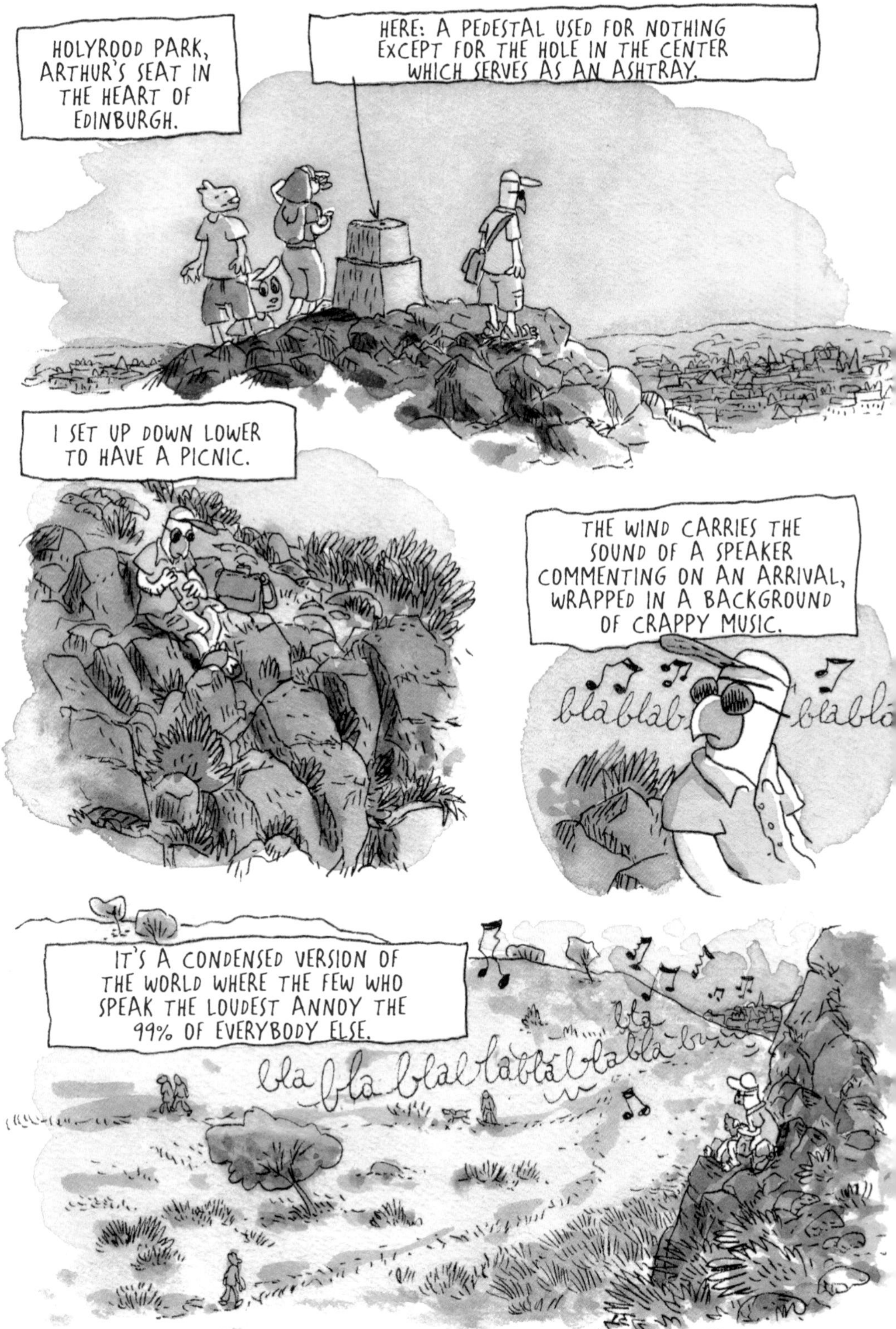
HOLYROOD PARK, ARTHUR'S SEAT IN THE HEART OF EDINBURGH.
HERE: A PEDESTAL USED FOR NOTHING EXCEPT FOR THE HOLE IN THE CENTER WHICH SERVES AS AN ASHTRAY.
I SET UP DOWN LOWER TO HAVE A PICNIC.
THE WIND CARRIES THE SOUND OF A SPEAKER COMMENTING ON AN ARRIVAL, WRAPPED IN A BACKGROUND OF CRAPPY MUSIC.
IT'S A CONDENSED VERSION OF THE WORLD WHERE THE FEW WHO SPEAK THE LOUDEST ANNOY THE 99% OF EVERYBODY ELSE.

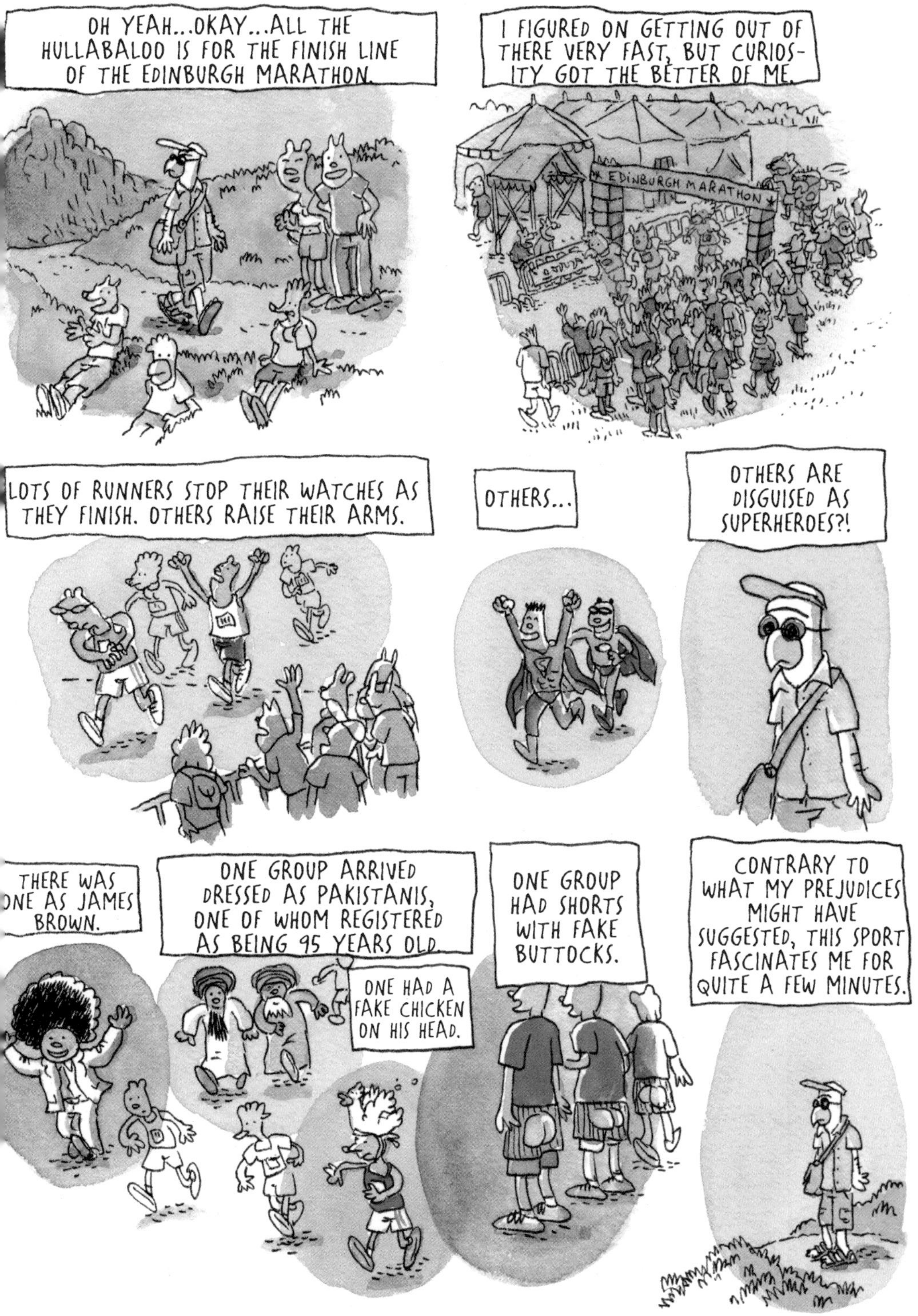

OH YEAH...OKAY...ALL THE HULLABALOO IS FOR THE FINISH LINE OF THE EDINBURGH MARATHON.
I FIGURED ON GETTING OUT OF THERE VERY FAST, BUT CURIOSITY GOT THE BETTER OF ME.
EDINBURGH MARATHON
LOTS OF RUNNERS STOP THEIR WATCHES AS THEY FINISH. OTHERS RAISE THEIR ARMS.
OTHERS...
OTHERS ARE DISGUISED AS SUPERHEROES?!
THERE WAS ONE AS JAMES BROWN.
ONE GROUP ARRIVED DRESSED AS PAKISTANIS, ONE OF WHOM REGISTERED AS BEING 95 YEARS OLD.
ONE HAD A FAKE CHICKEN ON HIS HEAD.
ONE GROUP HAD SHORTS WITH FAKE BUTTOCKS.
CONTRARY TO WHAT MY PREJUDICES MIGHT HAVE SUGGESTED, THIS SPORT FASCINATES ME FOR QUITE A FEW MINUTES.

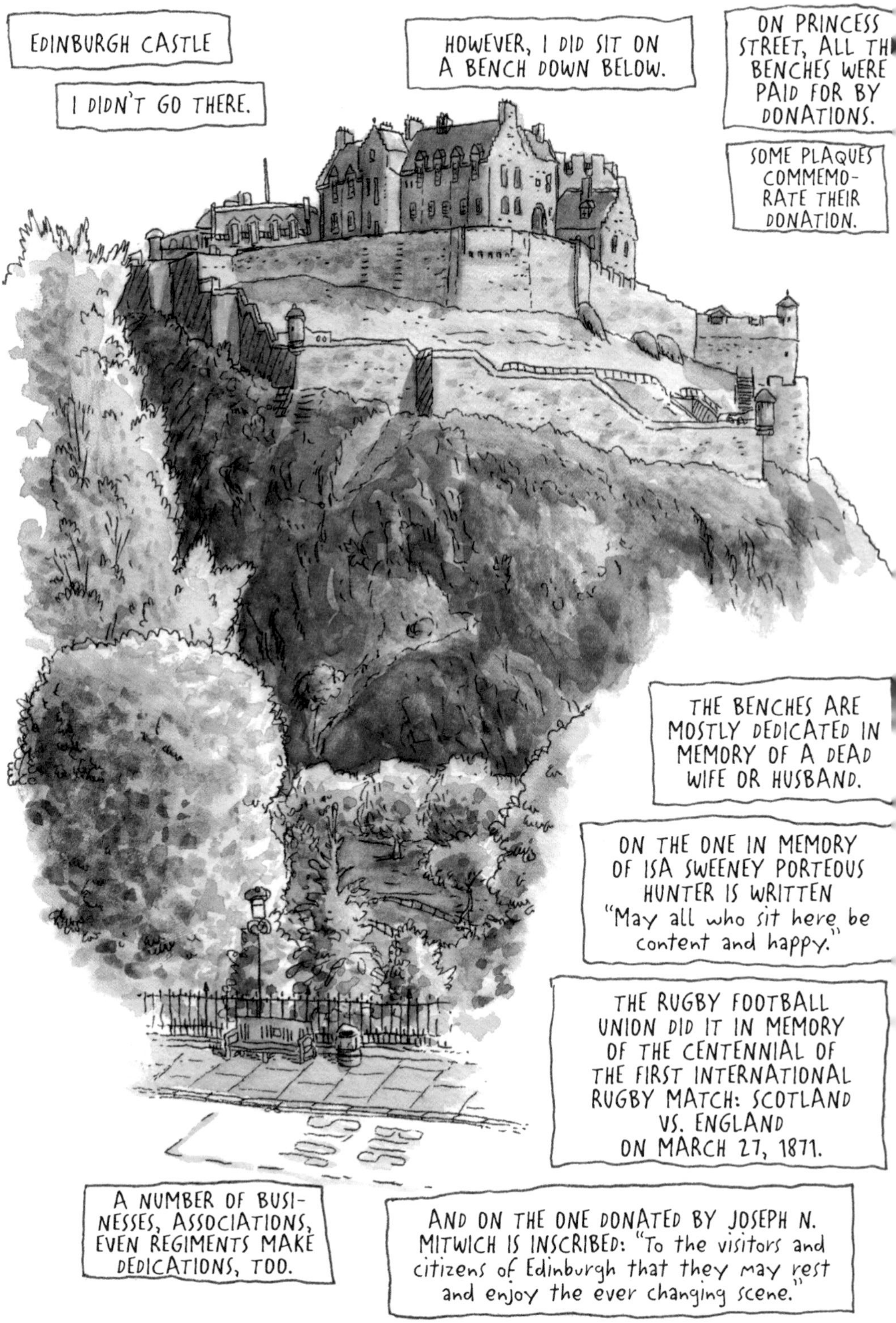
EDINBURGH CASTLE
I DIDN'T GO THERE.
HOWEVER, I DID SIT ON A BENCH DOWN BELOW.
ON PRINCESS STREET, ALL THE BENCHES WERE PAID FOR BY DONATIONS.
SOME PLAQUES COMMEMORATE THEIR DONATION.
THE BENCHES ARE MOSTLY DEDICATED IN MEMORY OF A DEAD WIFE OR HUSBAND.
ON THE ONE IN MEMORY OF ISA SWEENEY PORTEOUS HUNTER IS WRITTEN "May all who sit here be content and happy."
THE RUGBY FOOTBALL UNION DID IT IN MEMORY OF THE CENTENNIAL OF THE FIRST INTERNATIONAL RUGBY MATCH: SCOTLAND VS. ENGLAND ON MARCH 27, 1871.
A NUMBER OF BUSINESSES, ASSOCIATIONS, EVEN REGIMENTS MAKE DEDICATIONS, TOO.
AND ON THE ONE DONATED BY JOSEPH N. MITWICH IS INSCRIBED: "To the visitors and citizens of Edinburgh that they may rest and enjoy the ever changing scene."

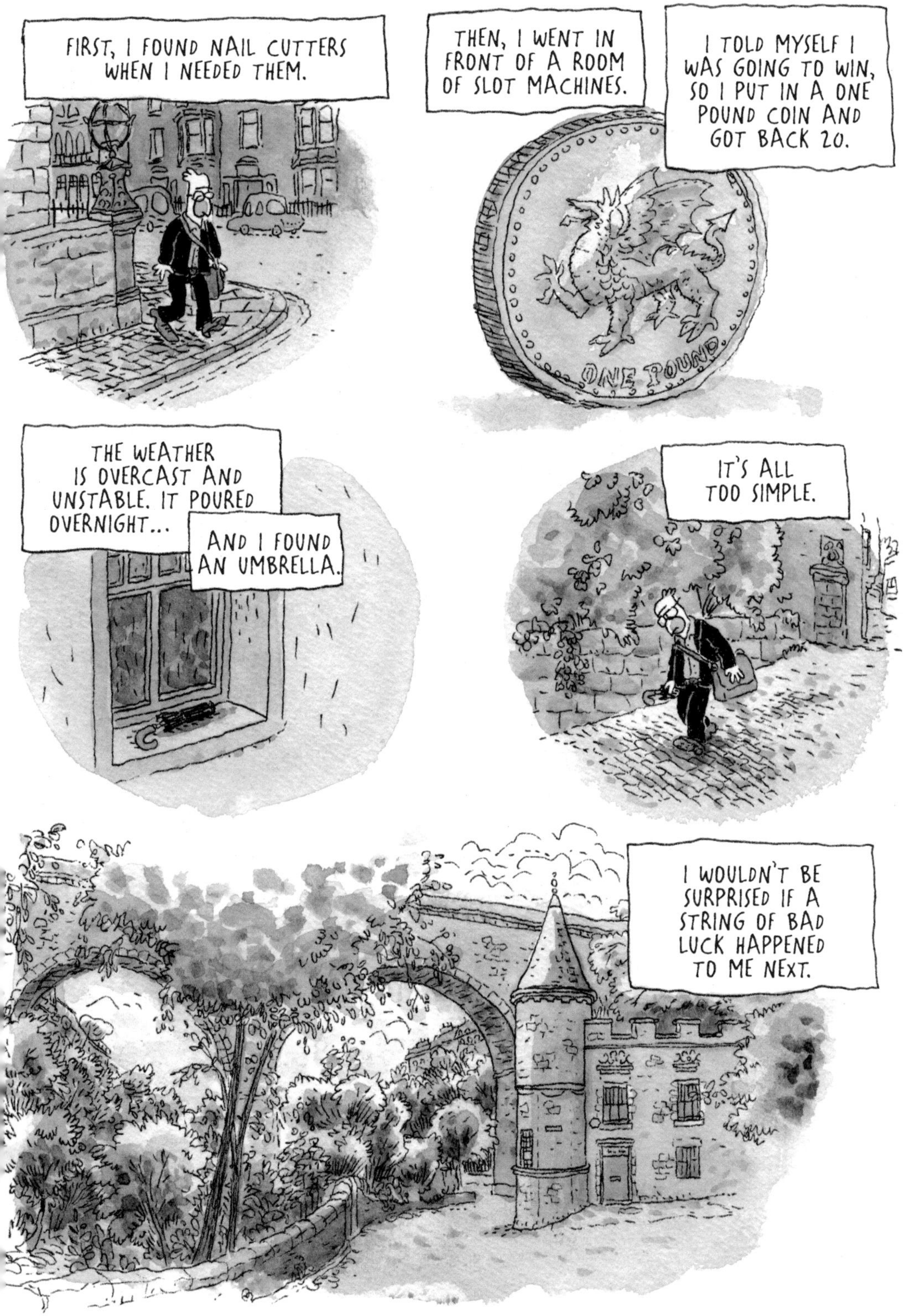
FIRST, I FOUND NAIL CUTTERS WHEN I NEEDED THEM.
THEN, I WENT IN FRONT OF A ROOM OF SLOT MACHINES.
I TOLD MYSELF I WAS GOING TO WIN, SO I PUT IN A ONE POUND COIN AND GOT BACK 20.
ONE POUND
THE WEATHER IS OVERCAST AND UNSTABLE. IT POURED OVERNIGHT...
AND I FOUND AN UMBRELLA.
IT'S ALL TOO SIMPLE.
I WOULDN'T BE SURPRISED IF A STRING OF BAD LUCK HAPPENED TO ME NEXT.

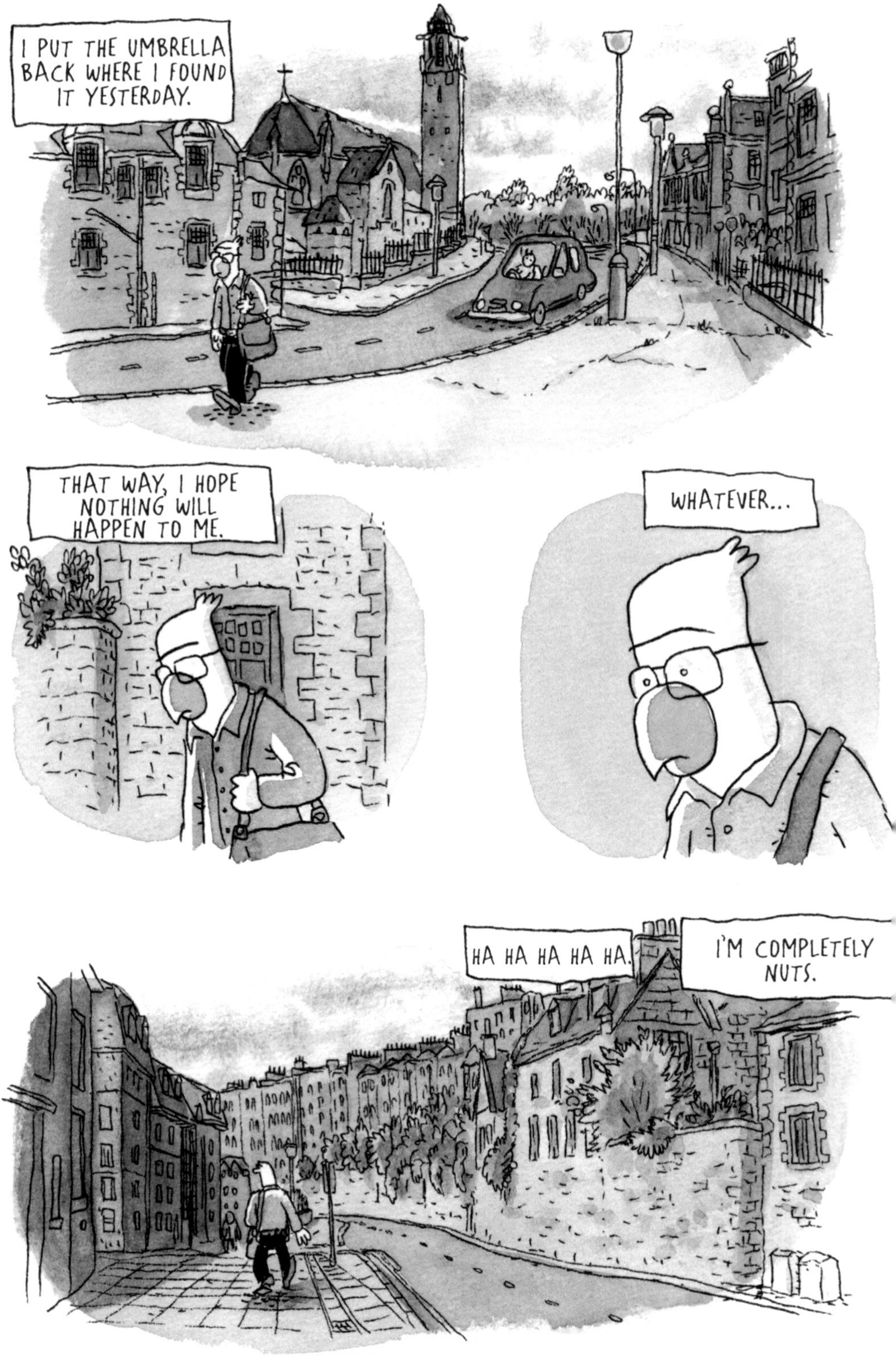
I PUT THE UMBRELLA BACK WHERE I FOUND IT YESTERDAY.
THAT WAY, I HOPE NOTHING WILL HAPPEN TO ME.
WHATEVER...
HA HA HA HA HA.
I'M COMPLETELY NUTS.

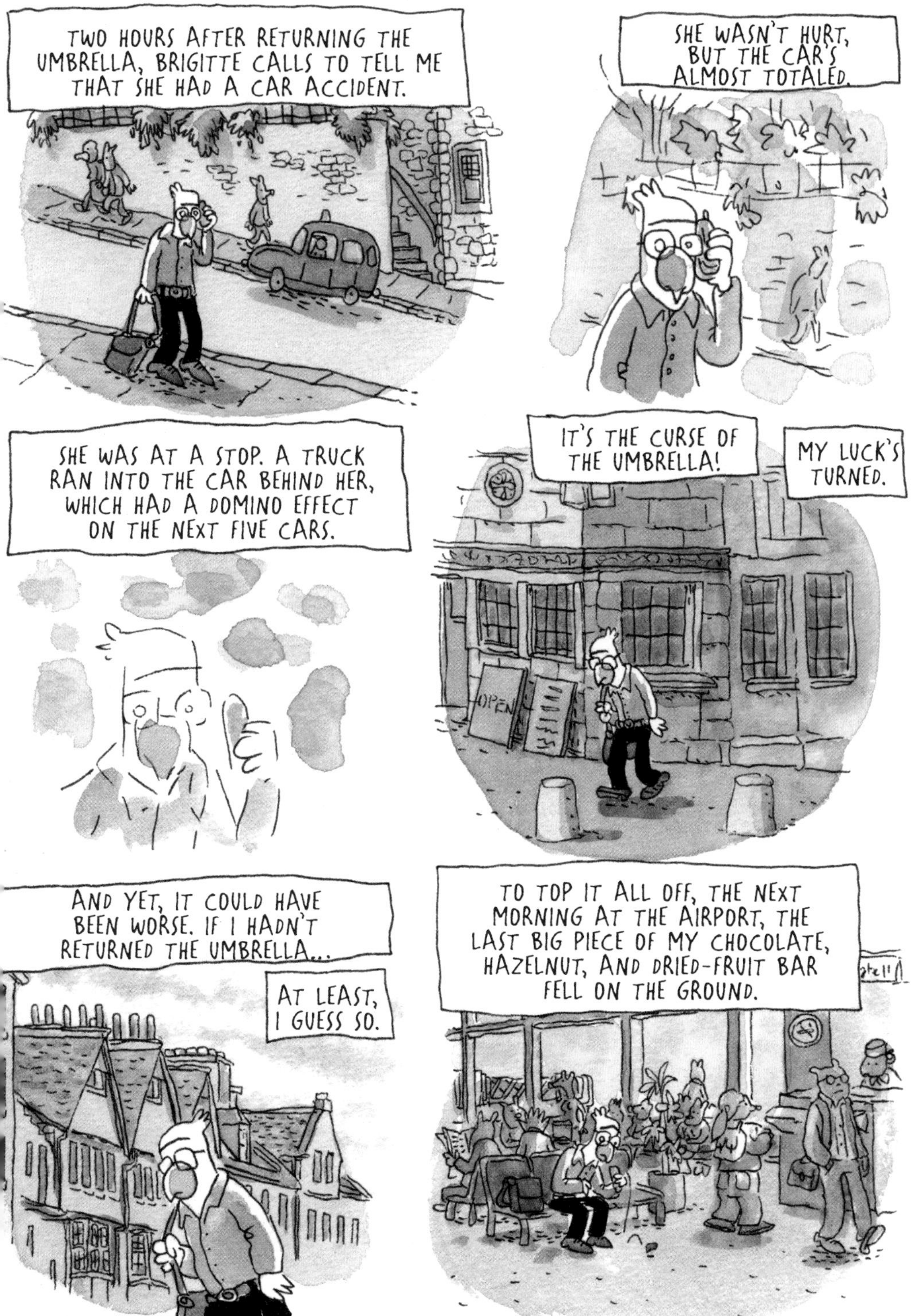
TWO HOURS AFTER RETURNING THE UMBRELLA, BRIGITTE CALLS TO TELL ME THAT SHE HAD A CAR ACCIDENT.
SHE WASN'T HURT, BUT THE CAR'S ALMOST TOTALED.
SHE WAS AT A STOP. A TRUCK RAN INTO THE CAR BEHIND HER, WHICH HAD A DOMINO EFFECT ON THE NEXT FIVE CARS.
IT'S THE CURSE OF THE UMBRELLA!
MY LUCK'S TURNED.
OPEN
AND YET, IT COULD HAVE BEEN WORSE. IF I HADN'T RETURNED THE UMBRELLA...
AT LEAST, I GUESS SO.
TO TOP IT ALL OFF, THE NEXT MORNING AT THE AIRPORT, THE LAST BIG PIECE OF MY CHOCOLATE, HAZELNUT, AND DRIED-FRUIT BAR FELL ON THE GROUND.

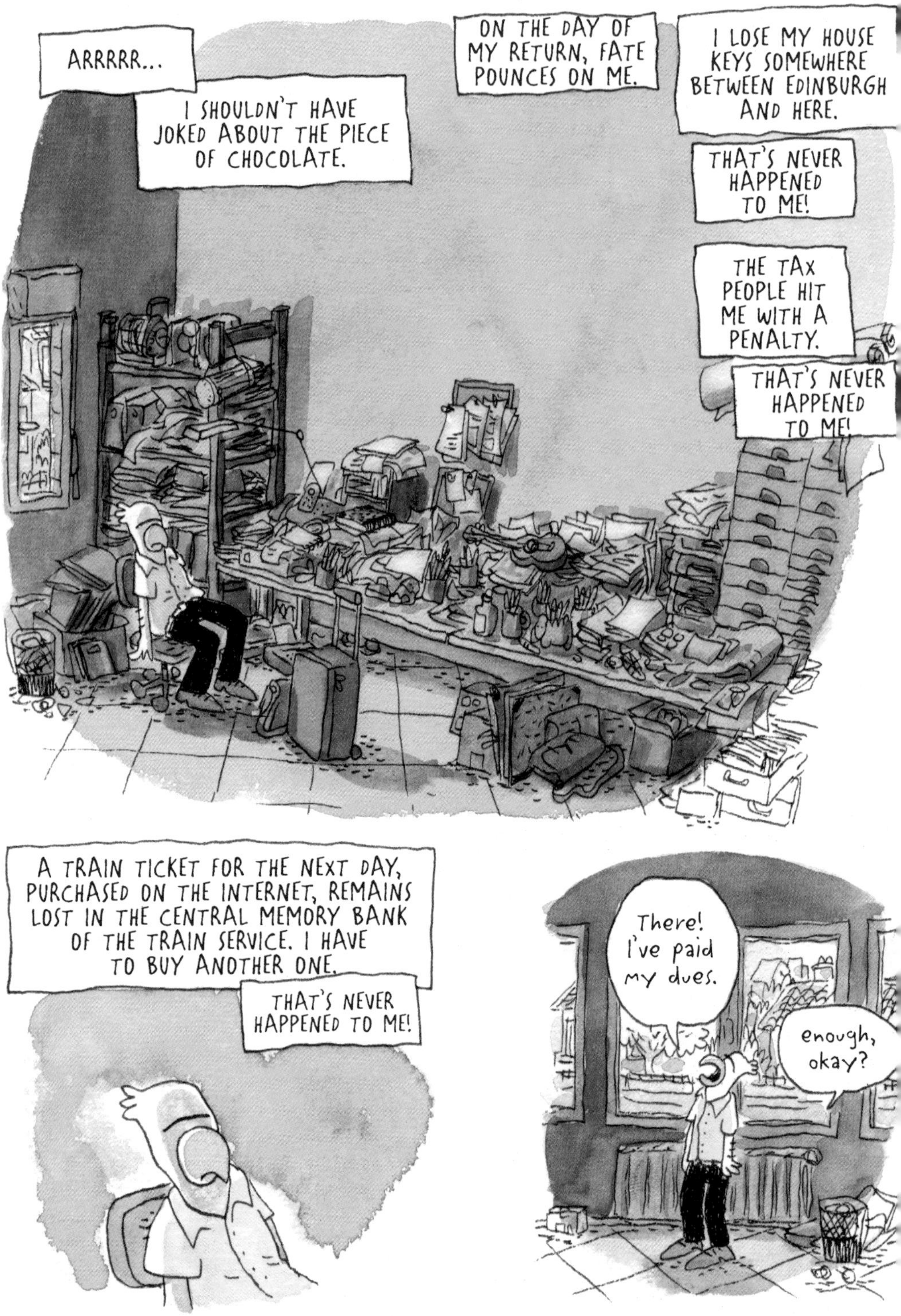
ARRRRR...
I SHOULDN'T HAVE JOKED ABOUT THE PIECE OF CHOCOLATE.
ON THE DAY OF MY RETURN, FATE POUNCES ON ME.
I LOSE MY HOUSE KEYS SOMEWHERE BETWEEN EDINBURGH AND HERE.
THAT'S NEVER HAPPENED TO ME!
THE TAX PEOPLE HIT ME WITH A PENALTY.
THAT'S NEVER HAPPENED TO ME!
A TRAIN TICKET FOR THE NEXT DAY, PURCHASED ON THE INTERNET, REMAINS LOST IN THE CENTRAL MEMORY BANK OF THE TRAIN SERVICE. I HAVE TO BUY ANOTHER ONE.
THAT'S NEVER HAPPENED TO ME!
There! I've paid my dues.
enough, okay?

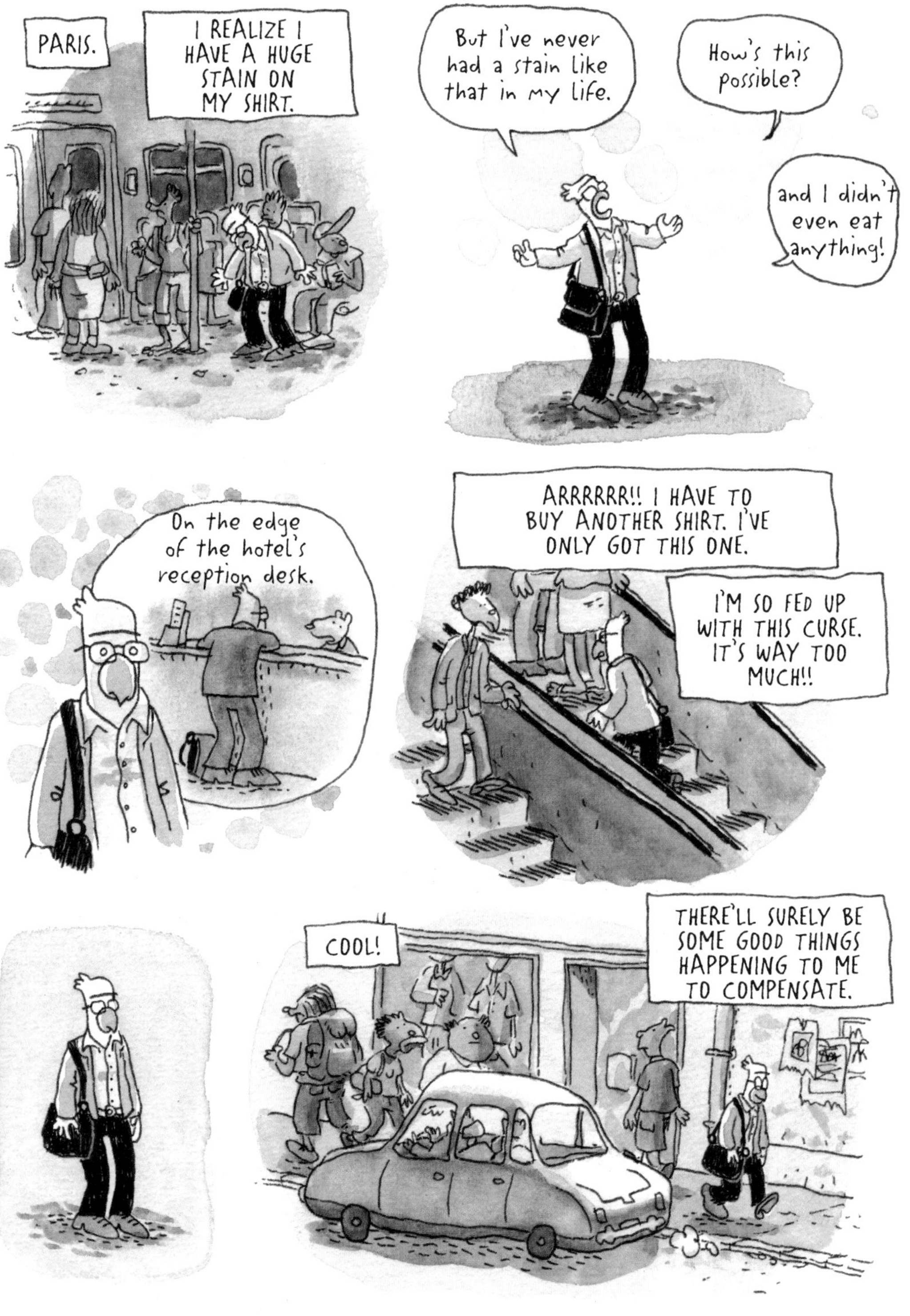

PARIS.
I REALIZE I HAVE A HUGE STAIN ON MY SHIRT.
But I've never had a stain like that in my life.
How's this possible?
and I didn't even eat anything!
On the edge of the hotel's reception desk.
ARRRRRR!! I HAVE TO BUY ANOTHER SHIRT. I'VE ONLY GOT THIS ONE.
I'M SO FED UP WITH THIS CURSE. IT'S WAY TOO MUCH!!
COOL!
THERE'LL SURELY BE SOME GOOD THINGS HAPPENING TO ME TO COMPENSATE.

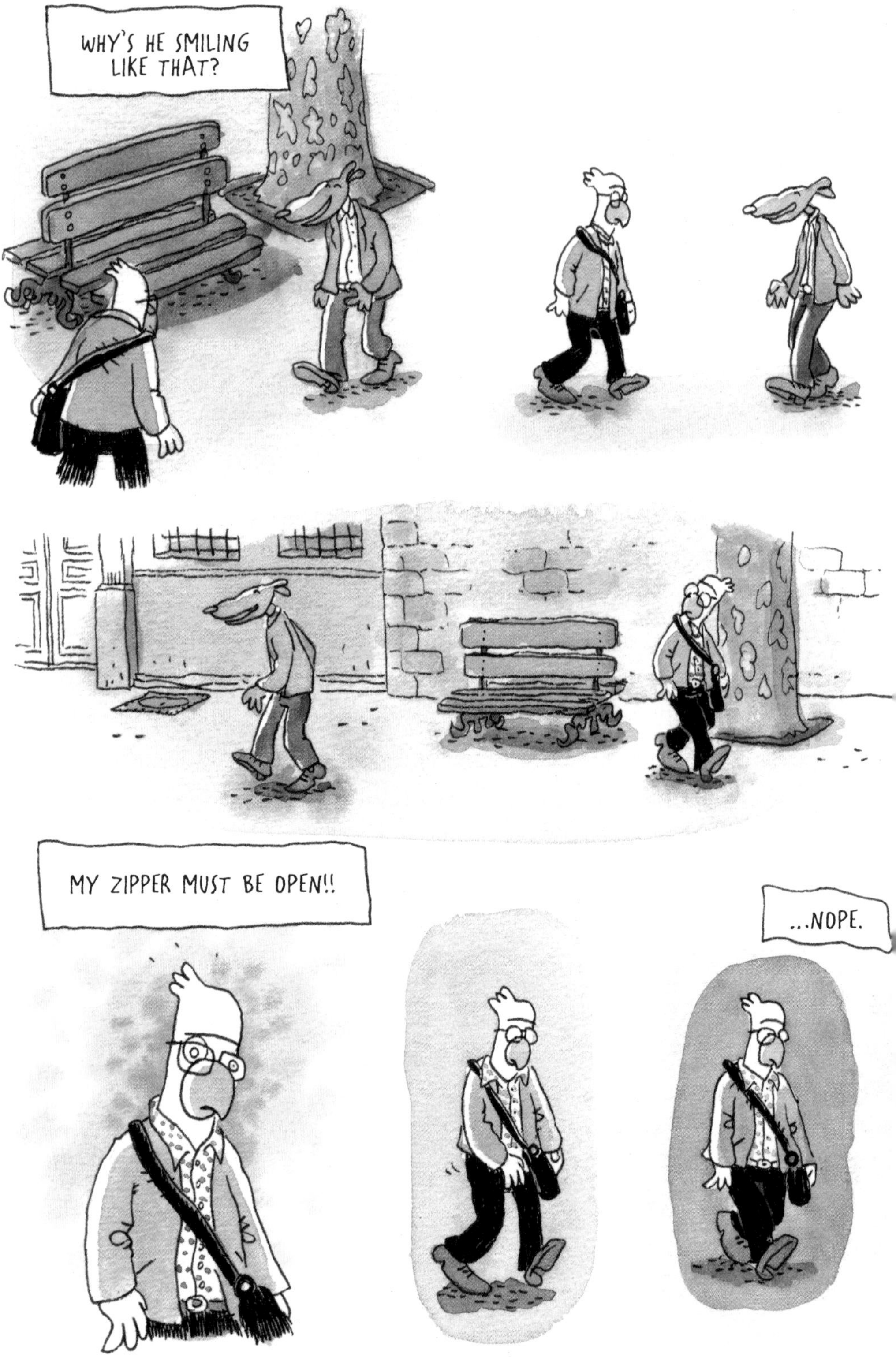
WHY'S HE SMILING LIKE THAT?
MY ZIPPER MUST BE OPEN!!
...NOPE.

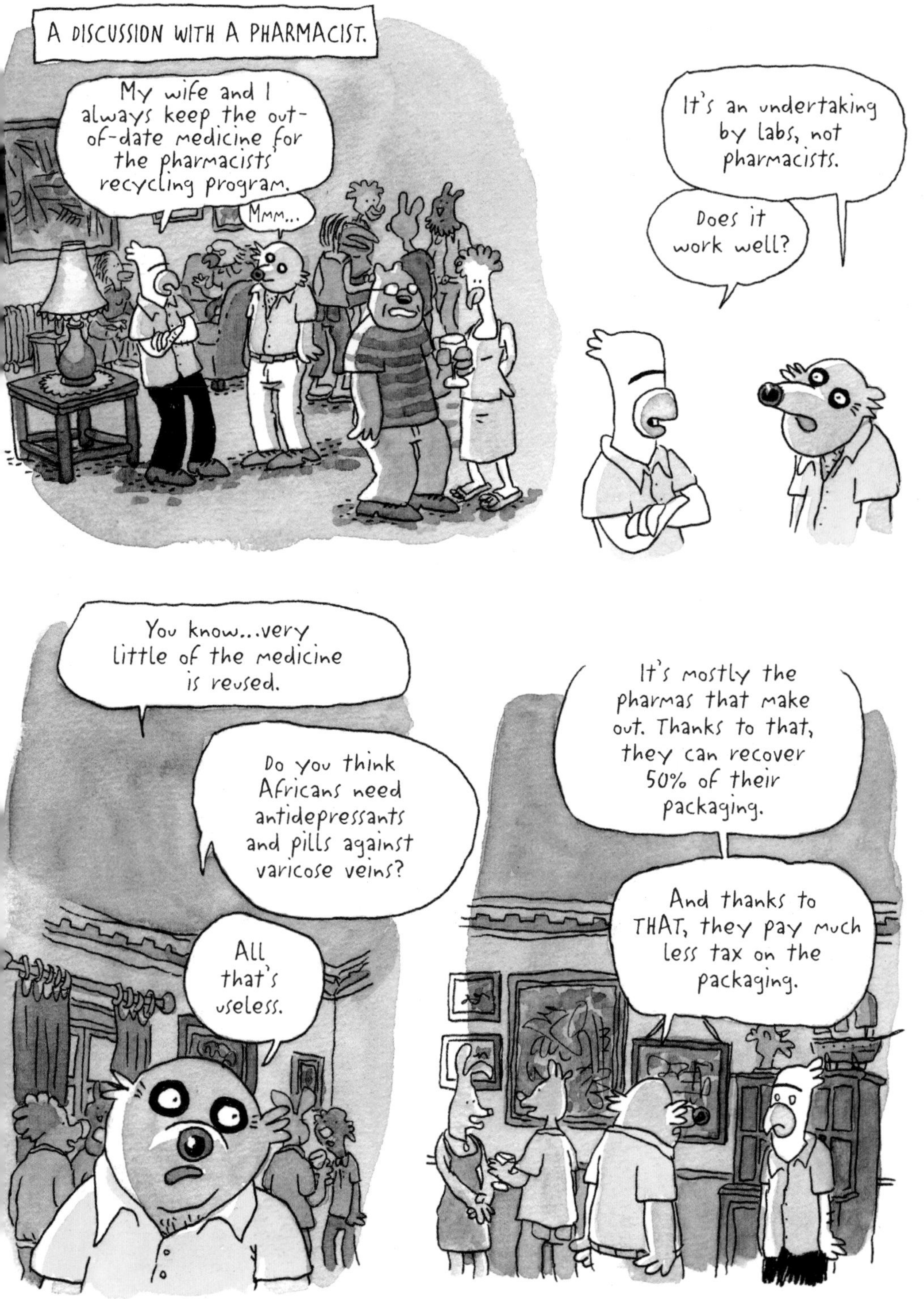
A DISCUSSION WITH A PHARMACIST.
My wife and I always keep the out-of-date medicine for the pharmacists' recycling program.
Mmm...
It's an undertaking by labs, not pharmacists.
Does it work well?
You know...very little of the medicine is reused.
Do you think Africans need antidepressants and pills against varicose veins?
All that's useless.
It's mostly the pharmas that make out. Thanks to that, they can recover 50% of their packaging.
And thanks to THAT, they pay much less tax on the packaging.

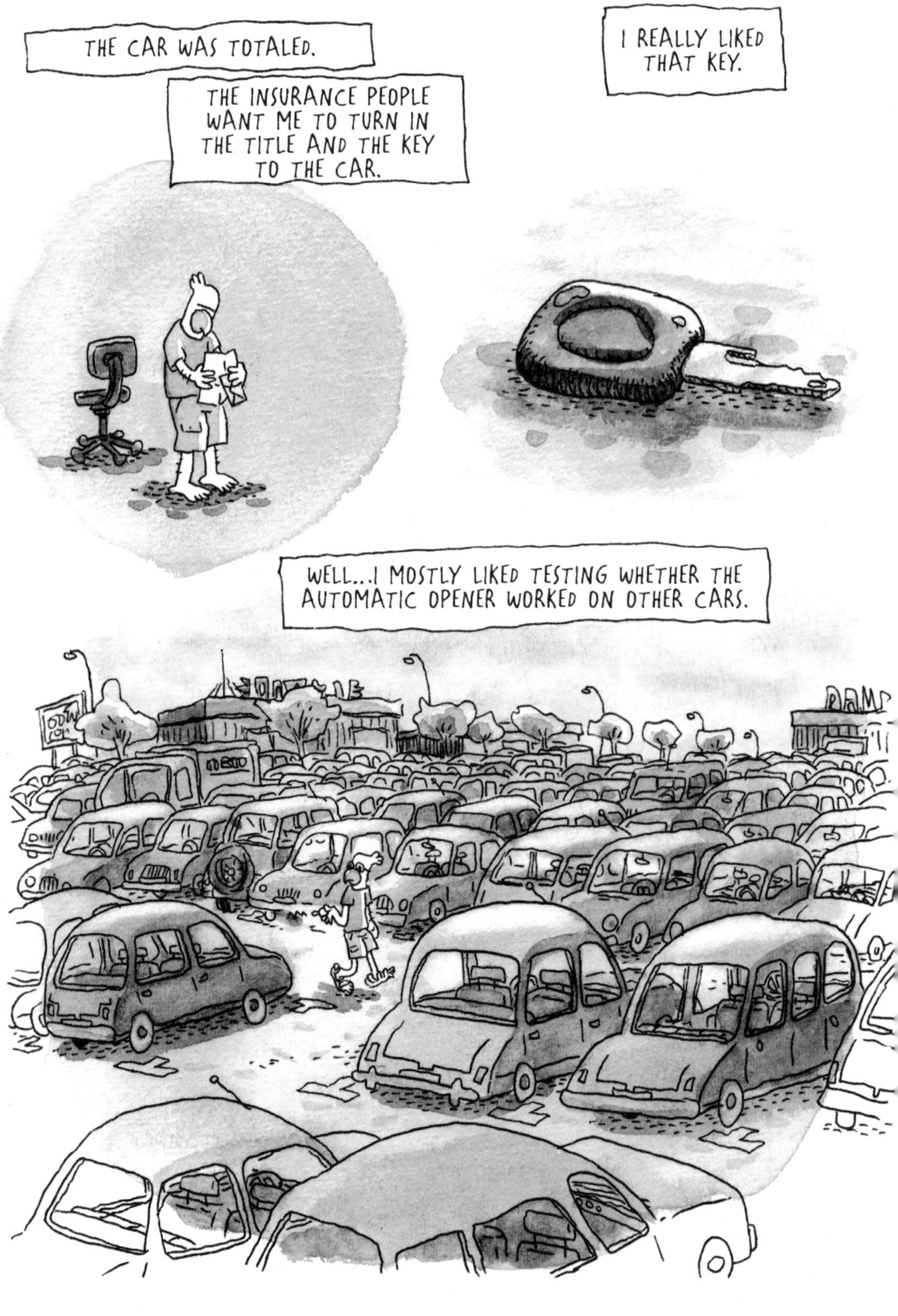
THE CAR WAS TOTALED.
THE INSURANCE PEOPLE WANT ME TO TURN IN THE TITLE AND THE KEY TO THE CAR.
I REALLY LIKED THAT KEY.
WELL...I MOSTLY LIKED TESTING WHETHER THE AUTOMATIC OPENER WORKED ON OTHER CARS.

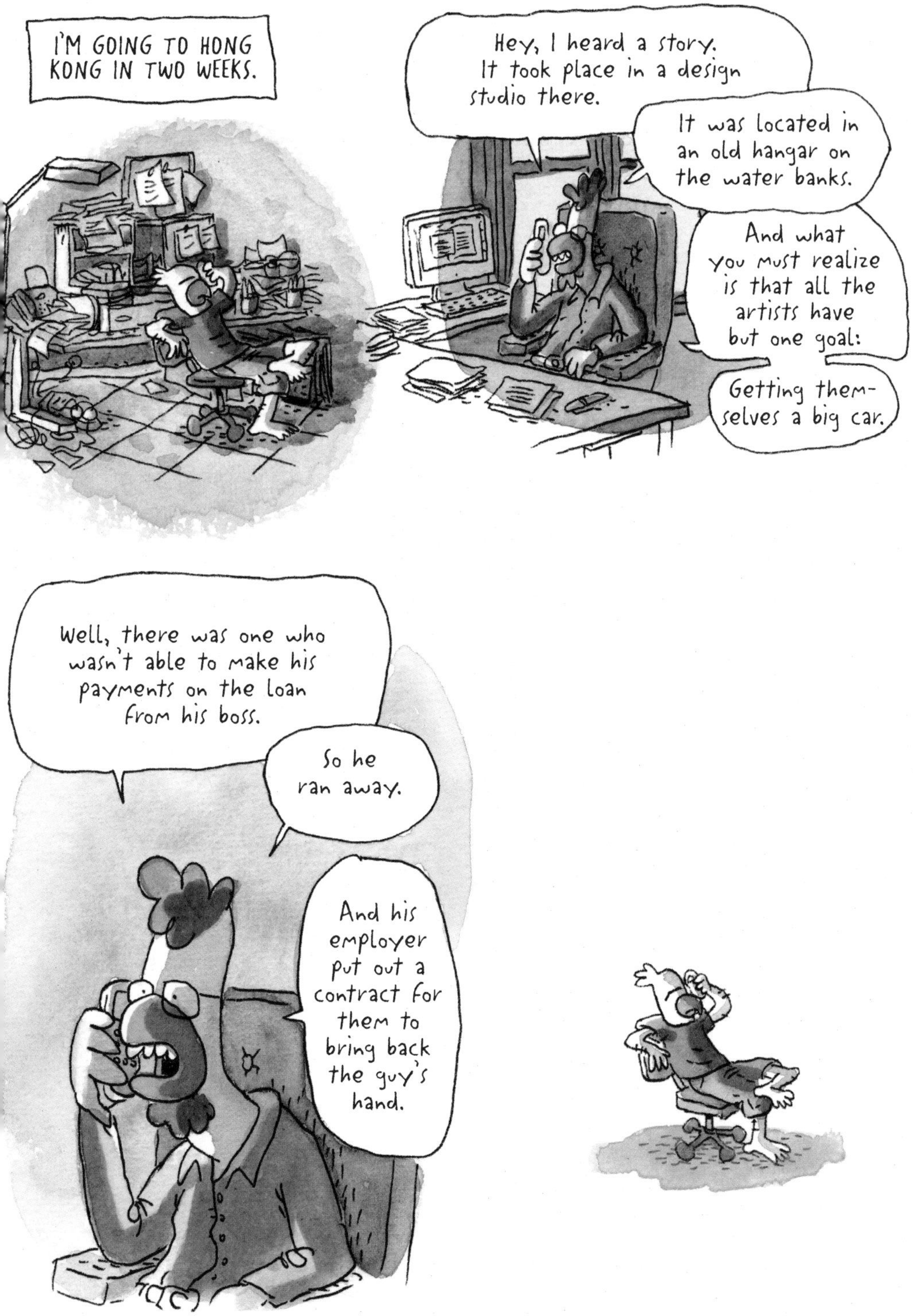
I'M GOING TO HONG KONG IN TWO WEEKS.
Hey, I heard a story. It took place in a design studio there.
It was located in an old hangar on the water banks.
And what you must realize is that all the artists have but one goal:
Getting them-selves a big car.
Well, there was one who wasn't able to make his payments on the loan from his boss.
So he ran away.
And his employer put out a contract for them to bring back the guy's hand.

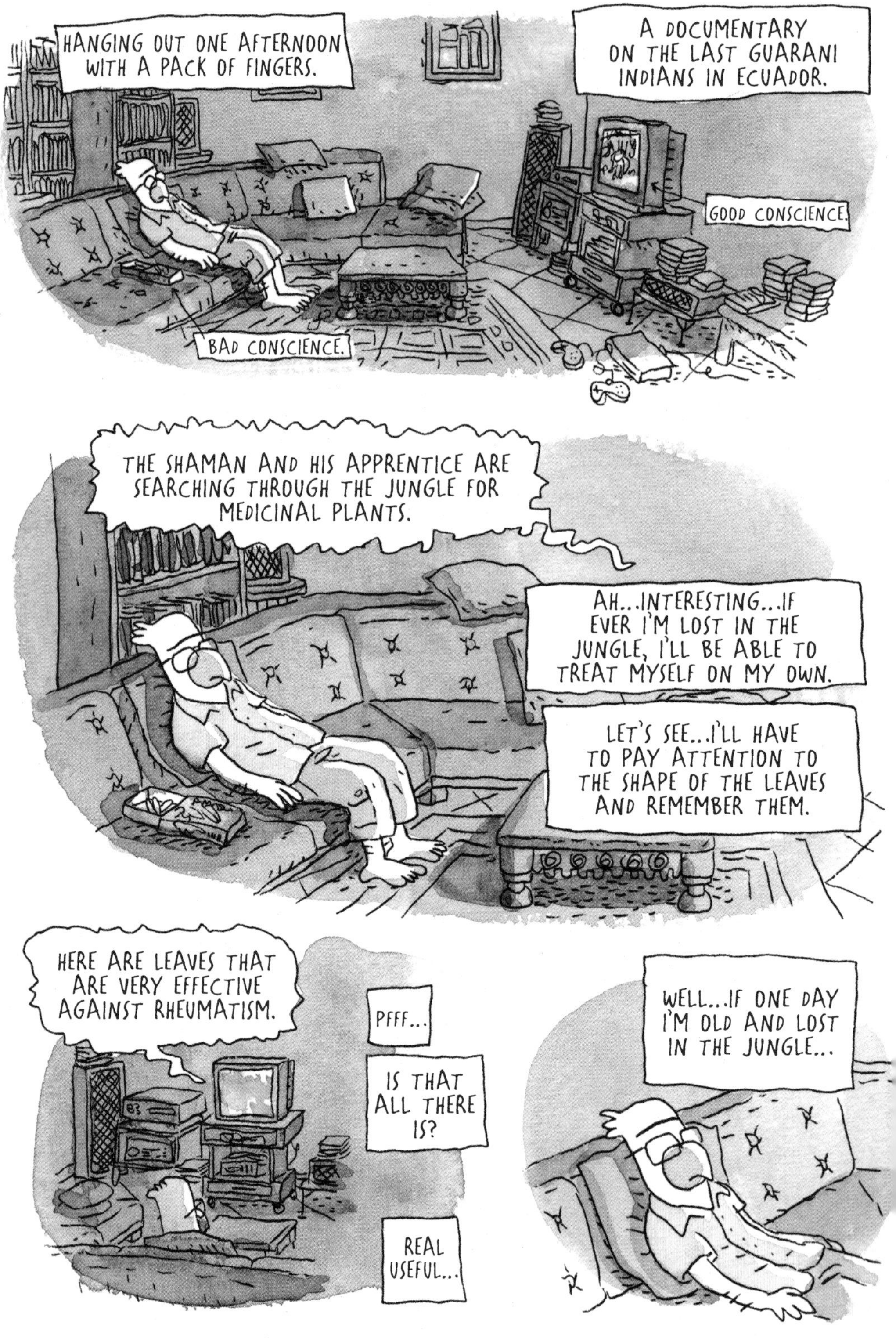

HANGING OUT ONE AFTERNOON WITH A PACK OF FINGERS.
A DOCUMENTARY ON THE LAST GUARANI INDIANS IN ECUADOR.
GOOD CONSCIENCE.
BAD CONSCIENCE.
THE SHAMAN AND HIS APPRENTICE ARE SEARCHING THROUGH THE JUNGLE FOR MEDICINAL PLANTS.
AH...INTERESTING...IF EVER I'M LOST IN THE JUNGLE, I'LL BE ABLE TO TREAT MYSELF ON MY OWN.
LET'S SEE...I'LL HAVE TO PAY ATTENTION TO THE SHAPE OF THE LEAVES AND REMEMBER THEM.
HERE ARE LEAVES THAT ARE VERY EFFECTIVE AGAINST RHEUMATISM.
PFFF...
IS THAT ALL THERE IS?
REAL USEFUL...
WELL...IF ONE DAY I'M OLD AND LOST IN THE JUNGLE...

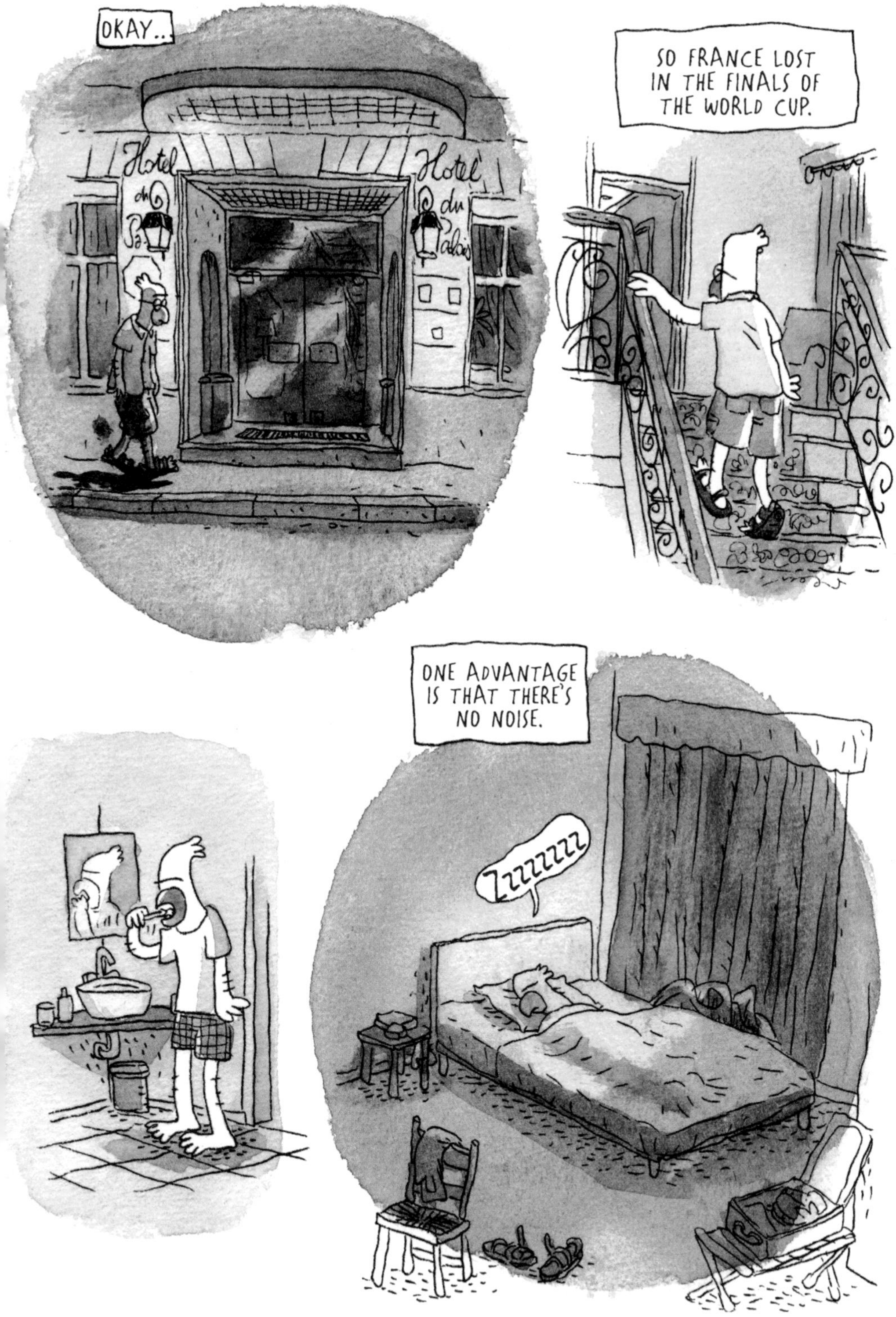
OKAY..
SO FRANCE LOST IN THE FINALS OF THE WORLD CUP.
ONE ADVANTAGE IS THAT THERE'S NO NOISE.
Zzzzzzzz

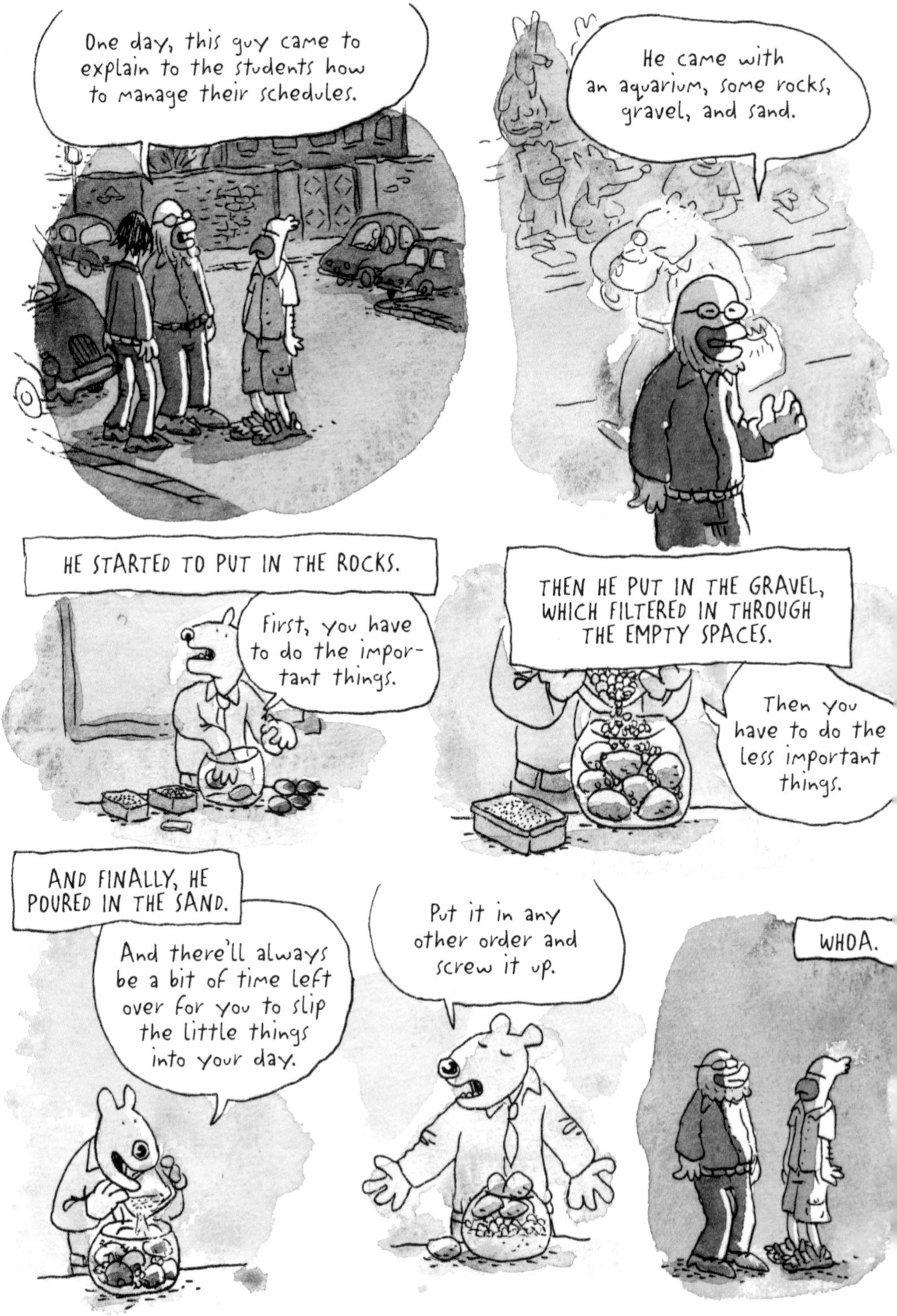
One day, this guy came to explain to the students how to manage their schedules.
He came with an aquarium, some rocks, gravel, and sand.
HE STARTED TO PUT IN THE ROCKS.
First, you have to do the important things.
THEN HE PUT IN THE GRAVEL, WHICH FILTERED IN THROUGH THE EMPTY SPACES.
Then you have to do the less important things.
AND FINALLY, HE POURED IN THE SAND.
And there'll always be a bit of time left over for you to slip the little things into your day.
Put it in any other order and screw it up.
WHOA.

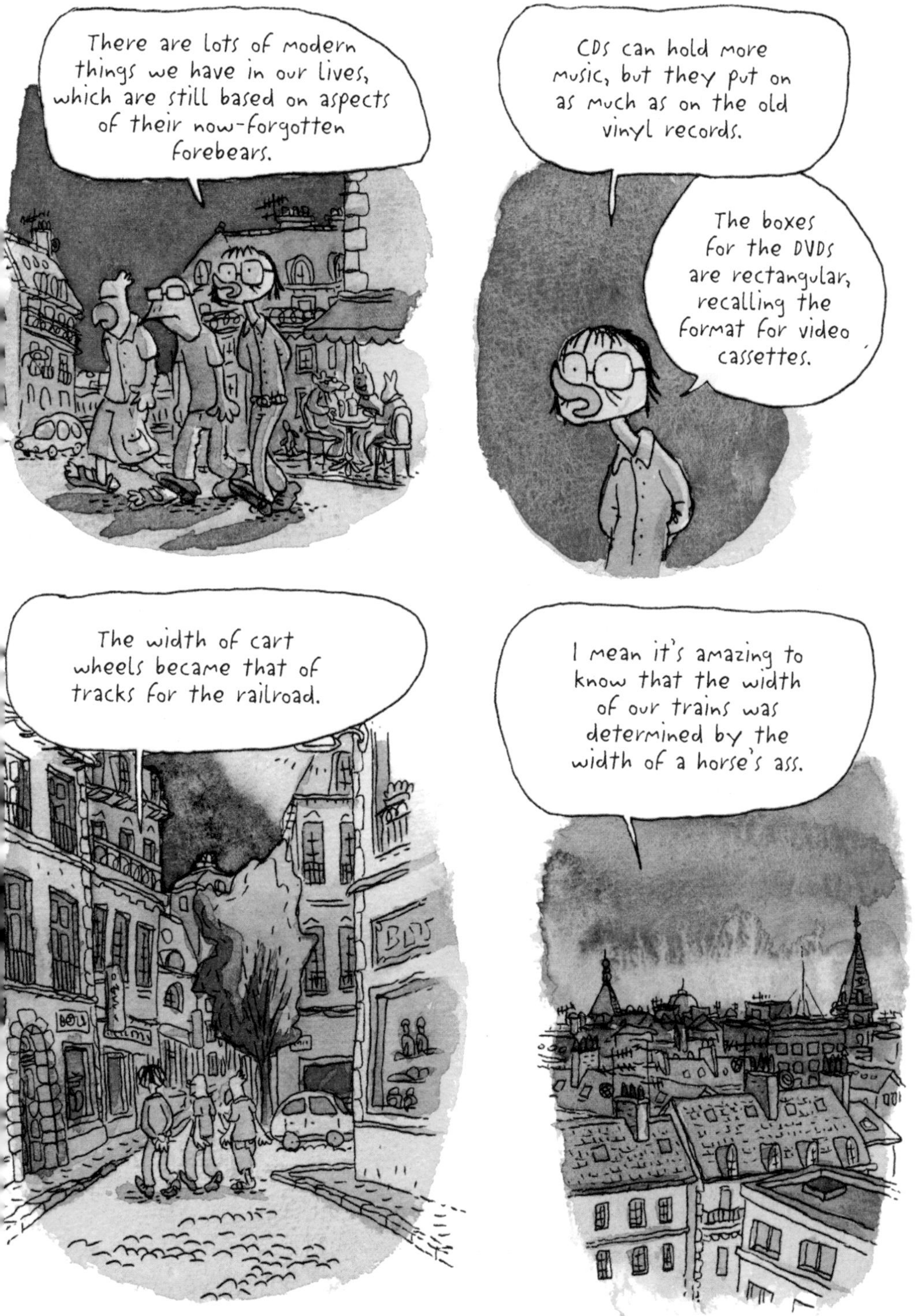
There are lots of modern things we have in our lives, which are still based on aspects of their now-forgotten forebears.
CDs can hold more music, but they put on as much as on the old vinyl records.
The boxes for the DVDs are rectangular, recalling the format for video cassettes.
The width of cart wheels became that of tracks for the railroad.
I mean it's amazing to know that the width of our trains was determined by the width of a horse's ass.

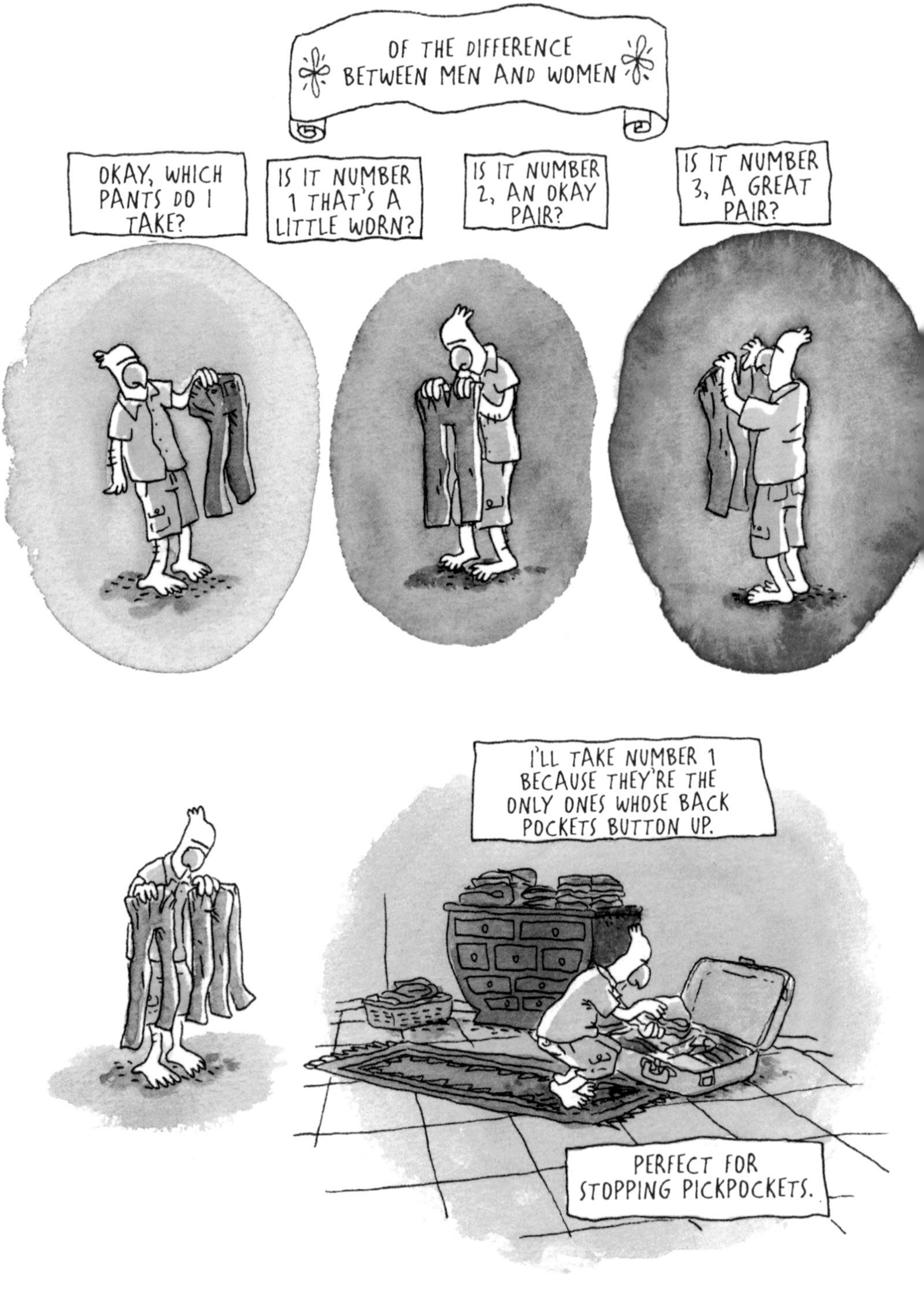
OF THE DIFFERENCE BETWEEN MEN AND WOMEN
OKAY, WHICH PANTS DO I TAKE?
IS IT NUMBER 1 THAT'S A LITTLE WORN?
IS IT NUMBER 2, AN OKAY PAIR?
IS IT NUMBER 3, A GREAT PAIR?
I'LL TAKE NUMBER 1 BECAUSE THEY'RE THE ONLY ONES WHOSE BACK POCKETS BUTTON UP.
PERFECT FOR STOPPING PICKPOCKETS.

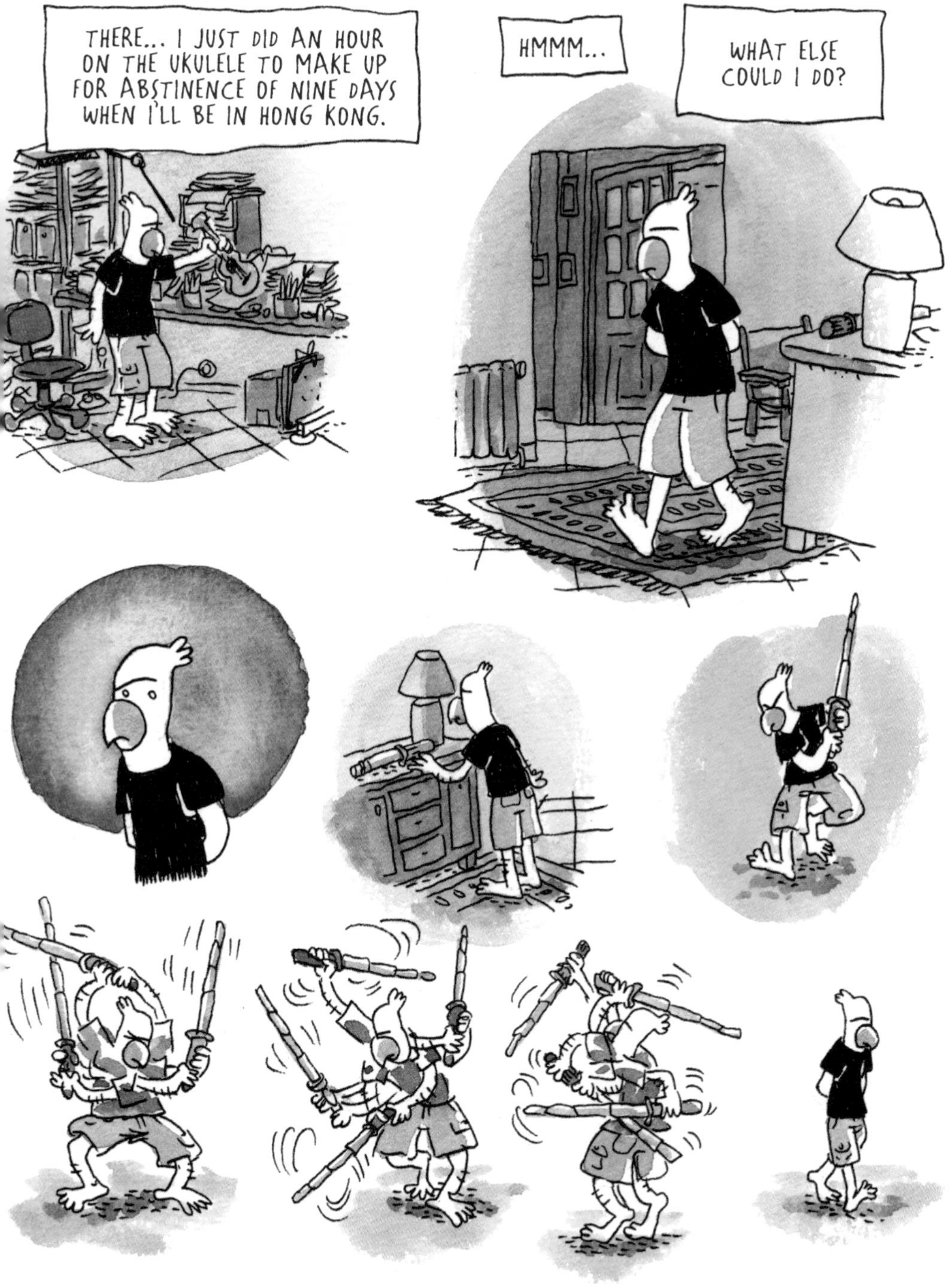
THERE... I JUST DID AN HOUR ON THE UKULELE TO MAKE UP FOR ABSTINENCE OF NINE DAYS WHEN I'LL BE IN HONG KONG.
HMMM...
WHAT ELSE COULD I DO?

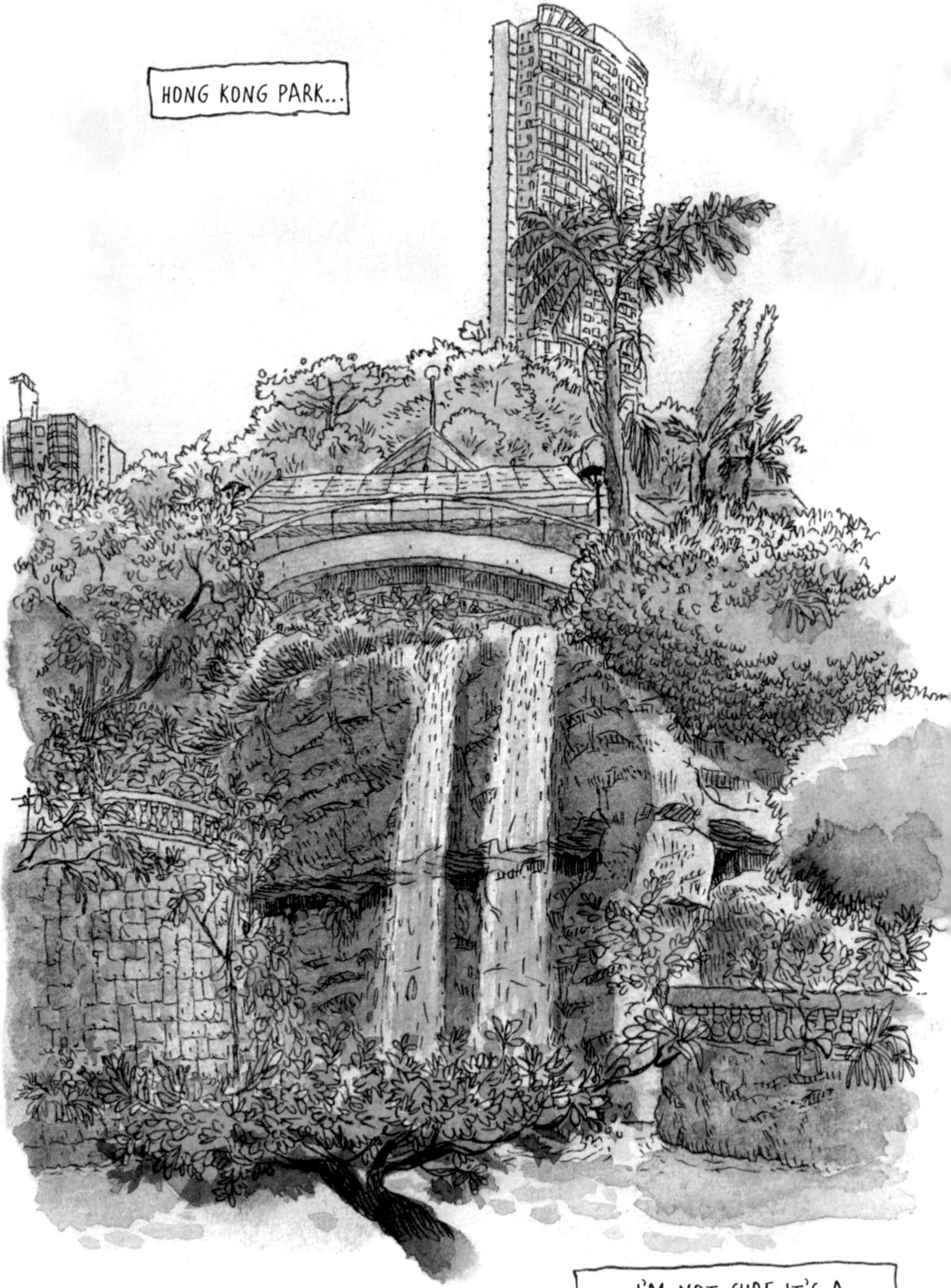
HONG KONG PARK...
I'M NOT SURE IT'S A NATURAL WATERFALL.

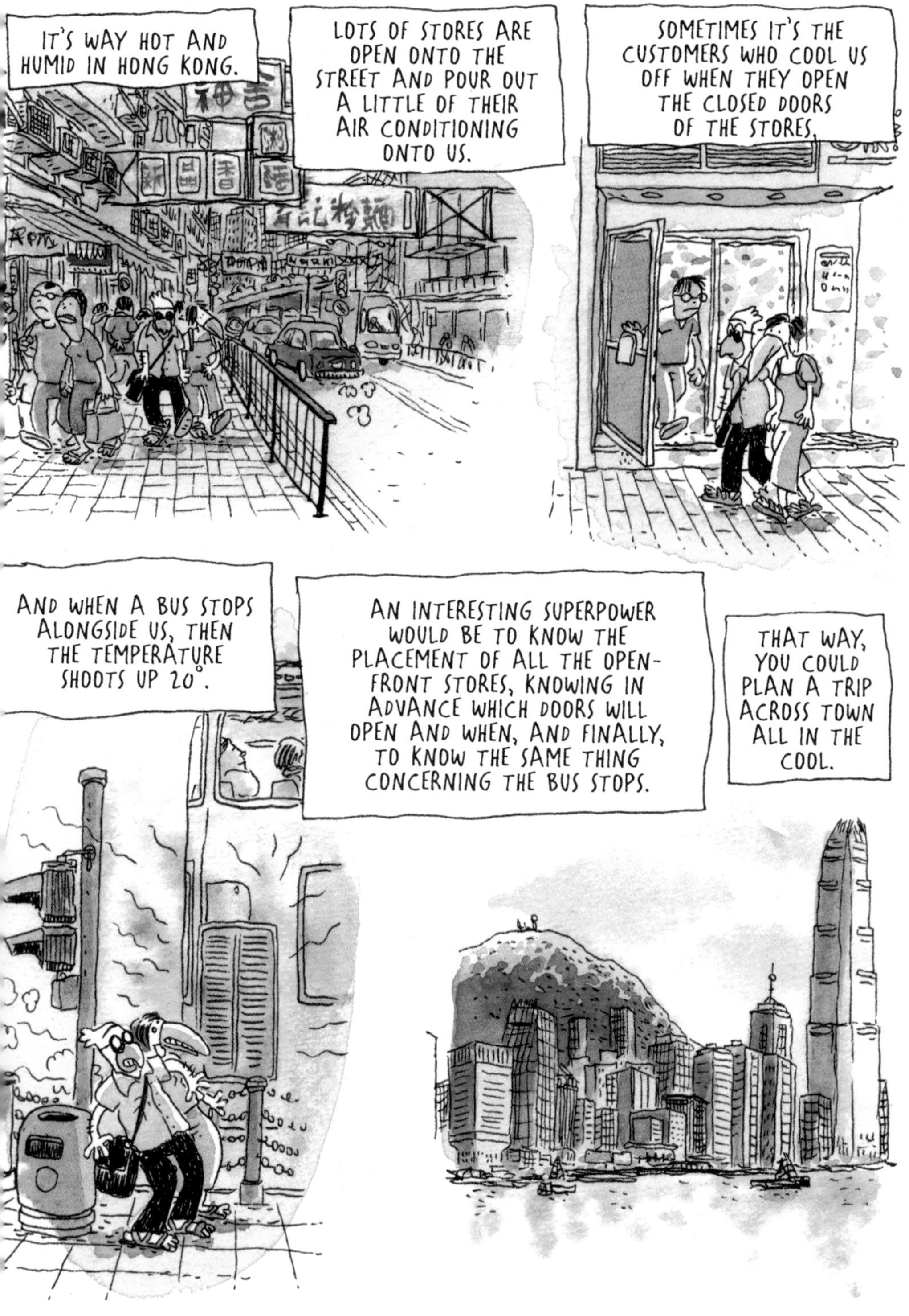
IT'S WAY HOT AND HUMID IN HONG KONG.
LOTS OF STORES ARE OPEN ONTO THE STREET AND POUR OUT A LITTLE OF THEIR AIR CONDITIONING ONTO US.
SOMETIMES IT'S THE CUSTOMERS WHO COOL US OFF WHEN THEY OPEN THE CLOSED DOORS OF THE STORES.
AND WHEN A BUS STOPS ALONGSIDE US, THEN THE TEMPERATURE SHOOTS UP 20°.
AN INTERESTING SUPERPOWER WOULD BE TO KNOW THE PLACEMENT OF ALL THE OPEN-FRONT STORES, KNOWING IN ADVANCE WHICH DOORS WILL OPEN AND WHEN, AND FINALLY, TO KNOW THE SAME THING CONCERNING THE BUS STOPS.
THAT WAY, YOU COULD PLAN A TRIP ACROSS TOWN ALL IN THE COOL.

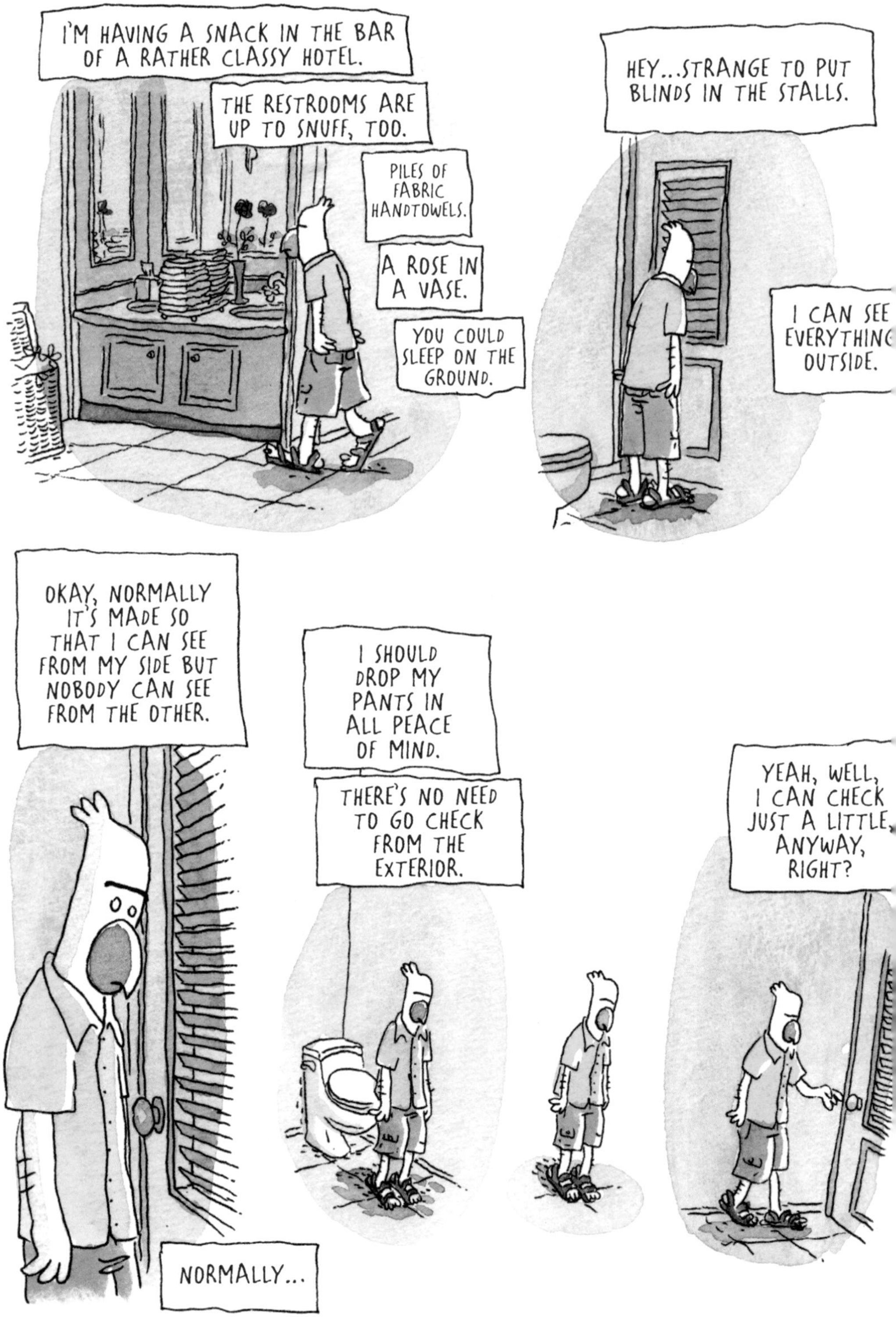
I'M HAVING A SNACK IN THE BAR OF A RATHER CLASSY HOTEL.
THE RESTROOMS ARE UP TO SNUFF, TOO.
PILES OF FABRIC HANDTOWELS.
A ROSE IN A VASE.
YOU COULD SLEEP ON THE GROUND.
HEY...STRANGE TO PUT BLINDS IN THE STALLS.
I CAN SEE EVERYTHING OUTSIDE.
OKAY, NORMALLY IT'S MADE SO THAT I CAN SEE FROM MY SIDE BUT NOBODY CAN SEE FROM THE OTHER.
NORMALLY...
I SHOULD DROP MY PANTS IN ALL PEACE OF MIND.
THERE'S NO NEED TO GO CHECK FROM THE EXTERIOR.
YEAH, WELL, I CAN CHECK JUST A LITTLE, ANYWAY, RIGHT?

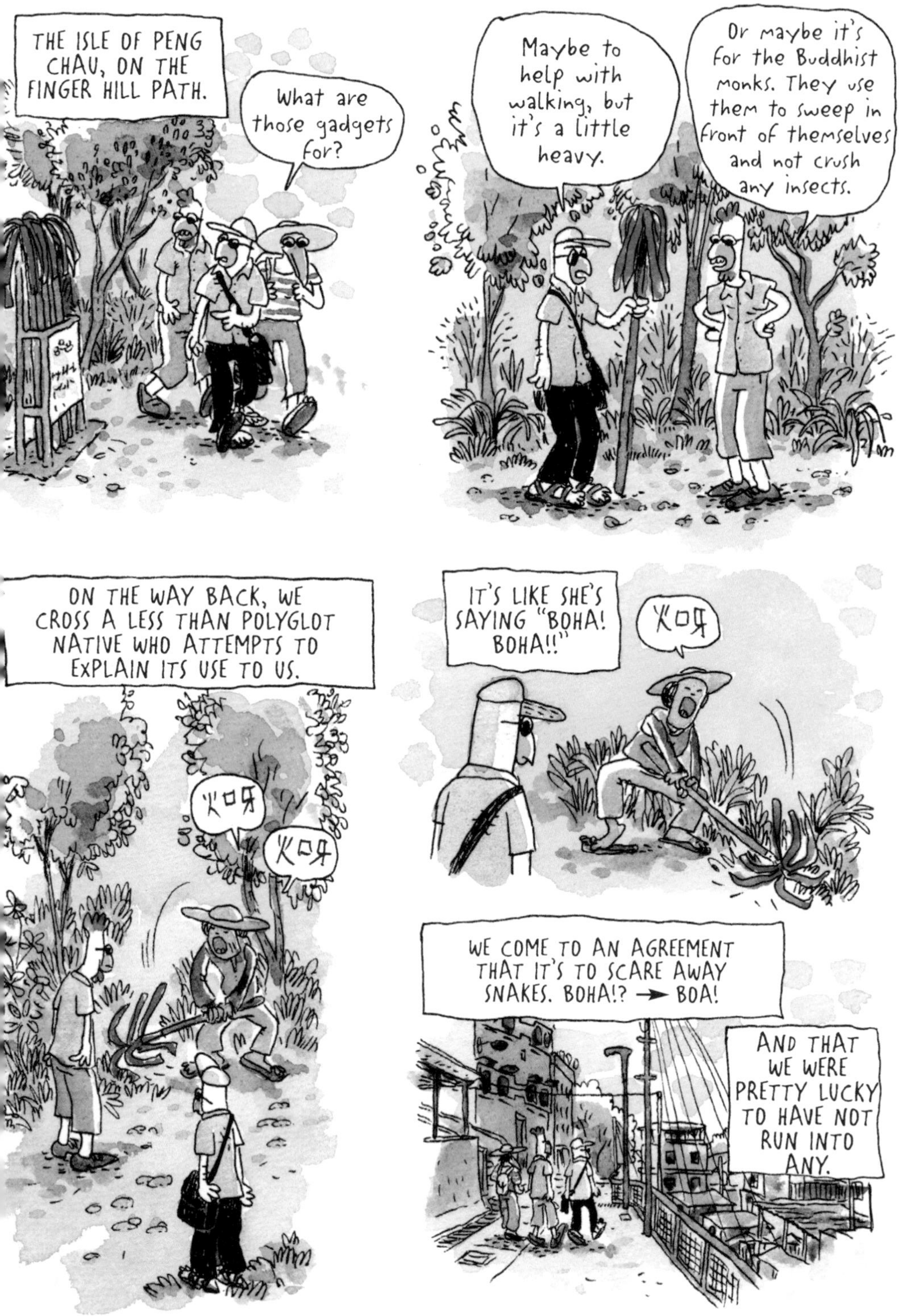
THE ISLE OF PENG CHAU, ON THE FINGER HILL PATH.
What are those gadgets for?
Maybe to help with walking, but it's a little heavy.
Or maybe it's for the Buddhist monks. They use them to sweep in front of themselves and not crush any insects.
ON THE WAY BACK, WE CROSS A LESS THAN POLYGLOT NATIVE WHO ATTEMPTS TO EXPLAIN ITS USE TO US.
火口牙
火口牙
IT'S LIKE SHE'S SAYING "BOHA! BOHA!!"
火口牙
WE COME TO AN AGREEMENT THAT IT'S TO SCARE AWAY SNAKES. BOHA!? ➞ BOA!
AND THAT WE WERE PRETTY LUCKY TO HAVE NOT RUN INTO ANY.

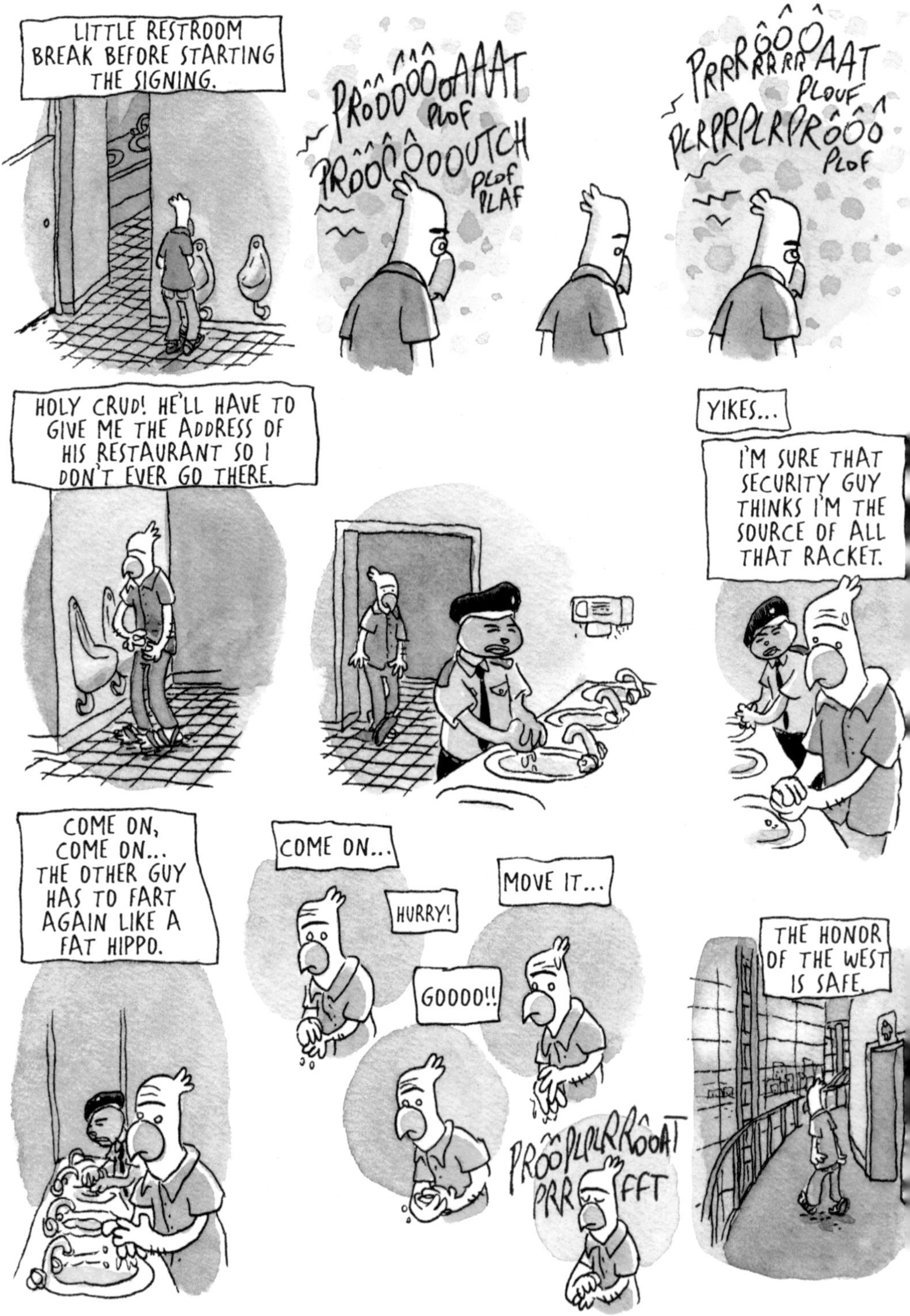
LITTLE RESTROOM BREAK BEFORE STARTING THE SIGNING.
PRÔÔOOOOAAAT
PLOF
PRÔÔÔÔOOUTCH
PLOF
PLAF
PRRRÔÔRRRRAAT
PLOUF
PLRPRPLRPRÔÔÔ
PLOF
HOLY CRUD! HE'LL HAVE TO GIVE ME THE ADDRESS OF HIS RESTAURANT SO I DON'T EVER GO THERE.
YIKES...
I'M SURE THAT SECURITY GUY THINKS I'M THE SOURCE OF ALL THAT RACKET.
COME ON, COME ON... THE OTHER GUY HAS TO FART AGAIN LIKE A FAT HIPPO.
COME ON...
HURRY!
MOVE IT...
GOODO!!
PRÔÔPLRLRRÔÔAT
PRRFFT
THE HONOR OF THE WEST IS SAFE.

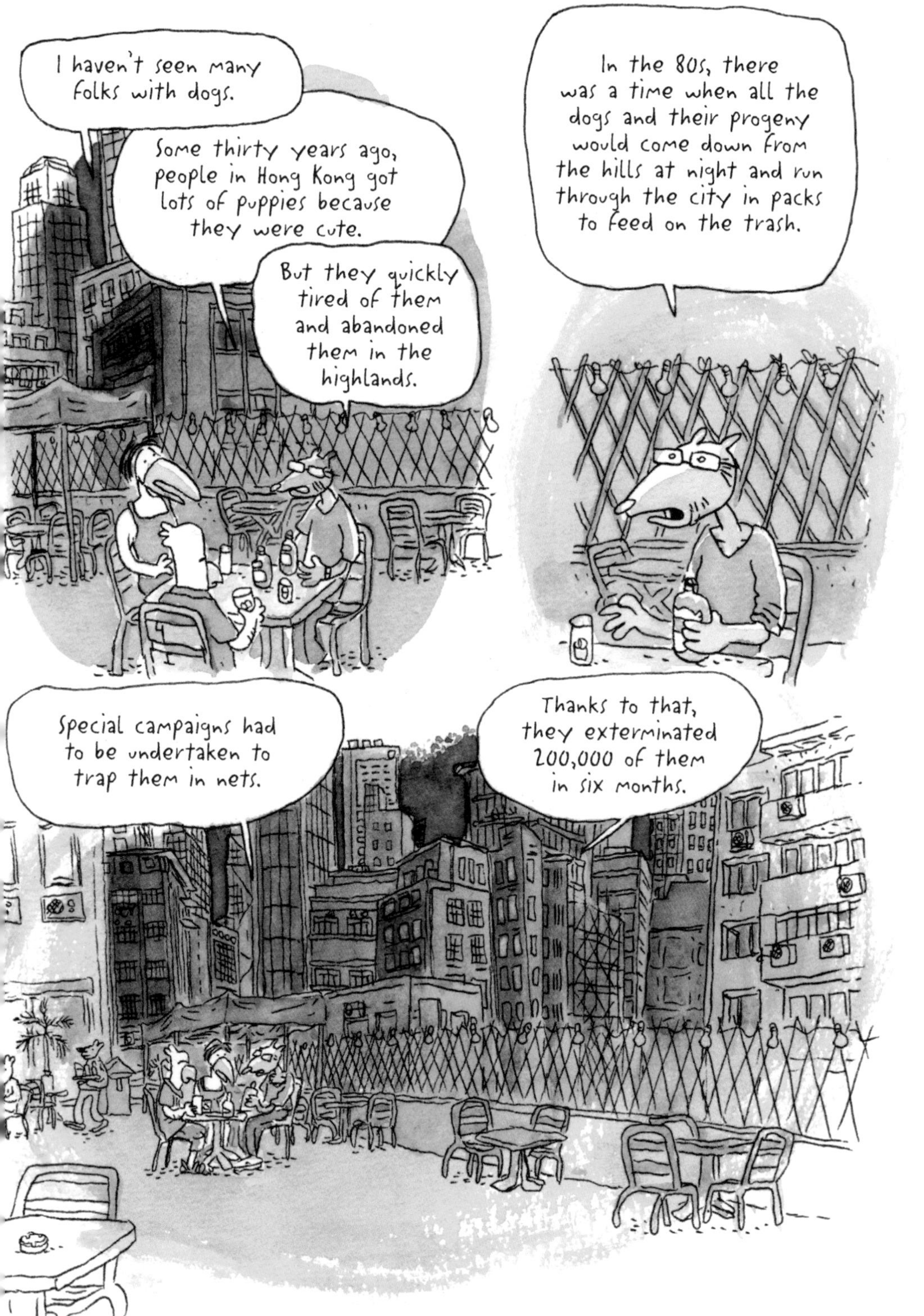
I haven't seen many folks with dogs.
Some thirty years ago, people in Hong Kong got lots of puppies because they were cute.
But they quickly tired of them and abandoned them in the highlands.
In the 80s, there was a time when all the dogs and their progeny would come down from the hills at night and run through the city in packs to feed on the trash.
Special campaigns had to be undertaken to trap them in nets.
Thanks to that, they exterminated 200,000 of them in six months.

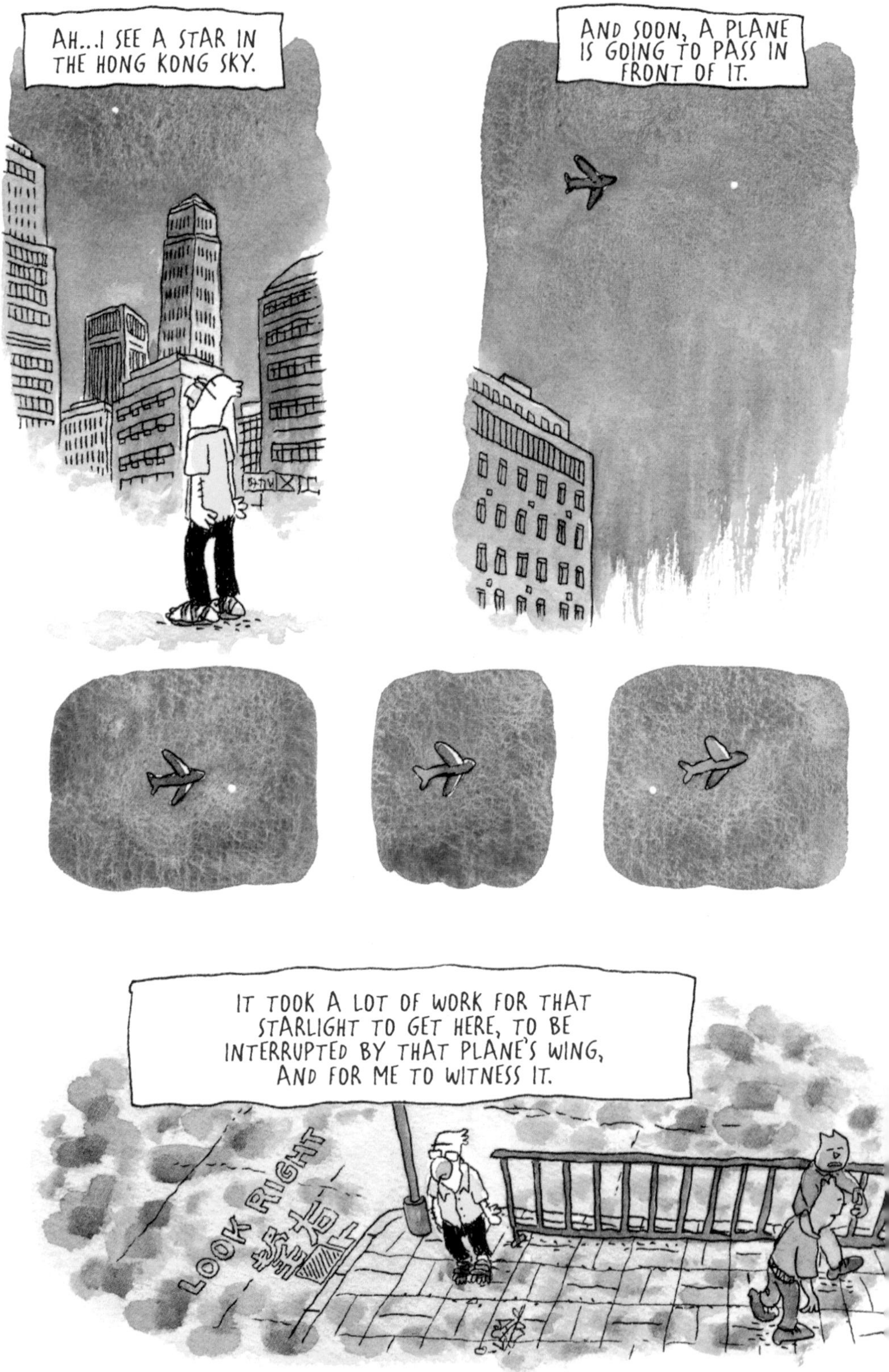
AH...I SEE A STAR IN THE HONG KONG SKY.
AND SOON, A PLANE IS GOING TO PASS IN FRONT OF IT.
IT TOOK A LOT OF WORK FOR THAT STARLIGHT TO GET HERE, TO BE INTERRUPTED BY THAT PLANE'S WING, AND FOR ME TO WITNESS IT.
LOOK RIGHT

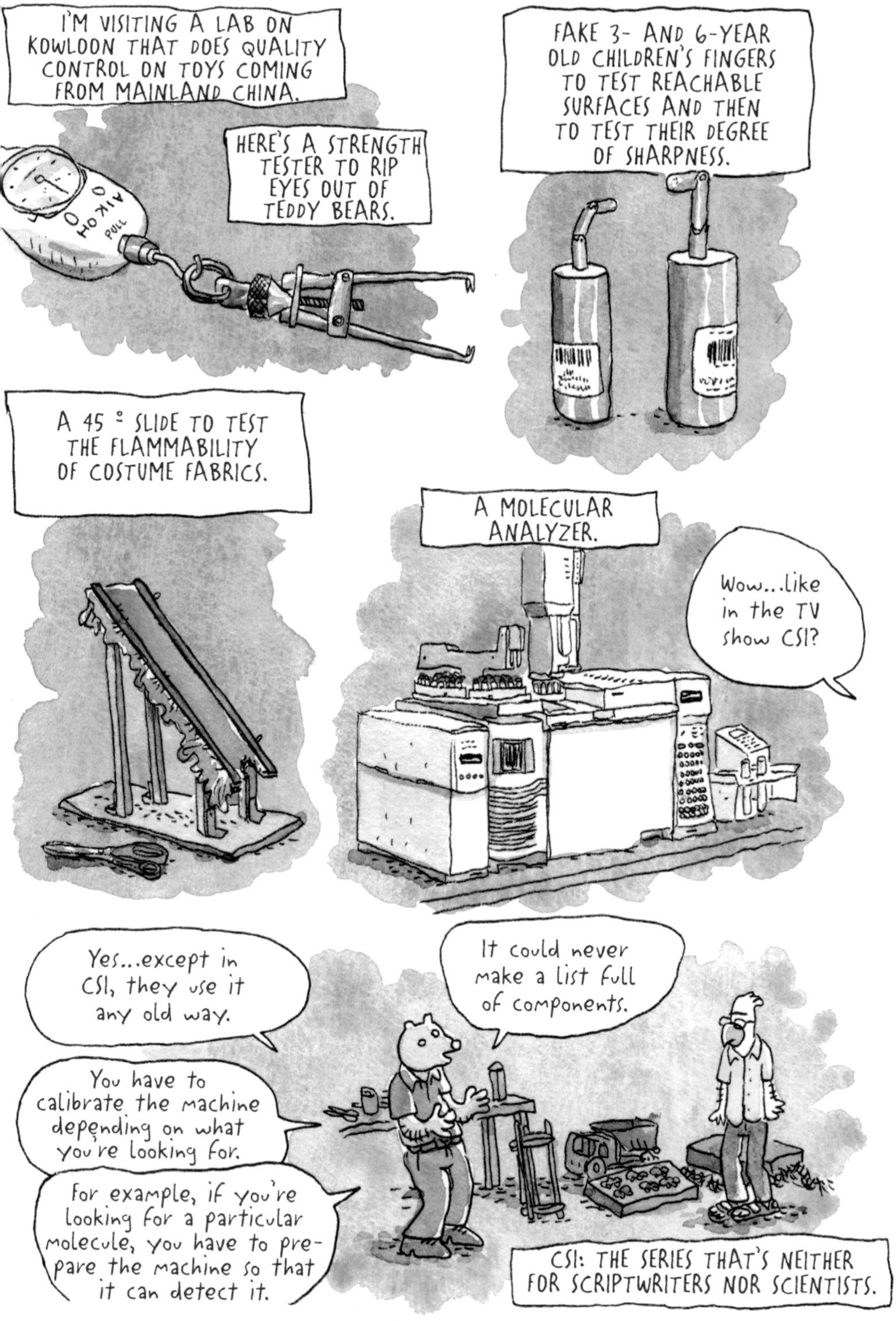
I'M VISITING A LAB ON KOWLOON THAT DOES QUALITY CONTROL ON TOYS COMING FROM MAINLAND CHINA.
HERE'S A STRENGTH TESTER TO RIP EYES OUT OF TEDDY BEARS.
FAKE 3- AND 6-YEAR OLD CHILDREN'S FINGERS TO TEST REACHABLE SURFACES AND THEN TO TEST THEIR DEGREE OF SHARPNESS.
A 45° SLIDE TO TEST THE FLAMMABILITY OF COSTUME FABRICS.
A MOLECULAR ANALYZER.
Wow...like in the TV show CSI?
Yes...except in CSI, they use it any old way.
You have to calibrate the machine depending on what you're looking for.
For example, if you're looking for a particular molecule, you have to prepare the machine so that it can detect it.
It could never make a list full of components.
CSI: THE SERIES THAT'S NEITHER FOR SCRIPTWRITERS NOR SCIENTISTS.

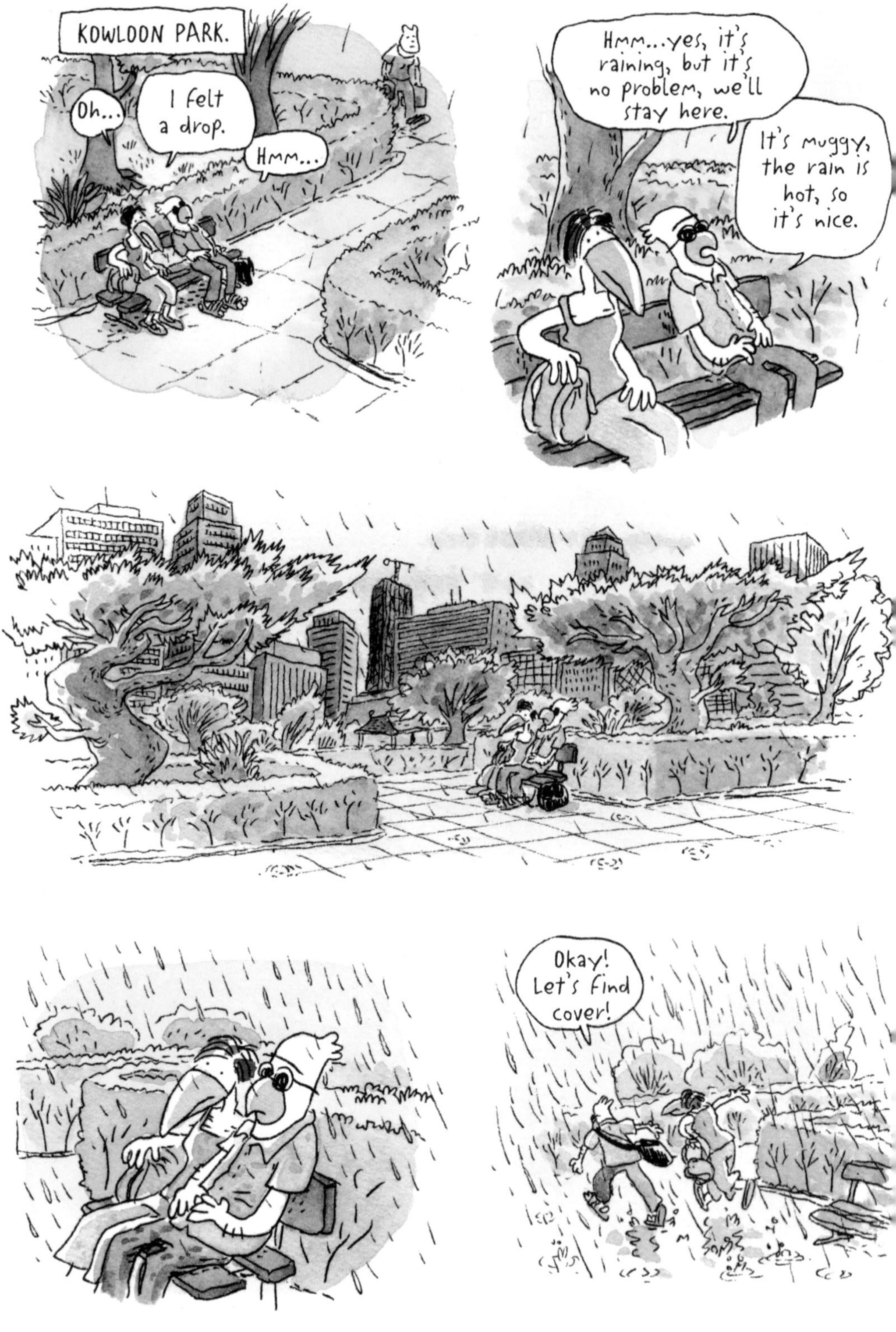
KOWLOON PARK.
Oh...
I felt a drop.
Hmm...
Hmm...yes, it's raining, but it's no problem, we'll stay here.
It's muggy, the rain is hot, so it's nice.
Okay! Let's find cover!

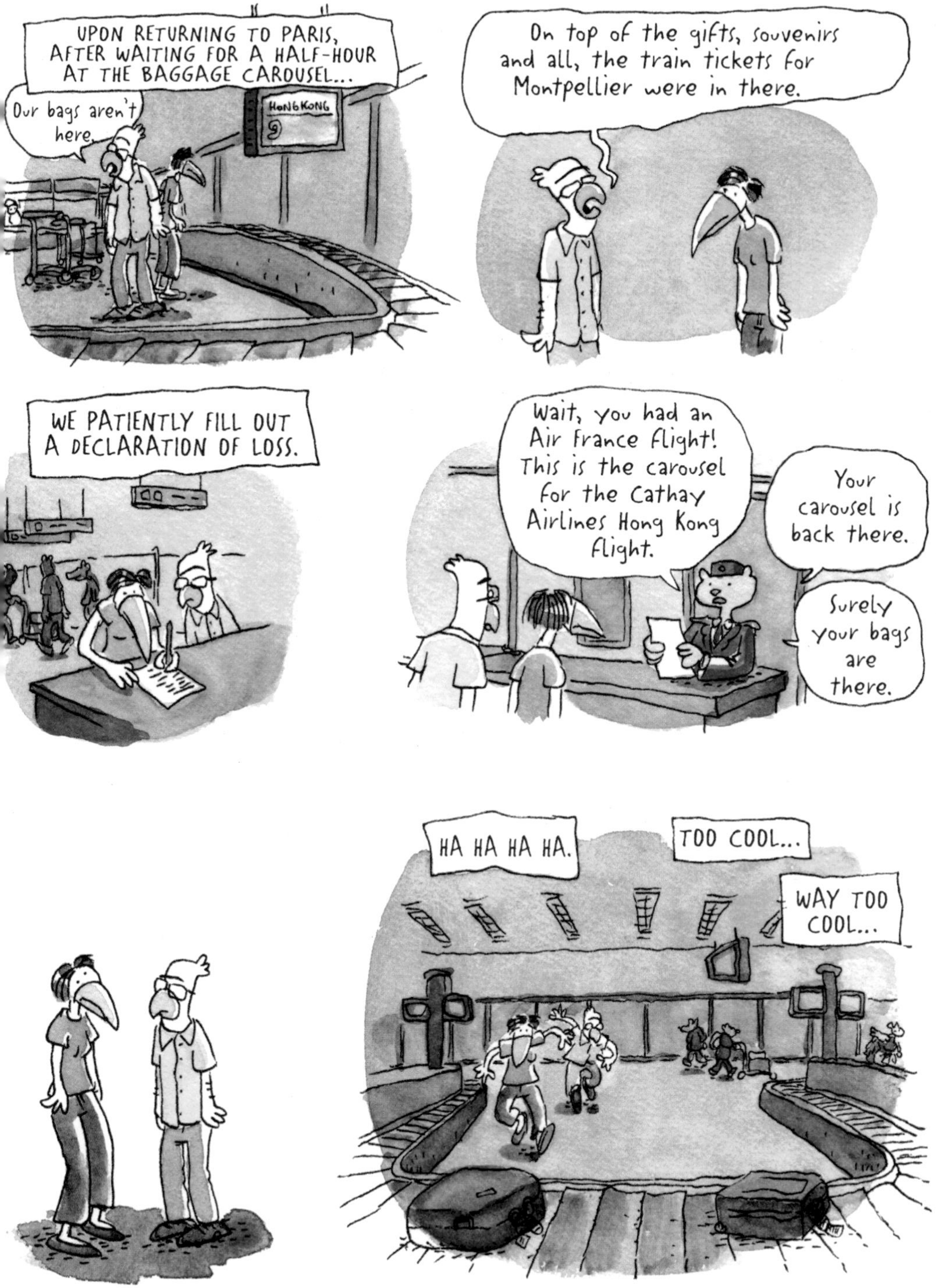
UPON RETURNING TO PARIS, AFTER WAITING FOR A HALF-HOUR AT THE BAGGAGE CAROUSEL...
Our bags aren't here.
HONG KONG
On top of the gifts, souvenirs and all, the train tickets for Montpellier were in there.
WE PATIENTLY FILL OUT A DECLARATION OF LOSS.
Wait, you had an Air France flight! This is the carousel for the Cathay Airlines Hong Kong flight.
Your carousel is back there.
Surely your bags are there.
HA HA HA HA.
TOO COOL...
WAY TOO COOL...

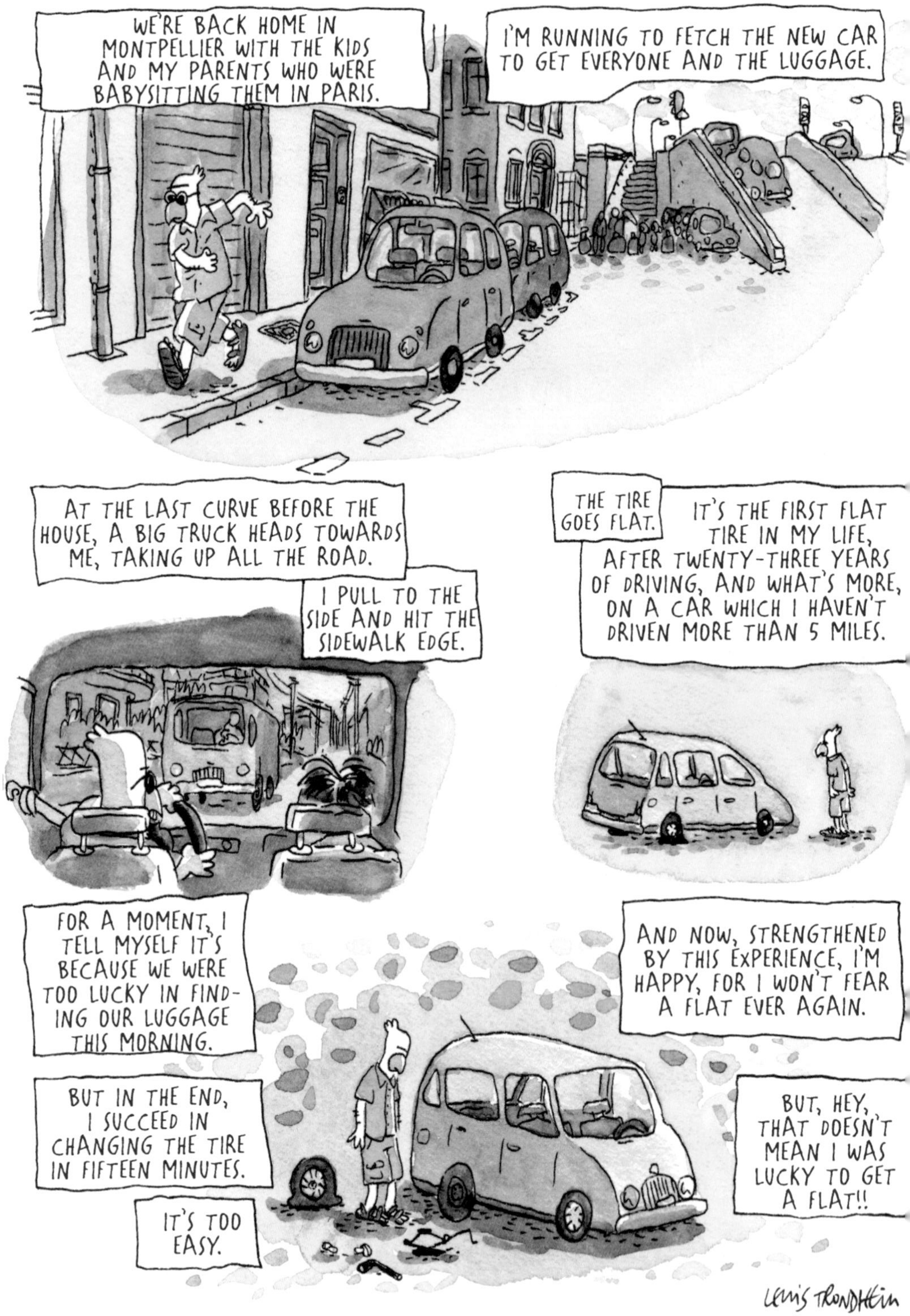
WE'RE BACK HOME IN MONTPELLIER WITH THE KIDS AND MY PARENTS WHO WERE BABYSITTING THEM IN PARIS.
I'M RUNNING TO FETCH THE NEW CAR TO GET EVERYONE AND THE LUGGAGE.
AT THE LAST CURVE BEFORE THE HOUSE, A BIG TRUCK HEADS TOWARDS ME, TAKING UP ALL THE ROAD.
I PULL TO THE SIDE AND HIT THE SIDEWALK EDGE.
THE TIRE GOES FLAT.
IT'S THE FIRST FLAT TIRE IN MY LIFE, AFTER TWENTY-THREE YEARS OF DRIVING, AND WHAT'S MORE, ON A CAR WHICH I HAVEN'T DRIVEN MORE THAN 5 MILES.
FOR A MOMENT, I TELL MYSELF IT'S BECAUSE WE WERE TOO LUCKY IN FINDING OUR LUGGAGE THIS MORNING.
BUT IN THE END, I SUCCEED IN CHANGING THE TIRE IN FIFTEEN MINUTES.
IT'S TOO EASY.
AND NOW, STRENGTHENED BY THIS EXPERIENCE, I'M HAPPY, FOR I WON'T FEAR A FLAT EVER AGAIN.
BUT, HEY, THAT DOESN'T MEAN I WAS LUCKY TO GET A FLAT!!
Lewis Trondheim

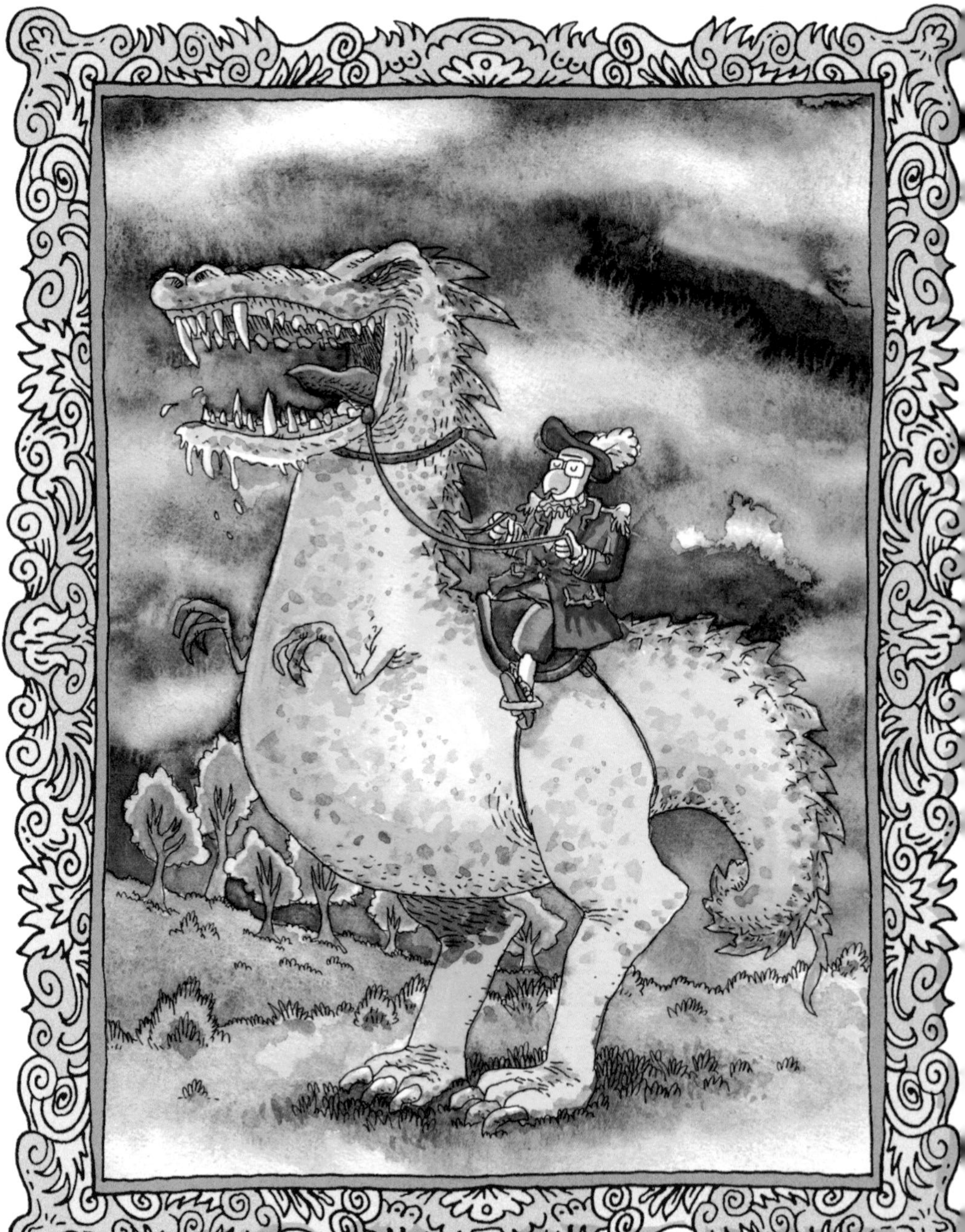

Other books by Trondheim from NBM:
Mr. O, $13.95
Mr. I, $13.95
with Joann Sfar:
Dungeon, Zenith, vols. 1, 2, $14.95 each
Dungeon Early Years, vol. 1, $14.95
Dungeon, Twilight, vols. 1, 2, $14.95 each
Dungeon, Parade, vols. 1, 2, $9.95 each
with Thierry Robin:
Li'l Santa, $14.95
Happy Halloween, Li'l Santa, $14.95

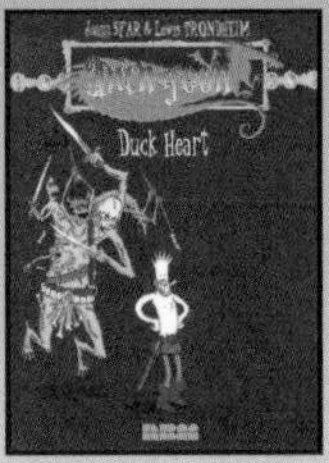
Duck Heart

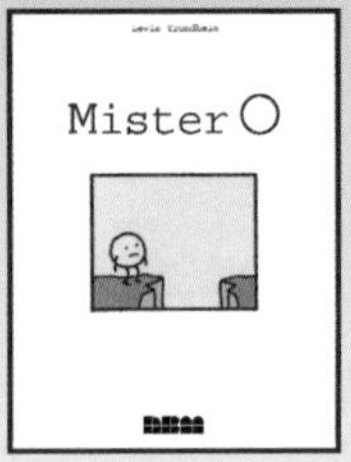
Mister O

Add $3 P&H first item $1 each additional.

Write for our complete catalog
of over 200 graphic novels:
NBM
40 Exchange Pl., Suite 1308
New York, NY 10005
www.nbmpublishing.com